a lotus grows in the mud

a lotus grows in the mud

goldie hawn

with wendy holden

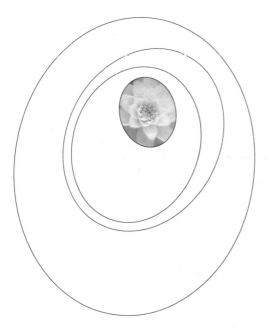

g. p. putnam's sons

new york

⫘P

G. P. Putnam's Sons
Publishers Since 1838
Published by the Penguin Group
Penguin Group (USA) Inc., 375 Hudson Street, New York,
New York 10014, USA • Penguin Group (Canada), 10 Alcorn Avenue,
Toronto, Ontario, Canada M4V 3B2 (a division of Pearson Penguin Canada
Inc.) • Penguin Books Ltd, 80 Strand, London WC2R 0RL, England • Penguin
Ireland, 25 St Stephen's Green, Dublin 2, Ireland (a division of Penguin Books
Ltd) • Penguin Group (Australia), 250 Camberwell Road, Camberwell, Victoria
3124, Australia (a division of Pearson Australia Group Pty Ltd) • Penguin Books
India Pvt Ltd, 11 Community Centre, Panchsheel Park, New Delhi – 110 017,
India • Penguin Group (NZ), cnr Airborne and Rosedale Roads, Albany,
Auckland 1310, New Zealand (a division of Pearson New Zealand Ltd) •
Penguin Books (South Africa) (Pty) Ltd, 24 Sturdee Avenue,
Rosebank, Johannesburg 2196, South Africa

Penguin Books Ltd, Registered Offices:
80 Strand, London WC2R 0RL, England

Text photo captions and credits can be found on page 447.

ISBN 0-399-15285-7

Printed in the United States of America

Book design by Stephanie Huntwork

For my beloved Kurt, who I believe was sent from above. He continues to encourage me to run the race, to live life honestly, to never forget to play and to love as if there is no tomorrow.

For my children, Oliver, Kate, Wyatt, and my stepson, Boston, who remind me each day that miracles do happen, and who have shown me that my heart can hold more love and joy than I ever dreamed possible.

For Deloris Horn, who has been my assistant for thirty years. Who has stood by me through the good times and the bad. Who has held my life in her hands and sometimes in times of sadness held me in her arms. I am more grateful to her than words can express. We have been together from the beginning, before our children, during the blessed birth of our children, right through to the time they fled the nest as young adults. She has my life tucked inside her heart. She possesses the rare human qualities of truth, honesty, integrity and honor. I love her with all of my heart, and without her my life would never have been the same. Never. I will miss you, De, for I understand that it is time for you to take time for yourself. You deserve that and so much more. I love you.

contents

preface

I don't have the answers to the big questions in life. I'm still on my own road to discovery. And, yes, I have been incredibly lucky. But everything is relative; everything has its story; and everyone has obstacles to overcome. They are our greatest teachers.

Each of us goes through transitions and transformations. The important thing is that we acknowledge them and learn from them. That is the idea behind this book. Not to tell my life story, but to speak openly and from the heart about episodes in my life in the hope of explaining how they changed my perception and how they helped me to look at the world more clearly.

I am no pundit. I have only my own life experiences to go on. And the obstacles I have overcome in life have been, in my way, difficult. There may be some who criticize me for not going into intimate details. But that is my decision. I have too much respect for the people involved, and some things are sacred. Some things we need to keep to ourselves. So I am not looking to exploit the story of my relationship with anyone in order to explain myself. I can speak about my feelings without details, and you can fill in the spaces if you wish.

Every relationship is a gift, and that is the theme of the book. What great gifts I have been given by each of the people I have encountered on my journey through life. How they have helped shape me into the person I have become and still hope to be.

Humans are the most extraordinary creatures, and a big part of me still wants to reach an even greater understanding about who we are. Not because I need to know more, necessarily, but because I am drawn to the process of discovery. If someone asks what makes me happiest, it is never anything I can quantify like a house or a possession or something I can touch. It is the spirit of the human being, which can fill me with more joy than anything in the world.

And that's what I've learned on my journey, that my spirit is uplifted by these encounters. Yes, I have met some bad people along the way. But I have also met some amazing souls, and their light fills me.

a lotus grows in the mud

be careful what you wish for

*I'd rather be standing at the bottom
of the mountain looking up than
at the top of the mountain
looking down.*

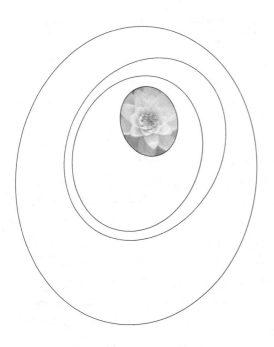

I waddle through the back lot of Paramount Studios, six months pregnant with my second child, Miss Katie. She kicks and rolls as I wend my way in the dark to the restaurant where I am meeting two young writers to discuss a possible new film project.

It is the winter of 1979. The air is cold and damp. I am tired. I gather my coat around my big belly as I approach this landmark eatery where the old ghosts of Hollywood hover and the new players meet, share ideas and gossip unceremoniously about one another.

I'm at the end of a long week spent on a dark looping stage, re-creating every word I spoke in my last film, *Trip with Anita*. I am sick of looking at myself day after day trying to make the words fit in my mouth as each scene moves along silently with just a click track in my headphones. Thank heavens it's almost over and I can just concentrate on having my second baby and returning to my so-called normal life for a while.

Maybe it's not too late to make my marriage work, I think to myself. Maybe if I spend less time working, doing films back-to-back, and more time at home with Daddy Bill and little Oliver, we'll be okay. If my new production company takes off, giving me a little more control over the movies I produce and can make for other people, then I can throttle back for a while.

I open the door to the restaurant and see Nancy Meyers and Charles Shyer sitting in a booth near the window. They are animated, energetic, inspired and full of youth. I like them immediately.

"Hey, thanks for coming all the way into Hollywood to meet with me," I say as I peel off my coat and slump heavily into the seat opposite them. "I've been looping all day on this film I did in Italy last year. They don't use sound over there. Go figure."

We laugh about the archaic way that that particular Italian director makes movies. The menu comes, and I order my weekly dose of liver while my companions jump right in explaining what they're up to.

"We've been working on this idea for a script and want to talk to you about it . . . to see if you and your company might be interested in helping us get it made. We'd like you to play the lead role."

I settle into my seat, ready and eager to hear.

"Okay, guys, shoot."

"It's a story of a spoiled Jewish girl named Judy Benjamin who joins the Army on an impulse after her husband drops dead on their wedding night," Nancy says.

"While making love," Charles chips in.

I laugh out loud. "Oh my God, that's funny. Really funny. Then what?"

"She hates the Army and can't wait to get out and be normal again!" continues Nancy.

I'm loving this pitch. I laugh and laugh as they tell me the rest of the story. The concept is so fresh, so brave and original. The female lead carries the whole movie, almost by herself. She embarks on a personal journey and becomes empowered and independent and strong. It couldn't be more different from my last movie.

I can feel a flutter of excitement in my belly that has nothing to do with my baby. This is a dream role for any actress. My fatigue melts away, and my heart races at being asked to play one of the best characters I have ever been offered.

"What's the film called?" I ask Nancy and Charles.

"*Private Benjamin*," they reply.

Feeling the warmth of my baby resting on the tops of my thighs, I shift in my seat, wondering, praying Judy Benjamin will wait for me.

Finally, I pop the question. "When do you plan on shooting this?"

"We aren't sure yet. We want to write the script on spec first."

"Oh, I see." I nod. "You haven't even written it yet?"

They glance at each other. "No, that will take some time. And, anyway, we wanted to find out if you were available first. When's the baby due?"

"In three months. She'll be born at the end of April, actually." I stroke my belly, happy at the prospect.

Charles and Nancy nod to each other and smile knowingly. "Well, that would work out really well."

"Great!" I exhale, over the moon, "then count me in. I would be honored to make this movie."

After dinner, we hug and say our good-byes as we walk in opposite directions to our cars. It's late, but I'm no longer tired. Reaching my car, I turn. "Who do you have in mind to produce, by the way?"

"No one yet," they call back across the parking lot. "We were going to wait until the script is finished."

"Well, you know what?" I yell back in the dark. "Maybe we could do this ourselves. Maybe we don't need another voice in the mix right now."

"That's what we were thinking."

I lower myself into the front seat of my Mercedes and start up the engine. Heading for home, I wonder what on earth I'm letting myself in for.

W arner Brothers bravely agreed to go with our triad as the only producers attached to *Private Benjamin*. The executives were not only trusting that two women and a man could produce this film, they were also banking on a story about a woman going into the Army bringing a good financial return. The Hollywood film industry at that time was still controlled by men.

But none of us even thought of that as a problem or perceived any glass ceiling at the time. Not at Warner Brothers, anyway. Bob Shapiro, the head of production, loved this movie and what it had to say. He told us from the outset, "If I can't make this film, then I want to be first in line to see it." He was a source of such support during the usual obstacles all films come up against in the long process of production.

It was an exciting time for all of us. We moved into our offices on the Warner Brothers lot and began to build the dream team that would, we hoped, bring this wonderful script to the silver screen. We needed everything from a director and cast to a cinematographer and set designer. We needed to look at actors and locations, costumes and line producers. All this just six months after I'd given birth to my perfect baby girl.

I drove joyfully to our offices almost every day, packing my tiny Kate in her little car seat, her bottles and cereal in my bag, along with a few rattles and toys and her fold-up playpen. Oliver was in preschool, and his nanny looked after him when I wasn't there. It was so great having Kate cooing away in the office with us in the midst of the hustle and bustle of pre-production.

We found ourselves a wonderful director, Arthur Hiller, who had directed *The In-Laws*. For reasons I was never sure of, he dropped out. He was a good man, and there were no hard feelings. It was difficult, however, to find another director at that stage of pre-production. As fate would have it, we were crossing the streets of the back lot on our way to lunch one day when we ran into a director friend of Nancy and Charles's: Howard Zieff. Throwing all caution to the wind, Charles popped the question.

"Hey, Howard, what are you working on these days?" Charles asked.

"Nothing right now."

The three of us looked at each other and smiled. "Nothing? Really? How would you like to direct our new movie?"

So there goes another Hollywood story. Howard Zieff became our new director.

Happy and fulfilled, I felt my life was almost perfect. I only wished there were two of me: the Goldie who could continue to be successful at my work and live the life I loved outside the home, and the Goldie who could be at home cooking and enjoying the domestic side of life that I also cared so deeply about. I battled with myself over these two roles constantly, trying to balance both, but somewhere deep inside I knew that I couldn't win this one. There was never enough time in the day to accomplish my dream of having it all.

Sometimes I'd get home much later than I might have wished and was unable to meet everyone's demands for attention. Some nights I raced home just to bathe my babies and tuck them in bed. I knew that my marriage was suffering as a consequence. The struggle of juggling all this was an enormous burden to bear, and the guilt relentless. The icing on the cake was the slight chance that this film would be a great big fat success. But I also feared that possibility. I knew that if it was a success, my obstacles would only be harder to overcome. The pressures that would put on my already fragile marriage would be almost insurmountable in this business where one party always feels left out of the parade.

But I was on this fantasy ride at Disneyland and I couldn't jump off. For one thing, it was way too much fun, and, second, the train had already left the station.

The film was a bigger, fatter success than I could ever have imagined. Not only was it the great creative collaboration of my life, it was the most thrilling time in my professional career. The movie opened at the theaters even better than anyone expected, and the only name above the title was mine. There was no male star to carry the picture, as they say, as was usually the case. If ever I had suspected how life-changing this movie would be for me, I could never have guessed how much.

Everybody suddenly wanted to interview me. I made the cover of *Newsweek*. I was touted as the Hollywood actress who broke the rules, broke box office expectations and blazed a new trail for women, especially for actresses who wanted to produce films for themselves and for others.

I was happy but at the same time worried at this superinflated image the media seemed to have created of me. I wasn't the only producer on the film. Nancy and Charles did as much, if not more, than I did. But because the media decided it would be so, I became the face of female power in Hollywood, even though Nancy is the one who has gone on to write, produce and direct huge box office hits like *What Women*

Want and *Something's Gotta Give,* and Charles Shyer has directed many films since.

My marriage finally cracked under the pressure, and the double-edged sword of my supposed new power in Hollywood stuck in my side. I'd only feared what success could do to destabilize my home life; I hadn't considered the reaction within the industry. It was increasingly difficult for me to be simply an actress for hire. I kept hearing things like, "But Goldie does her own films." Even though I met many wonderful, strong directors with great roles to offer, none of them hired me. I began getting a complex, thinking that they didn't want to work with me, when, in truth, they just didn't want the baggage of "Goldie Hawn." This realization was so crushing to me.

There were several fallow periods that followed, and many times I looked back and felt the bittersweet sting of *Private Benjamin.* Of the films I have made since then, some I have produced and some I have not. I've worked alongside some very good directors and some not so good. I have been fearless in arguing points I have felt strongly about with studio heads. I have made some friends and I've made some enemies trying to help make my films be as good as they can be. Sometimes I was right to share my vision, and sometimes I was wrong. My only hope was that a great collaboration would be sparked, and that ego and fear would be left outside the door.

But my passion and commitment to work was no longer tempered by the fear of not being liked. My tenacity and determination to be true to the person I had become were sacrosanct. I guess I came to know this about myself: for better or worse, I don't give up.

joy

The smile you give is
the smile you get back.

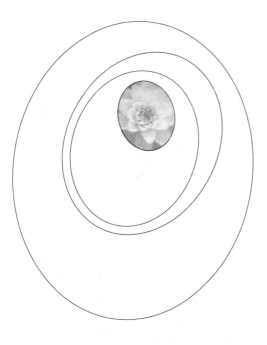

The walls are white and the day is yellow. The warmth of my new pink feet signals the beginning of a broadly sensuous life. The taste of my toe is sweet; I like it. Gazing through the sunlit bars of my crib, my mother appears from the yellow, her face shining white. Love is blazing from her eyes, filling my heart with beams of light. She is smiling down at me, and I feel completely adored.

She bends her body over mine and gently with her loving hands gathers up my freshly suckled feet. Before she can whistle Brahms's "Lullaby," I am naked as a jaybird. It is a state I will always relish.

My mother nuzzles her face into my belly and makes me laugh. I kick my legs playfully, for there is a sense of joy in me that to this day I find indefinable.

Then she picks me up and puts me in a tub of warm water. Her hands cup the water and pour it gently over my body. I feel her soft hands cleaning my legs, my arms, my back. It feels like silk. All too soon, I am lifted out of my bath and swaddled in a soft white towel. Mom snuggles me close, and suddenly I am on my back again. She rubs oil into my brand-new skin and then dusts my private parts with Johnson's baby powder. Its smell will always remind me of that perfect love.

My mother wrestles my moving arms and legs into a sleeper suit with feet and *snap, snap, snaps* me all the way up. With each snap cocooning me in, I feel a happiness inside, a safety that to this day I find difficult to describe, until I am wrapped right up to my neck in love. It is night.

Time for bed. The only thing I fear at that moment is the disappearance of her smile and the lights dimming.

They say a baby smiles an average of seventy-two times a day, and a toddler laughs or smiles six hundred times a day. We learn to smile very early in life. It is one of the first things we do, after we learn to cry. And how do we learn to smile? By how much we are smiled at. Does our smile live somewhere in the double helix of our DNA, or is it nurtured?

Somewhere in there lies the truth, which is—it is nature, but it must be nurtured. To understand our mother's smile is to understand our own smile, to know what triggers that physiological response.

A smile is an indication of a happy heart, and when you smile it changes your perception. It can create a better day. As frivolous as it might sound, studies have proven that even if you don't feel like smiling, if you force yourself to smile, you will change your state of mind. By doing so, you can actually raise the immune-system boosters in your blood.

The question is, Where does that smile go? Why is it that as we grow older we smile less? Could it be that we are looking for happiness and fulfillment in all the wrong places? Is it fear that stops us from being happy? Have we forgotten how to seek those simple pleasures that brought us such joy as children? To find the spaces between our thoughts that allow these joyful memories to flood back?

I suppose the key to holding on to that smile is to try to remember how much you smiled when you were young. Never forget, because that smile still lives in you, no matter how old you are.

growing pains

Here's to the kids who are different;
the kids who don't always get A's,
the kids who have ears
twice the size of their
peers', or noses that go
on for days.
Here's to the kids who
are different, the
kids who are just
out of step,
the kids they all
tease, who have
cuts on their knees
and whose sneakers
are constantly wet.
Here's to the kids who
are different, the kids
with a mischievous
streak,
for when they have grown,
as history has shown,
it's their difference that makes
them unique.

—*Digby Wolfe, for* The Goldie Hawn TV Special, *1978*

My toes find their footing in each hole in the chain-link fence as, step by step, I climb my way to the top. The smell of chocolate chip cookies egging me on, I pray that I won't snag my shorts on the sharp barbs of wire at the top.

I am making my daily assault on the barrier that separates me from my neighbor and first boyfriend, David Fisher. David lived a few houses away from our redbrick, three-bedroom duplex on Cleveland Avenue, in a suburb of Washington, D.C., called Takoma Park. To get to his house each day after school, I have to scale this fence in the yard of my next-door neighbor, Mr. Morningstar.

I could reach the Fisher house the easy way—by walking around the block—but that wouldn't be as much fun. Instead, I relish the challenge of climbing that fence, because the minute I have achieved my mission and landed with a thump in his backyard I will be leaving my empty house behind and entering a world that is very different from my own.

Mrs. Fisher stays home all day baking and cooking and keeping house for her four boys. Mr. Fisher comes home each night after work and doesn't go out again. Their home is filled with noise and school projects and fun. There is a miniature golf course they made in the backyard out of mud, complete with waterfalls, and, best of all, right next door to the Fishers lives my best friend, Jean Lynn.

Each afternoon when I return home from school to my dark and silent house, greeted only by Nixi, my pet Dalmatian, waiting for me on the front porch, I telephone my mom at the Flowers Gift Shop to let her know I'm home. My house always feels so empty, so lonely.

"Okay, honey, I'll come and pick you up just as soon as I close the store," she tells me. "Now do your homework, and be a good girl for Mrs. Fisher."

David has two sets of teeth. He has grown his second set, but his old set won't fall out, so his mouth is jam-packed. His lips can no longer meet. No one can understand a word he says but me. The teachers in school always sit me next to David. I have become his trusty interpreter.

My mom arrives on time to pick me up after work, sporting her straight skirt and pointy high-heeled shoes. She always looks so beautiful. She says hello to Mrs. Fisher and the boys. I can smell her perfume as she stands close to me, staring over my shoulder. She watches me color my elephants while David is reading his book.

"Why don't you have a reading book like David, Goldie?"

I shrug my bony shoulders and carry on with my drawing. "I don't know, Mommy. Maybe because I'm in the Purple Balls."

"The purple what?"

"The Purple Balls, Mommy," I say, proudly. "It's a special reading group, and it's really neat."

"Why is it neat, honey?"

"Because I'm the only one in it."

"David, why doesn't Goldie have a reading book?" Mommy asks him when she can't get a sensible reply out of me. He mumbles something, but my mother can't understand him, so she turns to me and asks, "What did he say?"

"He said, 'Because she's too dumb,' " I reply, without even looking up from my happy elephants.

"You're too what?" my mother asks, screwing her cigarette into the ashtray. "How come I don't know this?"

She gives me a strange look, and helps me pack up my things. "Come on, honey, it's time to go home."

The next day, Mom comes to the Silver Spring Intermediary Elementary School with me, something she never does. Instead of going straight to class as usual, I am taken to the principal's office for a meeting with my teacher, Mrs. Povitch. I sit silently listening to their conversation.

"Yes, Mrs. Hawn," Mrs. Povitch confirms, "the Purple Balls is the lowest reading group in second grade, I'm afraid. It's not that your daughter doesn't try, or that she isn't a good girl. She just gets easily distracted."

"Anything else I should know?" Mommy asks with a sigh.

"Yes, there is, actually." Mrs. Povitch laughs. "Every time we ask Goldie to color in the fruits in the coloring book—red for apples, purple for grapes and so on—she paints everything in yellow. When I ask her why, she says, 'Because I like yellow.' "

"Well, it is her favorite color." Mom bristles defensively.

"Oh, and she's such a sweet child," Mrs. Povitch says, throwing her head back and laughing. "She always signs her unfinished papers 'Love Goldie XX.' "

"Well, that's my Goldie," Mom replies. "She must love you very much."

Step, two-three, glide, two-three, pirouette and turn. The moves are etched into my brain in a continuous loop. Now balancé, two-three, and into the arabesque . . .

Dancing is my sport, my life, my purpose. Moving my body, challenging myself, sweat dripping from every pore, I feel the music vibrating within me, sending me to ecstasy. Competing with no one but myself, just moving molecules in the air, I reach such an emotional high in physical expression.

Everything goes away when I am dancing—schoolwork, boys and my loneliness. Dancing is something I can do. This is where I belong. I am good at this, and I know if I practice really hard I can make myself even better. When I am dancing, I am able to escape to my own little world. And, for the first time in my life, I realize that my unusual father is just the same; he dances to the beat of his own drum.

Picking me up from dance school one night, I overhear my mother talking to my dance teacher, Aunt Roberta.

"There's a talent show at Goldie's school next month," she says. "I thought she could do the parasol dance she did in her recital."

"No, Mommy," I pipe up as I peel off my tights and leotard and wriggle back into my school dress, "I want to improvise to 'Sleigh Ride.'" This is the song I whirl and twirl around the living room to every night when I get home.

"Don't you want to do your parasol dance?" Mommy asks. "You know it really well."

"I want to dance to 'Sleigh Ride,' Mommy," I insist. "It makes me happy."

Happiness was always important to me. Even at the young age of eleven, it was my biggest ambition. People would ask, "Goldie, what do you want to be when you grow up?"

"Happy," I would reply, looking in their eyes.

"No, no," they'd laugh. "That's really sweet, but I mean . . . what do you want to be? A ballerina? An actress maybe?"

"I just want to be happy."

And "Sleigh Ride" makes me happy.

The day before the show, all the contestants are gathered in the school gymnasium. "Wait here for Mrs. Toomey," a teacher tells us. "She'll be along in just a minute."

Mrs. Toomey is a very severe woman, with gray hair and bony fingers. I am a little scared of her, to tell you the truth. Sitting on the wooden basketball floor, I can hear her shoes clunking along the corridor toward us, and then, suddenly, she appears, standing over us ominously.

"Now, children, this is very exciting, and we are going to have a wonderful show. I am glad you are all here, but I want you to know that you must be absolutely perfect," she says, peering at us sternly with steel blue eyes.

Perfect? I think, the blood draining from my face. But I'm not perfect. I will be improvising to music. Anything could happen. I feel stricken.

"Your moms and dads and lots of people will be watching, and I don't want them to see any mistakes."

Panic-stricken, I keep thinking about what she said. Perfect? I won't be able to do that. To me, perfect is doing a pirouette without falling over, and I can't always manage that. My mind flashes hotly back to the maypole dance the previous year in this very gymnasium. I accidentally took a wrong turn and wound my ribbon on the outside instead of inside. Mrs. Toomey got so mad and started screaming at me, but I tried to hold on and not cry. The problem is that I can't control the tears that are streaming down my cheeks.

Walking home from school, I think long and hard about what she said, her words spinning round and round in my mind.

Perfect? I ask myself as I pass the old woman who always sits in her window crocheting. I wave and smile.

Perfect? What is perfect? I pass the man who constantly mows his lawn, with his pipe posted between his lips.

Perfect. Like Fred Astaire and Ginger Rogers?

I climb the front porch, where Nixi is waiting for me. We walk together into our home. I don't feel like climbing the chain-link fence to David Fisher's today. Instead, I go upstairs to my bedroom, where I sit staring at my dolls, waiting for Mom to come home.

Sitting at the kitchen table when she finally does, I plunk my elbows on it and rest my head in my hands. "Mommy, what is 'perfect'?"

"'Perfect' is when people don't make any mistakes, I guess." She purses her lips and looks at me askance.

"Okay, then I'm not doing the talent show."

"What? Goldie Jeanne, what do you mean you're not doing the talent show? Honey, you have to do the talent show; you're the only one up there who can do anything. You have practiced and practiced every night in the living room. You looked beautiful. You didn't make a single mistake."

"But I'm not perfect, Mommy."

"Well, nobody's perfect. Who said anything about perfect?"

"Mrs. Toomey said."

My mother raises her eyes to the heavens and shakes her head. "Oh boy. Here we go. Another trip to the school."

The next morning my mother picks up our precious copy of "Sleigh Ride" and escorts me to the school with it tucked firmly under her arm. We sit side by side in a small room with Mrs. Toomey, who seems a little panicked that my mother has come to see her. She leans forward in her chair and gives me a thin smile.

"Now, Goldie, I'm sure I didn't say 'perfect,'" she says defensively.

"Oh yes you did, Mrs. Toomey," I counter. "You said 'perfect,' and I'm not perfect."

My mother shakes her head in exasperation. "Now, Goldie, clearly Mrs. Toomey didn't mean you have to do everything exactly right."

Mrs. Toomey chimes in, groping for words. "Yes, that's right, honey. I just meant you have to be the best you can be. Goldie, I want you to be in the talent show."

"But I'm not perfect."

"Goldie, it doesn't matter," my mother insists.

After relentless pressure from them both, I finally give in. "Okay. I'll dance. But I'm *not* perfect," I add, under my breath.

My mother is so relieved she flops back down into a chair. Unfortunately, it was the wrong chair, because she sat on the only copy of "Sleigh Ride" we possessed. It shattered into pieces beneath her. There was a moment of silence before my mother wailed, "Oh my God! What did I just sit on?!"

"My record, Mommy. You sat on 'Sleigh Ride.'"

She pulls herself up, "Oh, for Christ's sake," she says, picking up the pieces helplessly.

Mrs. Toomey tries to comfort her. "Don't worry," she says.

My mother says, "What do you mean, 'Don't worry'? This is the only one. I have to go downtown and get another one." Bubbles of sweat lace her brow as she speed-walks down the corridor in her torpedo-shaped stilettos.

I pull my sequined costume up over my shapeless hips in a classroom next to the gym and listen to the music coming through the walls. The show has begun. Some of my classmates are singing, mostly off-key.

My mom brushes my hair away from my face, which I hate. As soon as she is done, I tease out some strands and pull them down over my forehead. As she fusses over me, fluffing the crinkles out of my tutu, she occasionally stops and stares into my face. I don't speak. I am too mesmerized by her heart-shaped face and her orangey red lipstick. I love to watch as she sits in front of the mirror each morning, with her big eyes and her auburn hair, and precisely follows the voluptuous contours of her mouth. Pressing her lips together, she always pouts and examines herself critically, one side and then the other, before slipping her feet into her high heels and trotting off to work.

Pushing my bangs away from my eyes again, my mother's face softens. "When you grow up, I want you to put my aunt Goldie's name up in lights."

"I will, Mommy," I reply dutifully.

Her eyes twinkle. "She was a wonderful woman."

I am still young but I will do anything for my mother, even the impossible. Great-Aunt Goldie Hochhauser, a jovial redhead—known in our house as "Tante" Goldie—raised my mother when she was orphaned at three years old in Braddock, Pennsylvania. She died a year before I was born. I was given her name, and I'm very proud.

"Okay, Goldie," my mother whispers in my ear as Mrs. Toomey signals that it is time for me to go on. "Remember, nobody's perfect." She takes the precious 78 and hands it to the stage manager before running to take her seat in the front row.

I walk to the edge of the stage, mimicking all the great ballerinas I have ever seen. My arms out in second position, my toe pointed in front of me, I am ready to be swept up by the music. Looking out at the audience, I feel my heart hammering on my ribs.

Somewhere out there is David Fisher and his brother, Jimmy. "Don't worry, Goldie, we'll clap extra hard," they assured me before I went on.

A few feet away from me, the stage manager places the needle onto the new copy of "Sleigh Ride," and the opening bars crackle through the loudspeakers. Closing my eyes, I allow the sound of my favorite song in the whole world to flood my head and my heart.

"Just hear those sleigh bells jingle-ing, ring-ting-tingle-ing too / Come on, it's lovely weather for a sleigh ride together with you . . ."

Before I know it, I am bouncing gently in time to the music, shifting my body this way and that, repeating the moves I know so well and have practiced so hard to get right. Improvising their sequence, I suddenly find my feet lifting me up and taking me flying across the stage, my arms and legs working in tandem, a big grin on my face and my head held high, completely forgetting about being perfect.

I catch a glimpse of my mom, her hands clasped together, nodding gently and moving her lips to the words of the song. Her big-eyed enthusiasm spurs me on.

As the music reaches its chorus, I am now completely lost, not knowing which move to make next and yet letting the music take me to uncharted territory. Whirling and twirling, I realize that we are now almost at the end of the piece. The music fades all too soon, and I find a way to end the dance in a curtsy on the final line: "These wonderful things are the things we remember all through our lives . . ."

Everyone jumps to their feet to clap enthusiastically, and I step timorously to the front of the stage to take a deep bow.

Looking down at the audience, I see my true friends on their feet, my only friends—Jean Lynn, David and Jimmy Fisher—smiling up at me with relief and happiness. My mother grins broadly from the front row and nods her head. My eyes scan the room for Mrs. Toomey and find her standing over to one side. To my surprise, she is sobbing openly, beaming up at me through her tears.

Gee, maybe not being perfect is what perfect really means.

postcard

Y ou ready, Go?" my dad yells from the driveway of our house, lifting a bucket of live bait and some fishing tackle into the trunk of his dark blue '49 Lincoln.

"Next stop, Chesapeake Bay!"

"Coming, Daddy," I cry, rushing excitedly across the front porch holding whatever he has rustled up for our lunch. I am eleven years old.

Settling into the front seat, I watch my father adoringly as he walks with his swaggering gait around to the driver's side. Slipping in next to me, his hair slicked back like Fred Astaire's, he glances over at me with those piercing sky blue eyes and smiles. "Ready to catch some fish, Go?" he asks.

"Yes." I nod, sliding across to cozy up to the first great love of my life.

I love sitting right alongside Daddy in the front seat. There is nothing better than to feel the warmth of his body against mine, and to inhale the unique scent of his skin. Watching his long, lean musician's fingers draped over the three-spoke banjo steering wheel, I sit very still and don't fidget, hoping that he won't shuffle those few inches away.

In less than an hour, we are sitting out in a little rental boat in that muddy old bay at the mouth of the Severn River, our fishing rods dangling in the water. He teaches me to hook the worms and net our catch. There aren't too many flounder, and sometimes we snag only a few small trout.

Whenever I catch one, he smiles at me proudly and says, "My daughter, the fisherman!" Mostly, we just sit there laughing and talking and eating our sandwiches and waiting for a bite. Neither of us is really there for the fishing.

Me, I am just so happy to steal some time with my father

by myself. Because he works every day, mending watches, and is out playing his music in Washington, D.C., almost every night, these fishing trips are my most precious moments. He is always different when he is alone with me, more childlike and free.

Out in the boat, facing each other on separate wooden seats, I sit quietly and listen to Daddy's soft, melodic voice. He's a dreamer with his own unique take on life, and I love to hear him talk.

"You know, Kink," he says, using the nickname only he uses, the one he calls me when he's really happy, "if you ever feel like you're getting too big for your britches, then come out here, or go to the ocean and stand on the shore and see how small you are."

Staring into the middle distance, he adds, "It's important never to lose sight of that."

"Yes, Daddy," I reply, nodding gravely. Little do I know that those are some of the most important words I will ever hear in my life.

Driving home from our fishing trip through the green rolling hills of Maryland, we make up nonsensical songs together—odd combinations of words and popular tunes. I sing, "The moon is bright . . . ," and Daddy adds, ". . . and the sun is yellow." We laugh and laugh as the sentences become more and more ridiculous.

The sun setting behind us, I announce, "I will always listen to the classics like you, Daddy, especially Bach." Gee, he loves his Bach.

"That's my girl."

"And I'll never, ever like rock and roll."

Giving me a sideways glance and a crooked smile, my father says, "We'll see about that."

Our journey home is never the same. Snuggled to his side on that long front seat of our '49 Lincoln, I see roads that look as if they lead nowhere.

I cry out, "Look, Daddy! Look at that neat road! It's like a roller-coaster ride. Let's go down it! Can we? Can we?"

"Okay, Kink, whatever you say!" Accustomed to our little game, and laughing his hee-haw laugh, he makes a sharp left-hand turn and steers the car down a bumpy track that throws up great billowing clouds of dust behind us.

Bumping and grinding down the dirt road with no destination in mind, the two of us become the wandering gypsies we've always secretly been at heart. I love him for his spontaneity, for his eagerness to take an unusual turn in life, regardless of the outcome. I guess it has always been his way.

Daddy's philosophy is, "Take a left-hand turn, Kink. See where it leads you." For him, the journey is always more exciting than the destination.

Hitting a rock on our ride home from the Bay, his old Lincoln's long-suffering suspension lifts me clear off the seat and brings me crashing back down to earth with a jolt.

My hand on my head, rubbing where it hit the roof, I look across at my grinning, free spirit of a father, and we both roll with laughter as our car follows the yellow brick road.

first steps

Life is a dance with the cosmos.

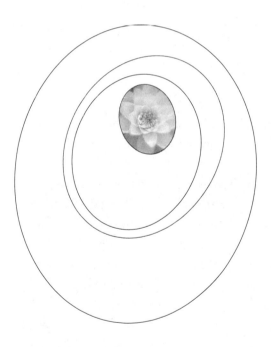

The bright lights of Washington, D.C., are reflected on my face as I press my cheek against the glass of the cab window. Butterflies dance in my stomach, and my skin feels clammy with fear.

"Don't be nervous, honey," is all my mother says as the yellow taxi drives us toward the Carter Barron Amphitheatre. It is a balmy June evening in 1956, and I am a last-minute understudy for the Ballet Russe de Monte Carlo.

"You'll be just fine," Mom adds with a confidence I don't altogether share. "The other girl will probably turn up and you won't even have to dance."

The Ballet Russe is performing Tchaikovsky's *Nutcracker Suite*. The star is the legendary Cuban ballerina Alicia Alonso. I am understudying the role of Clara, the little girl who receives the nutcracker as a Christmas gift. I am scared to death that I might actually have to go on.

"Here we are, now. Come along, Goldie, hurry up," my mother says, pressing a wad of dollar bills into the hand of the driver. "Quick, quick, out of the car, and grab your dance bag."

Where's the girl? Where's the other girl? is all I can think as we rush the stage door. Gripping my mother's hand so tight that my knuckles show white through the skin, we race inside.

The backstage area is all abustle with dancers and choreographers, costumers and makeup artists, running this way and that, speaking a language I don't understand. Everyone seems so strange to me, so exotic and extreme. I feel as if I have just walked into a play.

"Out of the way! Coming through!" someone yells as we are flattened against a wall by someone carrying a great gown of crushed red silk that rustles and whispers as he hurries past. A group of dancers, who look to me like exquisite swans with their long necks and white tutus, are stretching their limbs in the most amazing extensions I have ever seen. I gasp. As I do so, one girl draws deeply on a cigarette and stares at me fiercely, her huge eyes framed by stage makeup.

My mother pushes me forward and leads me down a winding staircase. "But where's the other girl, Mommy?" I ask, looking around wildly.

"I don't know," she snaps, and I stare up at her in open terror.

Led on in a trance, I am introduced by her to the director, who is excitable and flamboyant. This is not a world I know at all. I am definitely out of my element.

"It is a great pleasure to meet you," he says, bowing deeply and kissing my hand. I feel my face redden and my throat close. "We haven't much time."

"B-but where's the other girl?" I ask querulously.

"She is sick." He smiles. "You will be our Clara tonight."

I freeze and stare at my mother.

"You'll be fine," she tells me. Then, with more emphasis, "You'll be fine."

"*Eh bien*," the director says, clapping his hands together quickly. "Let's get you into your costume and show you what to do."

The next thing I know, I am whisked off to the side of the stage and squeezed into a starched Victorian outfit, a white silk dress with buttons all the way down the back and a big bow. Someone pulls some white tights onto my legs and puts a pair of white satin ballet shoes in front of me to slip my feet into. My mother brushes out my long blond hair.

"Do I have to, Mom?" I cry, finding my voice at last.

"What, now you want me to take you home? Dressed like this?" she says. "Keep still."

When she is done, and I am—to my mind—looking my ugliest with my ears sticking out, she places a large turquoise bow on top of my head, scraping my scalp with the comb.

Beyond the thick drapes, I can hear the orchestra tuning up. People are moving around, finding their seats and looking forward to the evening's performance. How many people are out there? I wonder, wringing my hands. Oh my God, I've got to go out onto that stage and face them!

The dancers I saw stretching earlier rush past me in a flurry of gauze and satin. The music strikes up and they are on, performing a short opening ballet by Prokofiev.

Now that they have all gone, my mother and I are left standing alone.

"Okay now, honey, just as soon as they are finished it is your turn," she whispers in my ear.

"B-but I don't know what to do!" I say, still looking around hopefully for the girl who does.

"It's okay, the choreographer is going to show you during the intermission."

He is called "Monsieur," and when the opening ballet has ended and the dancers have filed off he takes my hand and leads me quietly onto the dark and heavily curtained stage. Monsieur is a fabulous creature, like a bronze statue of a ballet dancer, muscular and demonstrative, his Frenchness oozing out of him. I feel like I'm on the caboose of a train that is moving so fast I can't get off.

Beyond the drapes, I can still hear the audience coughing and talking, moving about, stretching their legs and buying refreshments. Within a matter of minutes, there will no longer be the comfort of a red velvet barrier between them and me. With the pull of a rope, I shall be fully exposed.

"*Et voilà, ma chérie,* you come on here and you walk over there and then you bow deeply to the audience *comme ça,*" the choreographer tells me hastily, as I watch his steps and listen to his timed claps, desperately trying to take it all in.

"*Eh bien,* then you curtsy like this, and then make a turn and walk over to this side. You take Alicia Alonso's hand and you lead her onto the stage. I want you to walk with her like this, toes pointed, prancing almost, but not too fast. When you have brought her to her mark—see *ici*, the red dot on the stage floor—I want you to take a long walk around her and bow again deeply, before moving to one side and sitting here, *voilà*, to watch the rest of the ballet. *Comprends?* Do you understand?"

He might as well have asked me to recite the Gettysburg Address. My brain is aching with all I have to remember. I stand dumbstruck in the middle of the wooden floor, my entire body vibrating with fear. Just when I think my head will explode with the steps and the music and the bow and the perfectly timed moves—I suddenly realize what he just said.

Grabbing his arm, I ask, "I have to lead Miss Alonso out?"

"Yes, *chérie*," he whispers. "Of course, my darling. *Elle est aveugle.* She is, how you say? 'Blind.'"

He rushes off the stage in a flourish as the overture strikes up beyond the drapes. I stand there, staring after him, my mouth open. "Blind? Miss Alonso? She can't be! Holy banana cake!"

My knees are barely able to support my weight. Steadying myself in the darkness in the center of the stage, I wait for my signal. After what seems like an eternity, Monsieur waves a hand and the curtains fly open.

Alone in the spotlight, I swallow but find no saliva in my mouth. I blink into the glare of the lights but can make out only the first two rows of the audience; the area beyond is shrouded in blackness.

I can feel the expectation rolling in waves from the crowd. I can hear each chord being played by the musicians in the orchestra pit a few feet beneath me. There is so much energy in the air that I feel infused with its power, suddenly able to do everything I have been sent out to do. Every fiber of my being surges with the electricity of the moment.

Staring down at my white satin feet, I force myself to remember the steps Monsieur taught me. As I do so, Alicia Alonso, the goddess of my childhood adoration, appears silently at the back of the stage. She stands like a tree in the half-light, head bowed, hands clasped tightly together, listening to every note and to the sound of the music. Her legs and arms are willowy, and she exudes a heady mix of perfume and makeup. Her black hair is scraped back so tight on the top of her head that it pulls on her eyes. She looks like the most exquisite bird I have ever seen.

Somehow I find myself moving toward her as I was told, toes pointed, moving round in an arc to the back of the stage. As I reach her, she unfurls her impossibly long neck and her face comes alive with beauty and light.

I place my small hand in hers as the music rises from the orchestra like a harmonious flock of birds. The energy coming off her skin feels like a live electric wire and makes me jump physically. As the music rises, I feel her entire body lift up, as if she is weightless. My hand grips hers, for I fear that if I move it, she might float away.

Squeezing my hand back, Miss Alonso whispers, "It's all right, daahling, don't be afraid. You'll be magnificent."

As a burst of music wakes me from my reverie, she snaps an instruction at me. "Now!" she says, and tugs at my hand to lead her onto the stage. Even though I am supposed to be leading her, it is she who is leading me. Somehow her presence at my side infuses me with confidence. I am suddenly the most graceful ballet dancer in the world, just by being at her side.

Right foot, no, left foot first. Toes pointed, almost prancing, I remind myself, left arm out, fingers relaxed. And smile. I am pointing my toes that much better, and holding myself with more poise. For a moment, I become her, about to perform the dance of my life.

As if by magic, we float to our designated place, a spotlight following us wherever we go. She bows her head and adopts the stance she needs to prepare herself for her next move. I do exactly as I have been told and curtsy deeply to her. It is all I can do to stop myself from kissing her beautiful feet. Instead, I sweep round the stage to take my seat on a small stump to watch the "Dance of the Sugar Plum Fairy," toes pointed, posture perfect.

No sooner do I reach the stump than my legs start to shake. I can't imagine how they held me up for so long. The adrenaline rush over, I am only just able to sit without collapsing into a crumpled heap of white satin. My knees are knocking so violently that I feel sure people will see them. Placing a hand on each kneecap to settle them only makes my arms vibrate too. Watching the beautiful ballet unfold before me, I can't help but wonder what I am supposed to do next.

Trying to stay calm, my hands still firmly on my kneecaps, I look around for my mother. Nobody told me what I do now, I cry inwardly. When do I stand up? Do I just sit here? Or do I have to lead Miss Alonso back?

Despite my concerns, I am enraptured by the magical ballerina moving so fearlessly back and forth across the stage in front of me. I can hardly believe I am there, breathing the same air. I could sit motionless on that stage for the rest of my life, watching Alicia Alonso dance. She is dancing for me. For Clara.

Catching a glimpse of my mother in the wings, I am relieved to see she is smiling too. Mommy, my lips silently mouth. What do I do next? But she doesn't read my pleading eyes.

My gaze is dragged back to Alicia Alonso. She is dancing without fear, with complete trust that those around her will not let her down. How can she do it? How can she throw herself so forcefully into the arms of her leading man and be twirled high above his head, or pirouette so perilously close to the edge of the stage, when she is able to see little more than shadows?

The music seems to lift her, physically and emotionally, beyond her blindness. She is outside of herself somehow, lost to the sensation of dance. Her eyes may be ineffective for sight, but they radiate pure joy. Watching her, I think to myself: I know that feeling. I feel the same way.

Then all too suddenly, the music is over. Its vibration lingers in the air for a moment before fading to silence. The dancers stand like statues in the spotlights.

Applause roars like a sea in my ears. The air is now charged with a new electricity, that of adulation. As everyone claps madly, I soak up the tremendous energy while each member of the chorus walks to the front of the stage and graciously takes a bow, accepts the outpouring of praise. But I am lost. What do I do now? When am I supposed to get up? When am I supposed to take my bow?

Sitting there as prettily as I can, looking across at my mother, who is clapping wildly too, I try without success to elicit a signal from her as to when I should get up to take my bow. Should I wait till the next group, perhaps? I look in the wings for Monsieur, the director of the ballet, but

first steps

he is nowhere to be seen. The last line of the chorus takes their final bow and runs off the stage. It is only me and Alicia Alonzo and the premier dancer left on the stage. I'm panicked, frozen, lost as to what to do next. I can't possibly go now, I think, as Alicia and the male lead bow to a standing ovation.

I can see Alicia's chest rising and falling under her leotard as she tries to catch her breath. Those in the front row of the audience step up and throw long-stemmed roses at her. A single perfect rosebud lands near my feet and I cradle it in my hand. This must be my cue to take my bow.

I slowly rise, placing one foot in front of the other just like the prima ballerina. Stepping forward, I join the two stars at the front of the stage and begin my curtsy.

Alicia Alonso senses my presence. She smiles down at me, and hands me a rose. *"Bravo,"* she says, and kisses me on the cheek.

A cheer goes up from the crowd as I reach out and take it. A whole new roar of applause comes like a wave, enveloping me. I think to myself, Is that for me? For a moment, I am completely overwhelmed.

I glance toward the wings, beaming, and see the stage manager waving his hands about like a wild man, his face twisted into a grotesque mask, slapping his thighs repeatedly and yelling something at me. He must be pleased with my performance; after all, I did exactly as I was told. Behind him stands my mother, laughing openly. Emboldened by her expression of pride and joy, I stay right where I am, curtsying from the waist repeatedly to the crowd.

I flounce off the stage like the ballerina I now know I want to become. Running, grinning, crying, I fly into the open arms of my mother, the sound of applause still lapping against my ears.

"What were you thinking?" the stage manager screams at me as soon as my mother releases me from her embrace. "You weren't supposed to take a bow with *Madame!*"

My mother rounds on him. "Oh, for Christ's sake!" she yells. "You only gave the child five minutes to learn the whole routine! What do you expect?"

"Nobody told me what to do at the end," I pipe up anxiously.

My mother takes my hand and we walk past the stage manager. She shoots him a smile and says, "Get ahold of yourself. The audience loved her."

D ancing gave me something I very much needed as a child, especially as I was never going to excel academically. It allowed me to overcome my physical awkwardness as a little girl.

It wasn't a question of confidence; I had that in spades. My mother always told people proudly, "Goldie doesn't know a stranger," because whenever anyone came to our house I'd march straight up to them and kiss them.

And I always knew what I would become. "Goldie will dance, that is what Goldie will do," Mom would announce if anyone asked her what I would do when I grew up. She shared my unshaken belief in my life's path.

I owe so much of who I am to my dancing. I learned about timing and personal discipline. I learned about my own physicality. I pushed the limits of what I could or could not do. Through rigorous exercise in my early years I developed muscles, posture and, most important, I learned what it is to sweat.

When I danced, I felt absolutely grounded, at the peak of my physical strength. The music went right through me. It changed the way I felt about myself. It lifted my heart and made me want to fly through the air, slicing and dicing it all around me. That's what I lived for. That's what gave me everything. I was no longer disabled by my fear of being different, being out of step. Just as Alicia Alonso rose above her disability, so did I.

If we can give our children something other than a dependence on their social or academic life, we allow them to own something precious that is entirely their own. It can be dance or sport or art or singing or photography or anything that they can find themselves in. By giving them something to excel in and taking them away from the daunting peer group pressure of the playground, they can transcend the everyday slings and arrows of childhood.

For me, dancing provided a physical euphoria that nothing else would ever touch. Anything after that felt like a cheap trick. To push yourself to the physical and mental limits, to ask yourself to deliver more than you think you possibly can and to come through, is the greatest high there is.

compassion

*If we can cultivate compassion for those who have
hurt us, we have the possibility of over-
coming our anger, pain and fear.
Compassion is a great medicine.*

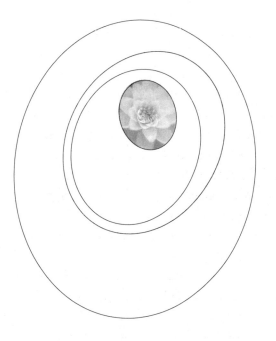

I can hear the tiny silver bells adorning my mother's cone-shaped hat tinkle each time she moves around the kitchen. Mouthwatering aromas fill the air, and the windows are steamed with cooking. It is Christmas Eve, 1956, that most magical of nights, and I am eleven years old.

"Goldie, honey, light the candles," Mom calls through the dining-room hatch. To my older sister, she says, "Patti, dear, would you please come in here and help carry something out?"

Christmas at our house is always special. Overlooking her Jewish heritage for this particular holiday, my mother relishes any excuse to have a party. The house is full of people, and, as usual, she is cooking up a storm. On her head is this year's creation, a homemade red felt hat with a strap under her neck and covered with dozens of hand-sewn-on bells.

Patti wanders through from the kitchen with a dish of scalloped potatoes to add to a dining-room table already groaning with vegetables, meats and different kinds of bread. In pride of place stands my mother's famous green dessert made with lime Jell-O and nuts. I light the candles and gaze happily into their flickering light, my stomach rumbling at the sight of my mother's huge ham, baked and honey-basted, bubbling with brown sugar and decorated with pineapples, cherries and cloves that look like perfect flowers.

I always want Christmas to be like this, but I know things are about to change. Patti, who is eight years older than me, is going off to college soon, and this will be the last Christmas I can really be a child. I am not ready to take the baton. I so want to remain the little girl, the funny, goofy, innocent little sister. I dread the idea of suddenly being older, which means to me that very soon Christmas would mean only having my friends over for the festivities on Christmas Eve. As much as I love David and Jimmy Fisher and Jean Lynn, the prospect of having just them in the house seems dull and empty. No matter how much I try to feel the excitement of this Christmas, something already feels strange.

My daddy is out working—he is always out working—playing his violin at a Christmas party for President Eisenhower in the White House. When he comes home late, he'll sneak in and put the same present that he buys my mother every year under the tree—a bottle of Shocking, a perfume by Schiaparelli, picked up just as the shops are closing on Christmas Eve.

Patti, whom I worship with her flaming hair, pinched-in waist and beautiful eyes, puts Frank Sinatra on the record player. The living room is filled with light and laughter as her friends gather round and share animated conversation. I love my sister's girlfriends. I love to watch them walk into our house one by one, covered in snow, holding gifts and stamping their feet. They peel off their overcoats to reveal pencil-straight skirts and matching sweater sets, perfect bobbed hair, perfect red lips. They all have beautiful hair, and they smell so good. Most impressive of all, they have breasts, when all I have are two little buds.

Come on now, boys," Mom cries as she emerges from the kitchen wiping her hands, "it's time to get the tree in."

Several of Patti's male friends put down their glasses of eggnog and go out on the front porch noisily to lift it up onto their shoulders and bring it in.

"Where do you want it this year, Mrs. Hawn?" one of them asks.

"Over in the corner by the side door, honey." Mom points. "Then, in the new year, I can just toss it out, and the hell with it."

Everyone pitches in, pulling and tugging and dragging the huge tree into the house, its thick, scented arms weighed down with snow.

"And, heave!" one of the boys shouts. "Heave!"

In no time at all, the tree is screwed into its holder and standing tall, its tip scraping the ceiling. Laughing like children, everyone gathers around to trim the tree, throwing sparkling strands of tinsel all over it.

I put the tinsel on strand by strand—my favorite part . . . my face buried deep in the tree's intoxicating needles that remind me of Christmases past, I peel each strand off and lay it on the floor, ready to replace it perfectly when the time comes.

Mom drags in a big old box full of the ornaments she and Daddy have had forever, each one with its own story.

"This was our first," she tells me, holding up a pretty glass bauble. "This was the one when we ran the boarding house on Thirteenth Street." One by one, we put them on the tree.

"There!" Mom cries with delight, as we all stand back to admire our handiwork and Dan, my sister's handsome friend, switches on the lights.

I gaze up in awe. I love the sparkly things, the glass baubles and the red and gold balls. But, best of all, I love the way the lights change the color of the room. Looking around, I see them reflected in the faces and eyes of everyone I know and love. All is right with my world.

Suddenly, the tree shudders, as if it is about to sneeze, and then topples headlong toward us all, crashing spectacularly to the floor.

"For Christ's sake, what was that?" Mom growls as we all gasp.

Someone forgot to lock the side door, and Jean Lynn's brother, Joey, barrels in, knocking the tree down in the process.

Everyone screams with laughter. "All right, now, let's get started over again," Mom laughs. Seeing Joey's red face, she says, "Okay, Joe. Lets have some eggnog."

Everyone laughs, and Patti's friends get the giggles with Joey while the boys hoist the tree back up. Before we can say Santa Claus, it is decorated perfectly again, the door locked securely behind it. People help themselves to the food my mother has so lovingly prepared, and someone puts on another Christmas carol.

"Deck the halls with boughs of holly . . ." I hear its familiar words and feel a lump in my throat.

Not wanting to let this piece of my childhood go for anything, I give in to the calling to go to bed early, while the party is at its peak. If I go to my room now, I can lie in bed and fall asleep listening to the sounds of music and laughter and Christmas below.

I make my way around the room, kissing Mom and Patti and her friends and our neighbors good night. Kissing, kissing everyone; always loving to be kissed back.

"Good night, Goldie. Do you still believe in Santa Claus?"

"Oh yes!"

"Are you ready for Christmas, Goldie?"

"Yes, yes, I'm so excited."

"Good night, Mommy."

"Well, off you go to bed now, honey. And, before you know it, Santa will be here."

I don't really believe in Santa Claus anymore, but I pretend to because I still want to play the surprised little Goldie in the morning. I want to come down and cry "Oh!" when I see my gifts piled up under the tree, the brightly colored Christmas lights illuminating the shiny wrapping paper.

I walk up the stairs slowly, step by step, looking back at all our friends and the food and the noise. This is such a special Christmas Eve; I can feel that, and I never want it to end. Taking another step, my fingers on the banister, I can't wait for the morning, when I wake up to a sleeping house and creep out of my bedroom. Taking my seat halfway down the stairs, I will sit and peer through the balusters at the pretty lights shining on the walls, filling the living room with an ethereal glow. With just the flick of my head, I will be able to see the tree itself, not just its glow, and see the gifts under it for the first time. But first, I savor the delicious sense of anticipation, wanting to hang on to the moment for as long as I can.

Reaching my little green room at the top of the stairs, I slip off my clothes and pull on my nightie. I tuck my favorite toy, a small turquoise dog, under his covers on the chair next to the bed. Then I slide into my own private envelope of crisp white sheets. Nobody has sheets like Mom's. She starches them and then hangs them out to dry in the cold eastern air. They feel cool and clean against my skin.

Sure enough, I lie awake for a while, watching the snow falling onto

43

compassion

the flat roof outside my window. Happily, I think of the little squirrels I love to watch, tucked up in the hollows of the oak trees, their winter hoard of nuts safely stored away.

I hear the chatter and the din from below, and I try to quell my tingling anticipation of the morning. Gradually, my eyelids grow heavy and my excitement abates. Finally, I drift off to sleep.

I awaken with a start, and for a moment I don't know where I am. "Wh-what?"

Shaking my head of sleep, I realize that someone is very close to me in the semidarkness, kneeling by the side of my bed.

The dark silhouette of a man is framed by the hallway landing light. He has slid his hands into my soft, warm bed and is fondling the new bumps on my chest. The presence of his cold fingers against my skin frightens me. Scarier still is when he moves farther down toward my groin.

"Don't! What are you doing? Stop it! Get out of here!" I cry, trying to push his hands away with both of mine. Then, "Wh-who are you?"

Sitting up and blinking in the half-light, I can just make out the face of one of Patti's school friends, a twenty-year-old guy I've known almost all my life.

"I'm just wishing you Merry Christmas, Goldie," he whispers, forcing his hands back under the covers. The smell of beer and cigarettes on his breath makes me feel sick.

"Don't! You shouldn't be here!" I splutter, squirming under his wandering hands. "Get away, get away from me."

He closes his eyes and rolls his head back on his neck and starts to moan softly.

Very frightened by his intensity, I cry out, as loud as I can, "Mom! Mommy! Help! Help me!" but no one answers.

Startled, the young man jumps to his feet. He fiddles with his clothing, then flies down the stairs and out the front door, slamming it shut behind him. In sudden urgent need of my mother, I leap out of bed. Standing at the top of the stairs, I call for her breathlessly. "Mommy! Mommy!"

One of the guests hears me and calls my mother. I look down through the balusters to see her smiling up at me from the foot of the stairs, my sister a few steps behind.

"Yes, Goldie, what is it?" Mom asks, her brow furrowing when she sees the expression on my face.

"Mommy," I wail, my face crumpling. "There was someone in my room, and he was touching me."

All the bustle and noise of the house suddenly seems to freeze. Everyone stops talking, and all I can hear is "Here Comes Santa Claus" playing merrily on the record player. My mother makes the first move. In moments, she is up those stairs, followed closely by Patti and several friends. I run back into my bedroom and hide under the covers, crying, as they come in and snap on the light.

"What happened, Goldie? Tell me what happened," my mother says, her face strange.

"He came into my room and he put his hands under my nightie and he touched me," I explain, frightened by the expressions on their faces.

"Where? Where did he touch you?"

Embarrassed, I point. "Here and here."

"Then what?"

"Well, I screamed and he ran off and I jumped out of bed."

Frank, one of Patti's male friends, suddenly points to a wet stain on the rug next to my bed. "Look at that!" he hisses. "The son of a bitch!"

Behind my mother, I see Patti clamp her hand over her mouth in shock as Frank turns red with rage. "Who was it, Goldie? Who did this?" he asks through gritted teeth. I have never seen anyone so angry in my life.

When I tell him, Frank rushes from the room and out the front door. The look of betrayal and incredulity on Patti's face scares me. I hear the sound of others running down the quiet street where we live, shouting the boy's name.

I sit there nodding on my little bed, trembling. An unknown fear, a strange sense of violation, fills me. I no longer feel safe.

My mother remains extremely calm. She takes me firmly by the shoulders and tells me to lie back down. In an urgent tone I've never

45

compassion

heard before, she banishes everyone else from the room. Downstairs, I can hear the party breaking up as people speak in whispers or disappear off to their own homes.

"Goldie, listen to me. That boy was sick. He's gone now. You're okay, that's all that matters. Turn over now, honey, and let me tickle your back. Now, go back to sleep, and, before you know it, Christmas will be here."

All I cared about was that my mom was there and everything was going to be fine because she said so.

She strokes my skin in rhythmic circles, rubbing and patting, rubbing and patting, just as I like it, and I begin to float off to the land of dreams, where nothing unpleasant ever happens.

For a moment, in my half sleep, I struggle with a restless thought.

"Mommy, are you still there?" I ask her, lifting my head to make sure she's still there.

"Yes, honey, I'm still here."

Sleep overcomes me and I drift away.

The next morning, I wake at five o'clock and lie in bed, staring up at the ceiling. A dark thought slides through my mind. Did something strange happen last night, or did I just dream it? I can't seem to remember. Looking out the window, I see giant flakes of snow softly bumping into one another beyond the glass. There is the oak tree, and there is the roof of the living room. But something has changed.

With a sudden rush of blood to my head, I sit bolt upright in bed. "It's Christmas!"

I try to imagine the day I'm about to have with Mommy and Daddy and Patti. I conjure up an image of the comforting rituals of Christmas with the family all around. I know that for the rest of the day, everyone will treat me like the little girl I desperately want to remain, giving me presents and being especially kind. Yet something inside doesn't feel quite so joyful.

Slipping out of bed as quietly as I can, and grabbing my turquoise dog, I pull on my bathrobe and tiptoe barefoot down the hallway toward the stairs. Settling on a step in the heavy silence of the sleeping house, I stare down at the Christmas tree lights in the living room, admiring the way their reflection colors the walls. It is, for me, the most magical moment of this, the most magical morning of the year.

Sitting in the chill air of the stairwell, spellbound with little-girl wonder for one last time, I face the same dilemma I face every year. Which color do I like the best? Is it the deep blue or the orange or one of the reds? Usually, I choose the yellow, but for some reason I don't feel like yellow this Christmas.

Whispering into the soft ear of my toy dog, I tell him sadly, "This year, I don't like any of them more than the rest. This year, I like all of them the best."

I t is proven that the more you remind yourself of a bad experience, the more damaging it can be because it imprints that experience indelibly on your mind and creates a new reality. Like wiggling a bad tooth with the tip of your tongue.

If you can tell yourself, Oh, forget about it, and if you actually can forget about it, then I believe you may be better off, because your mind doesn't store that memory and embellish it. This is one of the functions of the brain. With positive input, it creates new neural pathways that can alter your perception of reality.

Instinctively, my mother somehow knew this. Instead of using the terms "abuse" or "molestation"—words that would have lodged in my brain like a maggot—she explained to me that this young man was unwell in his own mind. I was never made to feel dirty, or that I had done anything wrong. I believed what my mother told me about his being sick, and I even felt a modicum of compassion for him.

If, as parents, we can assure our children that things are all right, if we don't constantly revisit a bad experience or are not overheard telling others about it, then it reassures our children and lets them know that there is no point dwelling on it.

That is not to say that there aren't some terrible things that can happen that inform our relationships, imprinting on how we feel about ourselves and others. Clearly, it is important to seek help in those instances—especially in the case of sexual assault—to try to understand what has happened and how it has affected the victim. So many women are victimized and never talk about it because they feel so ashamed.

To be afraid or ashamed is to lock the door on the experience. If we lock the door, then the psyche represses feelings, and, later, symptoms will begin to emerge. Sometimes, as time goes on, we can end up behaving in ways that we don't like, because we are allowing fears to keep us from having healthy, satisfying relationships. The fear of opening up that door is usually much greater than what lies behind it.

My mother opened that door immediately, before I was able to distort this event because of fear or failure to understand what happened to me. I learned to forgive by seeing my mother handle this, by putting my fears to rest. As a consequence, although this experience was horribly frightening, although it marked the end of my childhood, the end of my innocence, in many ways, it never marred me to the point that later I shied away from a man's touch, or had ugly flashbacks of being molested as a child. I never lost my trust in the male sex.

What is important here is how we attend to our children, and how we show our feelings. Our responses directly affect how our children's experiences are imprinted. This episode and its aftermath were such an important aspect of my growth in terms of sexual energy and understanding, and I will forever be grateful for the way it were handled.

The key is not to let these things fester. Worst of all, don't revel in being a victim. Don't become comfortable in your misery. Take back control. You may not be able to change what happened, but you can change your perception of it. All you need is the intention, and you have the power to change. Face up to what happened, admit it and try to move on. Through understanding, try to forgive not only yourself but the person who did this to you. This is truly another path to happiness.

postcard

My mother and I slip out of our cab on our way back from my dance class and walk up the narrow path to the front door. "What in the world is that noise?" Mom asks, stopping in her tracks and tilting her head to listen.

I can hear it now: a loud, white noise coming from somewhere deep inside our house. Running to the porch, I find Nixi cowering on the doorstep, ears flat. Flinging the door open, we rush inside. The house is in darkness, but the noise drones on from the kitchen.

"Rut? Rutledge? Is that you?" my mother calls.

"In here," my father yells from the back room.

We rush through the house and find him sitting in his big mohair armchair with a scotch in his hand, his customary TV tray by his side, and a strange smile on his face. A single lamp illuminates the room.

"What in the hell are you doing?" Mom asks. Like me, she stares wide-eyed at the long piece of plastic hose that Daddy is sitting in front of, legs crossed elegantly like a seventeenth-century count.

Following its course, I hurry into the kitchen to find the hose connected to the Electrolux vacuum cleaner, which is carefully positioned in front of the stove. All four gas burners are on, and there is some strange sort of contraption suspended over them, sucking the heat into the hose, along its length, right to Daddy's stocking feet. Mom has followed me, and, like me, her mouth drops open. Together, we wander back in to stare at Daddy.

"Have you seen our heating bill?" Daddy asks, waving a piece of paper in his hand. "I came up with a much cheaper method of heating the house."

"Are you completely insane?" my mother shrieks. Coming to her senses, she rushes back to the stove and switches off the gas. Hurrying back to confront my father, she barks, "Are you trying to blow us all up?"

I look up at her, confused for a moment, and then back at Daddy. His socks are peeled halfway off his feet as usual, to air them while he takes a break. It is six o'clock, and he can't have been in long from his day at work.

On his little TV table is his customary glass of bourbon, a jar of cut horseradish and bottles of A.1. and Worcestershire sauce. Like some fabulous fop, he embarks on an elaborate nightly ritual like another man might drink a martini with an olive.

First, he takes the bottle of Worcestershire sauce, inhales the contents deeply, puts it down. Then, he picks up the bottle of A.1. sauce and does the same. Finally, the horseradish, which blasts up his nostrils and makes his eyes water so much that only a sip of bourbon will clear things up. This is his way of unwinding. I don't think this is weird at all; I imagine this is what all fathers do.

"Rut? Did you hear me?" Mom asks, hands on her hips. "I said, 'Are you crazy or what?'"

"Just trying to save you some money, Laura," Daddy says, without looking up at her.

"Oh, for Christ's sake!"

Mom hurries back into the kitchen to dismantle the rest of Daddy's latest invention. She rattles around in there for almost an hour, cursing to herself all the while, noisily preparing supper. Wandering in, I sit at the table watching her, mesmerized by her hardworking hands holding a wooden spoon, beating and folding and mixing something. Nobody cooks like my mom. Nobody has better hands. She talks with her hands; she kneads with her hands; she loves with her hands.

Sitting at the table when dinner is ready, we bow our

heads and close our eyes while I say grace: "God is great. God is good. Thank you, God, for this food."

Before I open my eyes again, I inhale and try to guess what Mom has made. It might be borscht or her delicious brisket with French onion soup, chopped liver or chicken with dumplings, Hungarian goulash or noodles with cottage cheese.

"Thanks, Sergeant," Dad says, giving Mom a mock salute as she serves him his plateful. His mouth full, he begins to regale us with tales of his evening the night before. "President Kennedy and his wife hosted a dinner for King Saud of Saudi Arabia last night, and we played Strauss while the king danced all around the room in a long dress."

I laugh and laugh at his stories, rocking back on my chair. My mother, in spite of herself, has to crack a smile too.

Clearing away the dishes, she throws a comment over her shoulder, "By the way, did you go to the store last night and rearrange my show window?" Her eyebrows arched in suspicion.

"Yes, I did." My father grins, winking at me across the table. "I thought it needed my artistic touch."

"I spent half the day putting it back to normal, Rut."

"Normal? What's that?" my dad asks.

Daddy and Mommy are two separate people to me. Apples and oranges. I spend time either with one or with the other, rarely together. Whenever she rants at him in one of their one-sided arguments, he flicks the switch on the vacuum cleaner to drown her out. Once, when they were arguing while wallpapering the bathroom, he recorded every word of it, to play back to her later. He was hilarious. I helped Mom clear the table while Dad went upstairs to change into his tuxedo as he did almost every night, to play at parties thrown by various dignitaries in Washington, D.C. I was awakened late that night to the smell of hush puppies and chili-mac. I can just see my dad in the kitchen now, preparing his late-night snack in his tuxedo and the white blouse he borrowed from my mother because his white tuxedo shirt was dirty. I closed my eyes and laughed myself to sleep. There's nobody like him, I thought to myself, nobody like him in the whole world.

In the morning, I am the first up to fix eggs and cream cheese before school. The first thing I see as I come down the stairs is my mother's stuffed pheasant, which always stands on the living-room mantelpiece. It was a wedding present from my mother's eccentric father, Max. As usual, my dad always has the last laugh. He had dressed the pheasant with her glasses, her hairpiece planted firmly on its head. Beside it lay her purse. He had his own little private moment of mirth with his absurd take on life. I always think of that bird as a representation of his humor, his spirit and, yes, his anger. As I'm cooking my eggs, I hear my mother's footsteps coming down the stairs. I wait and listen as she stops and takes in my father's latest creation. I hear her deep and throaty laugh.

This is what Daddy does best. He makes her laugh.

fear

*It is what we don't know that frightens us,
and nothing stifles joy like fear.*

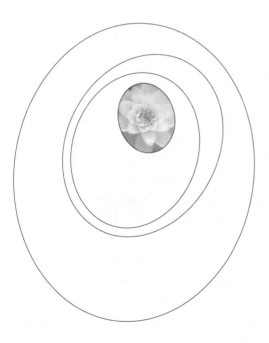

All is well with my world, or so I believe. It is a beautiful sunny day, and I am in the sixth grade at the school that is half a mile from my home in Takoma Park. The name of the town I grew up in derives from an old Indian word meaning "higher up near heaven." I love that. Nothing in my twelve years has ever caused me to doubt its truth. But I am about to learn, in the most graphic way, that death is just a heartbeat away.

I have been practicing my handwriting all morning with my best teacher, Mrs. Volmer. Robust and big-breasted, with perfect brown hair, she has taught me more than any teacher I have ever had. Gripping my pen firmly between the forefinger and thumb of my left hand, my tongue poking out of the corner of my mouth, I carefully draw circles within circles, making perfect loops every time, never allowing my hand to leave the paper.

The only left-hander in my class, I work very hard to hold my pen the way everyone else does. Thank heavens Mrs. Volmer doesn't force me to work with my right hand, or tie my left hand behind my back as some teachers do. Looping and looping, trying hard to keep within the lines, I can't help but feel like I'm dancing.

"Okay, class," she suddenly announces, clapping her hands together to attract our attention, "once you've finished your handwriting practice we're going to the Visual Aids Room to watch a film."

The class is all abuzz, excited about the chance to watch a movie about growing corn or New York City or maybe something about nature. Eager too, I finish my perfect loops, throw my pen into my pencil box and slam down the desk lid.

We all line up like little soldiers and snake our way out of the class. "Quiet down, children. Single file," Mrs. Volmer instructs. I start to do some balancés down the hallway but hear Mrs. Volmer from the back of the line: "Goldie, no dancing, please." Embarrassed, I fall back in step with the rest.

We file on through the cold, dark gymnasium, with its squeaky wooden floor and its bittersweet memories of the maypole dance and the talent show. We wend our way down the stairs to the basement. We call it "the Dungeon."

I scramble for a good seat in the front row and fidget next to my friends, staring up expectantly at the screen.

"Quiet down, now quiet down, kids. Hands in laps."

Mrs. Volmer flicks off the lights, and I whisper to the girl next to me, "I wonder what we're going to see." Staring into the inky blackness, I hear Mrs. Volmer make her way across to the projector, then click it on, and the 16 millimeter film starts running through the machine. Ever since I can remember, I have been scared of the dark. My mother always leaves my bedroom door open every night and the light on in the hallway. Now that there is a little light flickering on the screen, I feel comforted.

Then a bright white light on the screen suddenly illuminates the whole room. It is the face of a huge clock. A booming voice counts backward: "Ten . . . nine . . . eight . . . seven . . . six . . . five . . . four . . . three . . . two . . . one."

Suddenly, an enormous explosion erupts from the screen. The entire room vibrates. "This is what will happen when there is an enemy attack," a voice announces.

My whole being is shaken to the core. I gasp aloud, and press my back hard against the cold metal chair. The sheer noise and vibration level send me into a cataclysmic nosedive of fear.

The camera pans across images of total geological and human devastation. Flying debris. Windows bursting from buildings, flames and thick smoke billowing from the earth. Trees, whole areas of the earth, flattened.

Mothers sobbing, maimed and choking in the wreckage, their babies lying bleeding on the ground. I plug my ears against their agonizing cries.

My heart is pulsing in my throat. I feel dizzy, sick to my stomach. I begin to tremble from head to toe. I am in shock, unable to speak. This isn't a horror movie; this isn't a nightmare. This is real. Or is it? Could this really happen?

Mommy, I cry inside my head, rocking myself backward and forward in my seat. Mommy. I need my mom.

I try not to hear the words of the voice as it goes on to tell me the likelihood of such an apocalypse and presents me with chilling instructions about what I need to do to protect myself. Cringing as if every word were colliding with me physically, I listen to his ominous warnings of blinding flashes of light, flying glass and melting metal. Tighter and tighter, I curl into my body, and when the voice tells me to "Duck and cover" under my chair or school desk, or anywhere I can to save myself, I am already doing it.

Mrs. Volmer snaps the lights back on. My classmates and I sit blinking into the white glare for a moment, waiting for the images to fade. Jumping up, I run to the back of the class.

"I need to go home" is all I can say weakly, clutching my stomach. "I need my mommy. I don't feel so good."

Weighed down with an aching heaviness like gravity, I look up at my teacher, confident that she will see how shattered I am and do something about it. Strangely, she doesn't, which frightens me even more.

"But, Goldie, you never go home for lunch," she says, tilting her head and giving me a curious look.

"I know, but my mom is expecting me," I lie. Can't she see how upset I am?

"But won't Barney miss you?"

I think of Barney, my friend with cerebral palsy whom I have lunch with in the cafeteria every day, but I still need to go home. "I'll see him later," I reply.

"Well, all right, then, but hurry back."

I run up the stairs, push open the door to the gymnasium and tear across it. I rush out into the comforting daylight and head home. Sprinting toward my house, crying, the whole of my body heaving, I pick up the pace with each step. My feet pound the sidewalk as I fly through my neighborhood, past the crossing guard, who smiles at me strangely, wondering why I'm going home.

I can still hear the voice of the film in my head: "To avoid atomic radiation, be sure to use soap to wash it off your skin before it starts to burn." I run faster. I need to talk to my mom.

The voice continues in my ears: "Always remember the flash of an atomic bomb can come at any time. Go to the nearest safe cover. Know where you are to go, or ask an older person to help you. Duck and cover. That flash means act fast. Remember, duck and cover."

All my realities have shifted. Everything looks different. I can suddenly picture my ordinary neighborhood scorched and flattened.

We are all going to die, I tell myself. Of course we're going to die. I mean . . . we live so close to Washington, D.C. They'll drop a bomb and we'll all be dead.

I fly past the old lady who sits in her window and waves at me every morning on my way to school. Does she know that she's going to die? I fly past the man who is always outside mowing or raking his lawn; the boy who walks his dog. Everyone I know is going to die.

Running past them all, ignoring their stares, I turn onto my dead-end street. I run up the steps to my front porch. Nixi is surprised to see me and jumps up, wagging his tail and smiling, so happy I am home.

My next-door neighbor, Mr. Morningstar, is in his bathroom, as usual, looking out. "Goldie Jeanne ate a bean and now she's lean . . ." he begins to say to me, as if nothing is wrong. How can he not know that a bomb is going to drop on us any minute? He is a friend of ex-president Truman's. Maybe he can call him and stop this from happening?

I burst through the front door, which is never locked, and barrel into the empty hallway. Running right to the telephone, I call Mom at work. My hands are shaking so much I can barely rotate the dial.

"Mommy? You have to come home right now."

"What's the matter? Goldie? You're home? Why are you home?"

fear

"Because we're all going to die."

"What? What are you talking about?"

"We're all going to die, Mommy, because of the bomb. I'm so scared."

"What in the world are you talking about, Goldie?" my mother asks insistently.

"I saw a movie at school, and they said we're gonna die from an enemy attack. I ran straight home, Mommy, because I have to see you. Please come home."

"Oh, for Christ's sake! Okay, just let me lock up the store and call a cab."

Throwing my arms around Nixi's neck, I push my face into his black-and-white fur, feeling his chest rise and fall.

Running to the window, I climb on top of the radiator cover, waiting and waiting for the yellow taxi to pull into our driveway. It seems like an eternity. Suddenly, it appears from around the corner, and I am flooded with relief. I watch my mom step out, pay the driver and walk with quick little steps toward the house. She'll have the answers. She'll know what to say to make me feel okay. I run to the door, throw it open, hug her and begin to cry. "Mommy" is all I can manage.

She takes me inside, my arms tight around her waist, sits me in her lap on the sofa and waits for my tears to subside. In between hiccups, which I always get when I cry too hard, I start to tell her about the film. Bit by bit, I gather momentum.

"There were babies screaming and mothers crying, and dead dogs and cows. There was light busting out of windows, and all the buildings were ruined. Then there was this man, this man who said . . ." I try to catch my breath. "There was this man that said we were all going to die, and our skin would be burned away unless we used soap, and . . . and, Mommy, I don't understand." Sobbing, I hug her tighter. "Is Russia really going to bomb us?"

In my mother's inimitable fashion, she shakes her head. "All right now, Goldie Jeanne," she tells me, setting me down on the couch beside her, "we're going to straighten up and fly right here." She gets up and walks over to the bookcase and pulls out an atlas. Sitting down, she opens it on her lap. "Number one, this is Russia. And this is us," she says, pointing to two separate sides of the page. "We are miles and miles apart. If one person presses a button in Russia, it's going to take a long, long time for a bomb to get here. Number two, our bombs are bigger and faster than theirs, and they know that. Do you think the Russians want to be bombed any more than we do?"

I feel such relief. My breathing calms as Mom wipes the tears from my eyes. "Really, Mommy? Really?" I want to believe that she is telling me the truth.

"Yes, really. The fact that we have the same weapons, the fact that nobody wants to die—this is what's protecting us and keeping us safe."

I sit on the couch thinking about what she said, staring at the map. I hear Mom in the kitchen rattling around. I think she's putting on a pot of tea. She always does that to make me feel better. Sweet tea with lemon. When I was sick, she used to sit by my bed and spoon-feed it to me. But I'm a big girl now, sadly. She can no longer spoon-feed me tea. Just as she can no longer keep me from the fear of dying.

When the tea is brewed, I turn around and see my mother through the kitchen door. I watch her dial the telephone and demand to speak to the superintendent of schools.

"Hello, this is Laura Hawn," she says tersely. "My daughter Goldie is sitting here in our house in a terrible state because someone at her school was stupid enough to show her a film today about the A-bomb. I have had to come home from work to calm her down."

Her fury making the veins pulse in her neck, she asks, "What on earth do you hope to achieve by such propaganda? And what in the hell are they supposed to do about it? You are frightening the life out of them. I'd think twice before you show these films to other children!" Then she slams down the receiver.

Despite my mom's assurances, I continue to live in mortal fear of the atomic bomb. Every week in class, we have to perform a duck-and-cover exercise, flashing us back to that horrible experience in the Dungeon. I often skip school.

As the Cold War gains momentum and the propaganda fills our TV screens, ominous-looking sirens are erected on street corners and on the rooftops of every school. I can't even bear to look at them. And each time they begin to wail, I shift into a state of panic. For me, the sound of the siren is the sound of instant death and annihilation.

Even the noise of the firehouse siren sets me off. If I could call the president and ask him if this is the end of the world, I would, but instead I dial the operator.

"Excuse me, but are we having an enemy attack?"

There is silence at the other end of the phone. "Er, no, dear, I don't think so."

Afraid to be on my own, I climb the fence to the Fishers' or to my girlfriend Jean Lynn's house every night after school.

One afternoon, arriving at Jean's, I walk in and throw my school-books on the table, and she rushes out of the kitchen with a wicked smile on her face.

"Hey, look at this!" She grins and shows me an unopened jar of peanut butter. "Okay, who gets to go first?" she says as she unscrews the lid and reveals its shiny, swirly perfection. Satisfying our need to despoil it, we both stick our fingers in and mess it up badly, laughing so hard. Just as Jean goes to find another jar of peanut butter, or—better still—a jar of mayonnaise, the sirens go off.

The jar slips from her fingers and smashes onto the tiled kitchen floor. Shards of glass and globules of peanut butter splatter everywhere. Panic buddies, Jean and I lock eyes, and she runs for the door to her basement.

"Come on, Goldie!" she screams.

We race down the stairs, our feet clattering on the wooden steps, into a dark room filled with old scooters and art projects and caked mud pies we made as small children. In the middle of the room stands a table, piled up with freshly washed clothes and ironing.

"Here! Quick!" Jean cries, throwing me some of her mother's freshly pressed clothes. "Put these on."

I do as I am told, and watch as Jean rips the oilcloth from the table with one swift motion, tumbling the clothes to the floor. "They told us at school that if we cover ourselves in oilcloth, it will protect us from the fallout."

We wrap ourselves furiously as she pulls it over the top of us and we clamber under the table. Lying there together, huddled in the duck-and-cover position, arms over our heads, we look at each other and cry big, fat tears.

"We're going to die! I don't want to die!" we scream at each other, hyping each other into an hysterical state.

"Where's my Nixi? I don't want him to die by himself."

I cry and cry for my dog. I cry for the life I fear I won't have. I cry for the fact that I am never going to grow more than bumps on my chest. I cry over the double wedding Jean and I had planned in Takoma Park. I am so afraid of dying.

Looking at Jean under my arms, I say, through my snot and tears, "I haven't even been kissed yet!" Raising my face to heaven, I cry, "Please, God, let some boy kiss me before I die."

Just then, we hear an airplane fly low overhead, and we both fall quiet. Our eyes are as big as saucers; my fingers grip hers so tight that I can no longer feel them. "Oh my God! Oh my God! This is it!"

I hang my head in prayer and wait for the end.

"Hail Mary, full of grace," I repeat over and over, reciting the lines that I have learned from going to church with Jean Lynn. I have no idea what they mean. Just speaking them comforts me. Unknowingly, I am reciting my first mantra.

Without fear, we cannot evolve. It is a natural human emotion that protects us from harm or even death. It creates something called the "fight-or-flight response," where people either fight or run away. But fear is also one of the most destructive emotions we have. It can quickly manifest into anger. And, as we all know, anger can be poisonous. You must approach your fears with as much truth and courage as you can.

Fight-or-flight is very clearly embedded in us for survival, in the amygdala, a small area in the limbic center of the brain that becomes active only when people are emotionally aroused. It stems from the fight for survival; it keeps us from being annihilated. But fear can also override some of our other capabilities as humans, to live fully in a state of joy.

I once met a man who was a hundred and ten years old and very wise. "What is joy?" I asked him.

He smiled a toothless smile and replied simply, "It is the absence of fear."

I thought, My God, what would my world look like if I had no fear? When you look at that, you think of all the things you are afraid of in your life, and you suddenly realize that you spend so much time defending against them that you have no time to open up to fearlessness, to experience the greater potential of our gift—the wholeness of being human.

When I think about the people who run our world, I cannot help but wonder how much their brains have evolved. Now that we no longer have to kill for food or have to fear being eaten by saber-toothed tigers, we are honor bound to use every aspect of our remarkable evolution. The new brain—the prefrontal cortex that scientists have only recently discovered—has the endless ability to experience a full emotional life, and it is the only brain in the animal kingdom that has the ability to witness itself.

Unless we use that ability to look at ourselves, to rise above our situation and examine it from way up, we are going to get into trouble. In order to know that violence begets violence, that hatred is grown in the petri dish of fear, we must understand the ravages of anger and fear. Fear-based actions never end up well.

People get angry because they feel out of control. They are lost, they feel powerless, and so they lash out. Paranoia and polarization set in. If we can eliminate the negative emotions attached to fear—not necessarily the fear itself—if we can cultivate compassion and understand the root of our fear, then the experience itself will not control us.

Looking for answers to my own fear, I turned to God to try to find a sense of place, peace of mind and the nurturing of an inner life. I had such a sense of longing for a connection to the vastness. I used to look at the moon tangled in the trees outside my window and feel this incredible space and time in the universe.

Each night before I went to sleep, I read aloud the Twenty-third Psalm from a Bible an aunt gave me. "Yea, though I walk through the valley of the shadow of death, I will fear no evil: for thou art with me; thy rod and thy staff they comfort me." These words gave me immense solace, to know that there was a continuation of life, that death was nothing to fear.

From the time of the Cold War, I actively sought a spiritual life. It was this that helped me modulate to the next level of my being. It was one of the greatest teachers I ever had. I developed an inner yearning and a deep need to be grounded in some sort of faith. That need has continued to shape my entire life.

postcard

My eyes are too big, my nose is too flat, my ears stick out, my mouth is too big and my face is too small. The only thing I really like about myself is my hair. My body is as thin as a clarinet, and my ankles are so skinny that I wear two pairs of bobby socks because I don't want anybody to see how thin they are.

"The trouble is," I tell Nixi as I grimace into the bathroom mirror each night, "I just don't look like the other girls." Nixi licks my hand devotedly and thumps his tail on the floor to show me he doesn't care.

I can't say what exactly separates me from the rest of my classmates, but I just feel different—out of step somehow. I sometimes wish I could blend better with the other girls, who form tight cliques and pride themselves on how they look.

When I'm not practicing or rehearsing ballet, I go to the dances at the church every Friday night. Sneaking off to the bathroom, I stuff my double-A bra with lamb's wool that I use to pad my toe shoes, to make my breasts look bigger.

Every time a slow tune comes on, I wait around on the perimeter of the dance floor, hopeful that I might be asked, but when I realize I won't I find my way to the bathroom to put on more pink frosted lipstick and lift my ponytail higher. Unfortunately, the only thing I can see is my ears sticking out. If only I had some chewing gum, I could paste them back to the side of my head.

How can I stop looking so much like a ballerina? I groan inwardly as I grimace at my reflection.

Forgetting my childish dreams to become Alicia Alonso as I struggle with thornier issues of teenage hormones, I try in vain to slouch like the other girls in school, who all seem to walk around in groups, giggling, whispering secrets I can only guess.

At thirteen, I see my naturally ramrod-straight spine as one of the reasons for my exclusion from their cliques. It defines me as a dancer, the girl who can never come for tea or go out because her mother is always making her attend classes or rehearsals or theatrical productions.

I also hate my name. From as far back as I can remember, everyone has teased me about it. "Goldie-locks," they call across the playground. "Goldeeeeee-locks!"

I come home in tears and tell my mother, "I'm going to change my name to Jeanne. Nobody can tease me for being Jeanne."

My mother looks at me sternly over a bubbling pot of matzo ball soup on the stove. "I called you Goldie after the woman who meant most to me in my life," she reminds me. "I also gave you that name because I knew nobody would ever forget it. You mark my words, young lady, someday you'll thank me for it."

Now I am at the seventh-grade dance, and everyone seems to have forgotten my name. Not one boy has asked me to be his partner despite my attempts to dazzle them with my solo improvisational dancing. I can't understand it. I know I'm a good dancer. I'm just not the girl that anybody wants to be with.

Hiding in the bathroom as usual, I feel ugly and unloved. I poke out my tongue at my reflection, and pout sullenly as it pokes back.

Even David Fisher doesn't need me anymore. His first set of teeth finally fell out and the new ones grew in, and he is now understood by everyone. My translation skills are now redundant, even at Gifford's ice-cream parlor, where we go on weekends to eat Swiss chocolate sundaes with marshmallows.

David's brother, Jimmy, now seems to get the biggest kick out of me, by making me the butt of his practical jokes. Most recently, he made me stand on our street corner and call out repeatedly for an imaginary dog he told me was missing.

"Peeeeeee-nis!" I yelled, just as I was told. "Peeeeeee-nis!"

He laughed so hard the bubble he was blowing with bright

pink gum burst all over my hair. My mother was furious, and she had to cut great chunks of it out.

Anyway, I don't need David and Jimmy Fisher. Not when I have such an aching crush on a dark-haired Jewish boy at school named Ronnie Morgan. He has big, soupy black eyes and a full mouth, and he is so cool. My heart pounds every time I see him.

Mom has made me a beautiful green velvet skirt for the dance, full with crinoline, and a cream blouse. I know I'll never have a better chance of snaring Ronnie Morgan than I do tonight. Sadly, he doesn't even seem to know that I exist.

Standing alone with the rest of the wallflowers at the end of the evening, watching and waiting, I pray that at least one boy will ask me to dance. I want to grow up. I want boys to like me. I want to feel part of the crowd.

I nearly die of embarrassment when one boy yells across the dance floor, "I know what you have in your bra, Goldie Hawn, and you should be ashamed of yourself!"

"If I wasn't such a nice girl," I yell back, "I'd show you."

I am lying through my teeth. I can feel the sweat dripping from my armpits soaking my bra. I want to run and hide, but instead I laugh and twirl around, spinning my green velvet skirt, lifting the crinoline that in the privacy of my bedroom I secretly wear as a veil when I play at being a bride.

I nearly die a second time when I see Ronnie Morgan walking in my direction. Oh no! Is he going to ask me to dance? I think.

"Would you like a piece of cake, Goldie?" Ronnie asks, a glint in his eye.

I hardly dare hope the glint is for me, that maybe this is the moment I've been yearning for alone in my room at night. "Yes, please, Ronnie," I manage, flashing him my biggest smile. In my mind's eye, I can see myself twirling around the dance floor with him, like Ginger Rogers with Fred Astaire, perfectly in step, my green skirt kicking out between his legs as we float on air.

I watch him go over and cut me a piece of cake and carefully return with it resting on a napkin.

"Thank you," I say, and reach out both my hands. But before I can take the cake, he smashes it into my face, twisting it so that the cream and the jam squishes up my nose, into my eyes and mouth.

The cake slides off my chin to the floor, smearing greasily all down the front of the pretty green skirt my mother labored over to make me look like a princess. I stand there, staring at him through icing-encrusted eyelashes, a lump of misery in my throat. I can feel the corners of my mouth turning down involuntarily; I can't seem to control them.

Ronnie, and the friends who put him up to it, all stand around laughing uproariously and pointing as I feel my skin begin to heat up.

I have about two seconds to decide what to do next: run from the room, their laughter echoing hollowly in my ears; or join right in, and pretend that I think it is funny too. There was never even a choice. Extending my long pink tongue, I lick the cake right off all the places it can reach.

"Hmm. Yummy!" I cry, and laugh and laugh with the rest of them, while inside I'm dying.

Only when everyone has tired of my laughter do I rush to the toilet and, sitting in a stall, hold my head in my hands and cry. I wait there until the end of the dance and my ride home is ready. Rushing in through the front door, running upstairs and throwing myself on my mother's bed as she lies there reading, I bawl my eyes out.

"Mommy, I am so unhappy," I sob. "I am so ugly, and all the boys hate me. Why can't I look like Patti?"

My mother takes off her glasses and strokes my hair as I bury my face in her lap. "Oh, Goldie, don't be silly, honey," she tells me. "You're just a late bloomer, that's all. You wait and see. One day you'll have so many boyfriends you won't know what to do with them."

Crying myself to sleep in her arms, I don't believe her.

first love

*I believe that our lives are a series of concentric
circles, growing and growing like ripples
across water, connecting us all in
the same vast pool.*

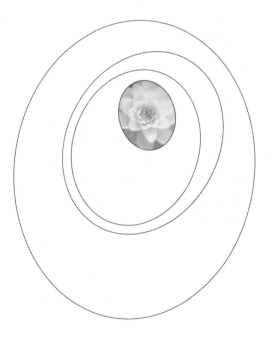

W hat does the future have in store for you, Goldie Hawn? I can't help thinking, as I lie on a four-poster bed in an old colonial guesthouse in Williamsburg, Virginia.

Outside, I can hear the sound of my mom and dad's car pulling away up the street. They are going home, leaving me to start my first professional job. I am seventeen years old and truly alone for the first time. Staring up at the flowery wallpaper, I am in a town I do not know, a long way from home. I have more questions than I have answers.

"What will happen to me here?" I ask aloud. "Is *this* the beginning of my path to the future?" Excited as I am to be joining the summer stock theater at the Lake Matoaka Amphitheater at the College of William and Mary, I imagine the distance my parents are putting between us as they begin their six-hour drive and I feel a flicker of panic.

I get up and look around at my surroundings. My fingers brush the unfamiliar antique dresser and the strange hurricane lamps. Needing the bathroom, I open a door, only to discover a closet. Tiptoeing downstairs, I find the old lady who owns the house playing solitaire in the living room.

"Excuse me," I ask shyly, "could you tell me where my bathroom is?"

"You have to share the one on the landing, dear," she replies, hardly looking up. "Make sure you lock the door behind you."

I'm sharing? With strangers? It all feels so odd.

Scurrying back upstairs, I use the bathroom and wash my face. If I don't hurry, I'll be late for my first cast meeting at five o'clock, the reason

I hurried from Takoma Park without even attending my high school graduation ceremony. Peering into the mirror, I think, Gee, I never got to say good-bye to my classmates. Well, I don't know if they ever really cared anyway.

Choosing an outfit, I run down the stairs and find my way through the streets of this picture-postcard colonial town to the college. The rest of the cast are milling around under huge oak trees just outside the amphitheater. My fellow performers comprise a few young hopefuls like me, but mostly they are professional dancers from New York City or classically trained actors in their mid-thirties from the Catholic university and local theaters. All far superior to me.

With relief, I spot the only person I know: Frank Cataldo, the choreographer who auditioned me in Washington. I go up to say hello.

"How nice to see you again, Goldie," he says, greeting me warmly. "Here, let me show you around."

He introduces me to some dancers from New York, who are friendly but distant. I happily link up with some other dancers I know from Washington, D.C. He takes me to meet Howard Scammon, the director— a large-bellied, ebullient, theatrical type of the old school. All he has to do is put a crown on his head and he could be one of Shakespeare's kings.

Compared to these gods and goddesses, I am just a gawky, wide-eyed yearling—the baby, fresh from high school in my bell-bottom jeans and midriff top, my belly button exposed.

"This is Willy Hicks," He tells me, as he pulls me up in front of a stranger. "Willy has been coming to summer stock for over ten years." Twenty-nine years old and a teacher at the Catholic university, Willy is short and stocky but has an interesting face, and it is instantly clear to me that everyone regards him as the kingpin.

"Nice to meet you," he tells me, extending his hand. His eyes are big and brown and sit deeply in their sockets. His face creases into a smile.

"And you," I reply, feeling suddenly more awkward. In my mind, I'm laughing and thinking, This guy is the cat's meow!

There is little time to get to know each other before we start rehearsals for our main show, *The Common Glory*, an historical drama on the signing of the Declaration of Independence. I link up with a girl

first love

called Donna, who will become a professional ballet dancer when the summer is over, and who is my new best friend.

As soon as the regular pupils have left for the summer, we move into the Ludwell Apartments. This place feels like a palace to me—gee, my very first apartment, with my very first roommate. I am no longer the odd one out—just one of the girls in the dorm, swapping clothes and makeup and having fun in one big party. I am part of a traveling show.

I quickly find my niche. As the youngest and definitely the wackiest member, dressed like a jazz dancer and endlessly full of mischief, I trade on my personality and adopt the role they expect of me: the giggly girl; the silly kid who doesn't know much but is good fun to have around. I like my new position; it suits me, and it doesn't put any pressure on me to compete, socially or intellectually.

"Oh, little Goldie," people usually say affectionately when they see me, "how lovely that you're here." They look me up and down, an innocent with a funny face and funny hair, and they laugh. "Oh, she's so cute," I hear someone say, and I know no one is taking me even remotely seriously.

All I have to do, it seems, is giggle and grin, wiggle and shimmy, always dressed in the snazziest outfits, and I get by. I've developed a ridiculous crush on Willy Hicks. One night at a party in our dorm, when we've all had too much vodka to drink, he grabs my face and kisses it.

I am blossoming into a young woman. My hormones are raging, and I think I am in love. I am surrounded by my new friends, in this beautiful place by the lake, and all is at peace with my world.

The Common Glory is such a great show to do. Each night, waiting backstage, I hear Vivaldi's *Four Seasons* start up as everyone is getting ready and my heart soars. This is all I ever wanted—to be a dancer, part of the chorus. I feel such happiness that I cannot bear to contemplate the end of summer and the end of this joy.

I see on the notice board that Howard Scammon is auditioning for *Romeo and Juliet,* along with the play's director, Donald Smith.

Romeo and Juliet? I say to myself. Hmm, interesting. I have this strange feeling that I might just be able to play Juliet. Leaning over to Donna, I whisper, "I'd like to have a go at that."

She looks across at me and laughs. "Well, good luck, honey!" she says. I can see she's thinking that there are at least twelve other girls, all professional actresses, who would play Juliet far better than me.

Taking a copy of the play nevertheless, I read and reread it in the quiet of my room until I have Juliet's part learned by heart. Despite being a C student my whole life, the task presents no problem to me. The language of Shakespeare is so beautiful; it is like a song with its cadence and rhythms. I especially love the potion speech and memorize that to perfection, reciting it endlessly in front of my bedroom window, which looks out onto the college's sweeping lawns.

On the morning of the audition, I dress in my usual white shoes, pedal-pushers hanging from my hips and a skimpy top, and stroll down to the open-air stage where the auditions are being held.

"Hi, Goldie!" pipe up some of the girls who share my dormitory. A few of the others, who are sitting around on the grass waiting their turn, wave and smile their hellos too. Willy Hicks, who is to play Friar Lawrence, nods his head in my direction. As usual, I can't take my eyes off him. He looks at me, and I look at him, and then I look away and he looks away, and we flirt with our eyes like that for a blissful few minutes.

"I've come to read for the part of Juliet," I tell the stage manager, the tremor in my voice belying my apparent confidence. Nobody says anything, but I see some of the girls laughing. One boy I know gives me the thumbs-up and whistles.

"You'll be the fifth on," the assistant director tells me, scribbling my name onto his clipboard. "Wait to be called."

I stand to one side and watch with interest as those before me read for the role. They are all classically trained actors, each reading different scenes, and each one better than the last. Every time they complete their audition, their friends and fellow performers give them a rousing reception.

"Goldie Hawn," the assistant director calls too quickly for me to prepare, and I clear my throat and step forward. He offers me a script, but I refuse. I know my lines so well I don't need one.

Moving to the center of the stage, I can see and hear my friends and fellow performers wishing me well.

"Good luck, little Goldie!" one whispers, grinning.

"Break a leg!"

Everyone has big beaming smiles on their faces, and all of them are being troupers for me. They seem to be enjoying the fact that I am willing to try out for this role. Like me, they believe it highly unlikely that I'll get it, but they applaud me for trying. I am grateful for their support.

Waiting for a lull, I take a deep breath and open my mouth to speak. The lines I know deep in my heart, recited over and over in my bedroom, fall from my lips word-perfect.

"How if, when I am laid into the tomb, / I wake before the time that Romeo / Come to redeem me? there's a fearful point! / Shall I not be, then, stifled in the vault, / To whose foul mouth no healthsome air breathes in, / And there die strangled ere my Romeo comes? . . ."

Focusing hard, I try to give the best performance I possibly can. Ignoring a jet growling overhead and a car backfiring on a nearby street, I carry on. Glancing up, I can't help but notice that the grins have been replaced with serious expressions. Trying not to think about what that might mean, I pick my way through the highly charged potion speech and reach the catastrophic climax.

When it is over, there is nothing but stony silence all around me. No one speaks. No one claps. There is a pause in time, as if an angel has flown overhead. Composing myself, I try to gauge the reaction of the director and producer. Did I go too far? Are they embarrassed for me?

As I look up, I see Willy Hicks beginning a slow handclap that the others gradually pick up. I find it difficult to figure out the astounded looks on people's faces. I always knew I could do it, and the fact that they apparently didn't until I stood up and opened my mouth confuses me. Falling back into the role that I feel most comfortable in, I laugh and giggle my way off the stage, slipping through the crowd and hurrying back to my dorm.

The following morning, I am sleeping late when Donna comes running into my bedroom. "Wake up! Wake up! They've just posted the list for *Romeo and Juliet!*" she shrieks, her whole body jumping up and down with excitement.

"What?" I say sleepily.

"You got the part!" she cries. "You got Juliet!"

"I got what?"

"Goldie, you're our Juliet!"

Throwing on some jeans and a T-shirt and running barefoot across the campus, I push my way through the cast gathered around the notice board, each one hoping to see his or her own name. Darting in and out between their shoulders, I can finally read the notice. There they are, the words I never expected to see.

Romeo...............................Lee Smith
Juliet....................................Goldie Hawn

My friends congratulate me, shock written on their faces.

Now it is the opening night—a sultry Virginia August evening. I am alone in my tiny dressing room, powdering my face, readying myself for this awesome experience I feel like I've spent my whole life preparing for.

I smooth down my long-sleeved green silk dress with its little train and try to calm myself by playing the music for the ballet *Romeo and Juliet* by Tchaikovsky. It is one of my father's favorite pieces, and I imagine him standing in the corner of the room playing the violin parts just for me.

Leaving my dressing room, I wander backstage and peep behind the curtain. Beyond, I can see three thousand people waiting to see us, the Williamsburg Shakespearean Players. They are using their programs as makeshift fans in the steamy heat, while the cicadas sing in the background. Oh, good, there are Mom and Dad. Oh, and Patti and her new husband. The sweeping lawn at the front of the stage is dotted with little children sitting on the grass. Oh no! Is that a good idea? The last thing I want is cartwheels in the middle of my potion speech.

The play opens, and I begin the slow mental countdown to the part where I first appear. First there is the bloody fight between Capulets and

Montagues on the streets of Verona. My pulse thumping in my ears, I watch from the wings as the players battle it out. Oh my God, how am I going to remember all my lines?

My young costar Lee Smith, in the guise of Romeo, takes the stage for his set piece with his friend Benvolio. They are followed by the actress who plays my nurse and another who plays my mother.

Then, in scene III, I'm on. I step lightly onto the stage, speaking the words, "How now? Who calls?" Oh my God, thank God I remembered my first lines. Now I'm home free.

I feel completely at ease. My nerves drip away. I become Juliet. There is no longer any separation between us. Our words flow in perfect juxtaposition, and I feel like I'm singing.

And then something strange happens. I am sitting in an Elizabethan chair, deeply involved in a scene with the nurse, who is going on and on as Shakespeare intended. It is my role, as the fourteen-year-old Juliet, to be exasperated with her and beg her to stop. So I put my elbow on the arm of the chair and my chin in my hand and roll my eyes petulantly. Sighing, I say, "And stint thou too, I pray thee, nurse, say I."

Suddenly, a laugh rises up from the audience like a hot-air balloon. I feel a flicker of panic. Oh God, you're not supposed to laugh in Shakespeare, are you? Juliet isn't supposed to be funny. Uh-oh, what did I do? I pull myself together and continue with the scene. When I leave the stage, Howard Scammon doesn't seem to have noticed. "Very good, my dear." He smiles, nodding. "Very good."

The play carries on as Romeo, Mercutio and Benvolio sneak into a party at their rival Capulets' house. There, Romeo spots Juliet and falls in love. Then it is time for me to rush up a rickety spiral staircase to get to my most cherished part: the balcony scene. I want to fulfill every teenage girl's dream. I reach the top and the spotlight flicks on. I am illuminated high over everybody's heads, up in the trees. I can't wait to deliver the lines "O Romeo, Romeo! wherefore art thou Romeo?" secretly hoping nobody will laugh. I so want to get it right. The good news is I don't fall off and the scene goes well.

Later, in the most tragic scene of all, I awaken from my potion-induced sleep to discover that my beloved Romeo has needlessly taken his life. I know this scene like the back of my hand, and I go down deep inside myself and pull out everything I've got.

Willy Hicks shares the stage with me as the friar as I waken and stir. "O comfortable friar! where is my lord? / I do remember well where I should be, / And there I am. Where is my Romeo?" His eyes urgent, he grabs my hand and tries to pull me away. "Lady, come from that nest / Of death, contagion, and unnatural sleep . . ." and then runs off the stage, afraid of being discovered.

"What's here? a cup? . . ." I begin, my eyes alighting on the goblet drained of its poison by my beloved, ". . . closed in my true love's hand?" Sniffing at it, my eyes strange with grief, I murmur, "Poison, I see, hath been his timeless end."

Just as I begin to really lose myself in the moment, I feel a spot of water on my face. Then one on my hand, and another on my head. Looking up, I see that it is beginning to rain, soft summer rain. I feel it settling on my hair, my clothes, my skin. For a moment, I don't know what to do because no one is moving. Should I stop talking or go on?

"O churl!" I cry, "drunk all, and left no friendly drop / To help me after? I will kiss thy lips; / Haply some poison yet doth hang on them, / To make me die with a restorative . . . Thy lips are warm."

I kiss the lips of Romeo as the rain gets heavier. In panic, I look across at Willy, now standing in the wings, and he motions to me with his hands and mouths the words, Keep going, keep going.

Nobody moves, not even the children on the lawn looking up at me with their heads in their hands, so I carry on. Kissing Romeo's lips again, I start at the noise of people approaching and look around in fear.

The rain comes harder now and a few people put up umbrellas. Some get up and leave, but most just sit there. Willy is still nodding at me, encouraging me on. Keep going, he continues to gesture. Through the light drizzle, I carry on through to the dramatic conclusion.

Cupping my hand over my right ear, "Yea, noise?" I cry, "then I'll be brief O happy dagger! / This is thy sheath"—plunging it deep between my breasts, I slump forward and gasp finally—"there rust, and let me die . . ." Rising up as if in pain, I allow my body to go limp and collapse.

first love

Lying across Romeo's warm body, the dagger in my chest, I peek up to see the guards arrive, and then Willy Hicks comes onstage in his friar's robes to speak some of the play's most poignant lines. The rain dripping off the hood of his habit, he catches my eye and winks before speaking his last line: ". . . if aught in this / Miscarried by my fault, let my old life / Be sacrificed, some hour before his time, / Unto the rigour of severest law."

The prince and the Capulets and Montagues flood onto the stage, united in their grief. As they stand around in shock, the prince declares: "For never was a story of more woe / Than this of Juliet and her Romeo."

There is nothing but silence. It seems interminable. Opening an eye, I see that some of the children on the lawn in front of me are weeping.

One by one, the members of the audience stand until nobody is left sitting. Their applause increases in volume and intensity until Willy Hicks lifts me by the hand and leads me to the front of the stage to take our bows.

I am experiencing my first standing ovation. I never want it to end. The experience feels so pure, so perfect. Something magical is happening.

Out of the corner of my mouth, I say to Willy, "I didn't know whether to go on when it started to rain."

"Goldie," he replies, his eyes bright, "I don't think anyone would have noticed if the sky had fallen in."

Out in the audience, I spot my father walking straight toward me. A few paces behind him are my mother and Patti, both beaming. Daddy's eyes are fixed on mine, an expression on his face I don't recognize, and he weaves his way through the departing crowd and walks, backlit, right up onto the stage.

Staring at me as if he has never seen me before, his piercing blue eyes burn right through me. "Go," he says finally, "where in the world did you learn to do that?"

The last word lodged in his throat, he turns his head away quickly, spinning away from me so that I won't see his tears. Throwing my arms around his waist from behind, I rest my head on his back. "Oh, Daddy, I don't know."

·   ·   ·

I t was never my intention to become an actress, least of all a comedic one. That wasn't what I lived for. I wanted to be a prima ballerina or a Broadway chorus girl but never the goofy, crazy Goldie Hawn most people think of today. That comedy just happened, unintentionally, and I think it all began with a desire to be liked and to fit in.

Well, that and the fact that some people just seem to look at my face and laugh. In one of my earliest dramatic roles, a high school production of *Bye Bye Birdie*, I played the mayor's wife but it wasn't really acting. My character had to keep fainting over a handsome young man, and each time they picked her up she had to faint again. Using my dance training, knowing what a funny move was and what wasn't, I made my body loose like the cartoon character Olive Oyl, and it worked.

That was the first time I knew I could make people laugh, really laugh, and the reputation followed me throughout high school. Kids used to say, "Remember the time when you brought the house down?"

Later, when I was in a comic play called *Shot in the Dark* in Maryland, every time I came onto the stage and opened my mouth the audience began to howl. My mother saw the show, and she came backstage afterward and stared at me in a curious way.

"You know, Goldie," she said, cocking her head to one side, "I don't think you're funny."

"I know," I said, so relieved that someone finally agreed with me. "I don't either! I mean, what *are* all those people laughing at?"

It was many years before I realized that much of what made people laugh was my own physicality—my big smile, my giggle, the way I rolled my eyes and all the things I hated about myself as a young girl that combined to create something infectious.

I learned at Williamsburg that I could act in the toughest Shakespearean dramas if I wanted to, but I also learned that I didn't have to— there were plenty of other people who could do it far better than me. It was a long time before I really understood that what I ended up doing actually had its own value.

first love

We are all in service. Making people laugh is what we do. We're jesters; we help people forget their troubles. We're there to depict certain aspects of humanity, to mirror some truths. This was a lesson for me in authenticity, about finding my strengths and honoring them.

There have been times in my life when I have longed for Juliet and all that she meant to me. I have wanted to go back to her simplicity, to the beauty and value of what she gave me. There was an alchemy about that special night; a mysterious blending of people and place and time that led all of us who were there to drink from it deeply. I know I have never forgotten how it felt to have my father stand there and look at me for the first time as an adult.

The key is to look at our gifts, understand their power and modulate them realistically. Understand how important it is to honor them. Accept responsibility for them.

I feel so fortunate to have been put in the limelight and allowed to shine. I don't own this thing I do. It's not mine. It's what I was given. I try to hold this gift lightly and thank God for it.

postcard

Before that Williamsburg summer is over, Willy Hicks and I become lovers. He is my first love, and he gives me a blessed entrance to womanhood.

Willy takes care of me. He explains what is happening. He doesn't leave me, and he is so very tender. I waited and waited for this to happen, and, when it does, he is so kind and loving that he makes everything all right.

He makes me understand that sex is beautiful; that it is now part of my life. I am fortunate enough to have had such a nurturing environment in which to learn that.

My new plan, apart from to be happy, and to build on the weekend dancing school I began at seventeen, now includes marrying Willy Hicks and having his children. I can clearly see myself as a housewife, mother and dance teacher, living in a lovely little house with a white picket fence somewhere in Virginia.

I imagine us continuing to do summer stock together year after year, with all our friends in the cast, growing old and raising children together. I am head over heels in love, and nothing would make me happier than to be Mrs. Willy Hicks.

But Willy is a lot smarter than that. Much as he enjoys every day of our love affair that first summer, much as he enjoys resuming it the following year when I return to Williamsburg for another languid semester, he understands much better than I do that we have no future together.

Leaving Williamsburg after that second summer of love breaks my heart. I cry and cry for the friends I'll miss, for the good times we had, the shows we did, the sweaters we knitted, the people we laughed with, fought with and loved. I feel as lost and sad as I have ever felt.

When I return home reluctantly and arrange to meet Willy again, eager to introduce him to my parents and Jean Lynn and to show him where we shall be married, he doesn't show as much enthusiasm as I had hoped. Then, when I do pin him down to a rendezvous, he stands me up.

Calling him long-distance, I burst into tears when he answers the telephone.

"Willy," I cry, my mind full of unquiet thoughts, "you weren't there where we said. I waited and waited. What happened?"

There is a long silence, which he eventually breaks with a sigh. "Goldie," he says, in a voice that sends slivers of ice into my heart, "I can't see you anymore."

"Don't talk crazy, Willy, of course you can. What are you saying?"

"You're too young."

"I'm almost nineteen."

"And I'm almost thirty-one."

"That doesn't matter. You know it doesn't, not to me."

"Well, it does to me."

Tears slipping silently from my eyes, I try to speak but can only make a strange choking sound in the back of my throat.

"Listen to me, Goldie Hawn," he says tenderly. "You have a big life to lead, and all I will do is put a box around you. I can't do that. Not to you."

"But you *are* my big life," I plead. "You're the only big life I want."

"No, Goldie," he tells me firmly. "There's a whole world waiting out there for you, and you have to go and find it. You'll understand one day, and you will thank me."

Dear Willy Hicks. He broke my heart and left me in mourning. For months, I carried around a little lump of clay that I had sculpted into a bust of his head.

I went back to Williamsburg a few years later to find him, and he was happily married with a baby. He didn't seem at all surprised, it seemed, by what had happened to me. He lived contentedly there with his family for many years, playing at the summer stock theater and, I feel sure, continuing to inspire others.

I heard recently from some old friends that he had died. His family lost him way too soon. I hope he knew how much I once loved him and what an important person he was in my life.

And, Willy, if you can hear me up there in heaven, thank you. Thank you very much for being so wise and loving and tender. I will never forget you.

integrity

*The wonder of this life is that people, even the
worst kind of people, can surprise you.*

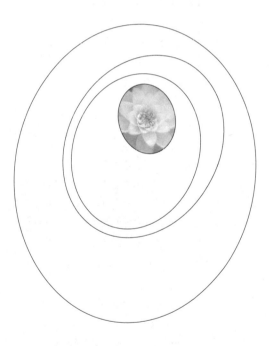

A cockroach scuttles across my arm. In my sleep, I find myself standing in the middle of a room I don't recognize. Where am I? Oh yes, I remember. As my brain begins to focus, I realize I am in my one-room apartment in New York City. Opening my eyes, I watch the cockroach scurry across the floor and disappear through a crack in the wall. It is May 1965, and I am in my first apartment on West Seventieth Street, an area known locally as "Needle Park."

Cringing at the cockroach and wondering how many others share his space beneath the floor, I feel homesickness flooding my heart. On the dirty white walls I summon a comforting image of my old bedroom on Cleveland Avenue, my street of hopes and dreams. In my waking dream, I can see the oak tree that stands tall outside my window, the azaleas, dogwoods and hydrangeas in the yard that my mother planted. Catching sight of myself now in a cracked mirror that hangs on the wall, I look no better than a long-necked baby bird fallen from the nest, waiting for its mother to rescue it.

My mother. The image swirls and I can see her warm brown eyes cradling pools of tears as she waves good-bye to me in front of our red-brick home just one month ago. My throat tightens and I choke back a sob inching its way up my gullet.

"Mommy, please don't cry," I tell her. "New York City is only five hours away."

For a moment, she looks more like a child than I do. Is she crying for me or for herself? For the mother she lost as a child? Or her first child, a baby boy who died in his crib? She sheds tears so rarely, but, when she does, her face is etched with the hidden pain of her life. When Laura Hawn weeps, so does the world. Or maybe just my world. I don't know.

Daddy's comic appearance slinking through the front door saves the day. Determined to be upbeat, he gives me the wide grin that always lifts my heart. Sharing the special little dance we do that makes us both giggle, he glide-steps, dip-steps and whirls me around. Leaning against the hood of his old black Cadillac, he offers me some lofty pearls of wisdom.

"Hey, Kink. Whatever you do, stay real in the big city," he advises. His arm is draped loosely over Mom's shoulders in a rare show of affection that steadies them both. "Show business is a fake business, so don't let it fool you. Don't walk around looking up at all the buildings, people will know you're a newcomer. Always look like you know where you're going even if you don't."

"Anything else?" I laugh.

"Yes. Don't pick your nose in public."

He and Mom couldn't be more different. But standing side by side, they are a monolith of strength. By uniting their own amazing proteins of life, they have manufactured their own petri dish of creation in which Patti and I have grown.

The cab pulls away from the sidewalk on our dead-end street with me sitting in the backseat. Twisted round, never taking my eyes off them, I wave and wave at the two people I love more than anything in the world, and who love me back more than anyone ever will again. I only turn away when the cab rounds the corner and they are lost from my sight, severing the invisible umbilical cord that holds me so close.

If I knew then that I would never live with my parents again, I don't think I would ever have left.

The school bell rings across the street, shattering the image on my wall and dispelling the nostalgic postcard from my past. This was the reason I took this crummy apartment in the first place: the school.

The sound of the children playing makes me feel a little easier about being a stranger in a strange town.

Realizing the time, I rush around the room, pick out a dress for my first modeling audition, stuff my big white vinyl dance bag with swimsuits and hope I won't be late. Poking a tongue out at myself in the mirror before I tackle the four heavy locks on my front door, I think to myself, I wish I didn't look so much like a parakeet.

Come on now, Goldie Jeanne, I tell myself sternly as I dash out the door and run down the stairs. This could be your lucky day.

But I am stopped at the entranceway to my building. Blocking it is a woman who has passed out.

"Excuse me, miss!" I cry. "Excuse me. I'm sorry, but you can't sleep here."

She looks up at me, her eyes rolling inside her head. Mumbling something unintelligible, she dribbles saliva down her chin before slumping back to the floor.

Hearing the creak of a hinge, I turn to see the door to the basement apartment opening. Inside sits a bald man in a grubby, darkened room. He is half dressed, sitting in dirty old shorts with his legs apart. He glares at me so ferociously when I meet his gaze that I gasp. Where the hell am I living? I ask myself. Under my breath, I close my eyes and repeat, There's no place like home. There is no place like home.

But no magic spell transports me back to Takoma Park, and I realize that this is the reality Daddy spoke about. Looking up, I spot a uniformed police officer strolling past the entrance to our building. Leaping over the woman at my feet, I run outside.

"Excuse me, officer!" I call. "Please, can you help me?"

"Sure," he says with a twisted grin. "What can I do for you?"

"There's a woman passed out in my hallway and she doesn't belong there. Could you help me? I'm a little scared."

"Not a problem, ma'am," he says, and follows me inside.

"Come on, Deidre, let's go," he yells, reaching down and picking her up by the scruff of her neck.

"You know her?" I ask.

"Yeah, she's harmless enough. She's a junkie. Come on, Deidre. I said, Let's go!"

He drags her through the front door and out onto the street. "Her dealer lives in that apartment." He points to a door that is still ajar. The man inside, watching everything that is going on through the gap, looks perversely pleased as he slams the door shut.

The police officer hurls Deidre unceremoniously into the street, and we both watch as she ricochets from car to wall, stoop to railing, toward Central Park. He dusts off his hands and bids me farewell.

Feeling sticky and icky and wanting desperately to be away from this place, I rush down the street away from my apartment building and try to clear my mind.

This is just a little glitch, I tell myself. You won't have to live here forever. I listen to the sound of my shoes *tap tapping* along the sidewalk, and I allow the brightness of the sunny New York day to lift my spirits. The air is warm and yellow, and the birds are chirping so loud I can actually hear them above the din of the city.

As I approach the corner of Seventy-first Street and Broadway, where I have to mount my chariot—the subway—I spot a handsome young man in his mid-twenties. He is wearing white pants and a sky blue shirt. He appears to be backlit with divine light. He flashes me a smile, and, involuntarily, I smile back.

"My, don't you look nice today!" he says as I walk past.

"Thank you." I blush coyly.

"That bag is bigger than you are," he says, getting into step with me. "Can I carry it for you?"

"No, thank you, I'm fine," I say, flattered. "It's my dance bag. I carry it all the time."

"You're a dancer? With legs like that, I should have guessed."

We reach the corner and he stops. "Listen," he says, "my name is Bobby."

"And I'm Goldie."

"Oh, I have an aunt named Goldie!"

"Really? That's an old Jewish name."

"I know. I am Jewish."

Perfect. Mom would approve. "You wouldn't by any chance be a dentist, would you?" I laugh.

"No." He laughs.

As it turns out, he wants to introduce me to a man he knows—a famous cartoonist named Al Capp.

"Have you ever heard of him?" he asks.

"Yes, of course."

"Mr. Capp is a national institution. He created the cartoon character Li'l Abner, the most popular comic strip of all time."

"I know!" I reply, putting down my bag. "Of course I know L'il Abner. I danced in the chorus of the school play."

Bobby hesitates. "Listen," he says, "I'm really not trying to put the make on you. In fact, here, look at this, I have a girlfriend, she gave me this gold watch." He peels off his watch and shows me the inscription: I LOVE YOU. DOLLY. He adds, "You can trust me."

"Oh, I do," I reply, when all I can think is, Lucky Dolly.

"Good, Goldie. Now listen. Al Capp's created a new character for a TV series for NBC. She's called Tenderlief Ericsson. She is not classically pretty, but she's interesting-looking. You'd be just perfect for the part."

Interesting-looking? Yes! Now he has my attention. If he had said I was pretty or sexy or beautiful, he would have lost me.

"Hey, my car's just around the corner. Let me give you a lift to wherever you're going and we can talk about it some more. I have a script for the show on the backseat."

Before I know it, I am scooped up in Bobby's green 1965 Cadillac convertible, the top down, being chauffeured to my audition. It all seems too good to be true. Here I am, living my dream: being discovered on the street by the cutest guy I've ever met, just a month after arriving in the Big Apple. I flop back, stare unashamedly at the giant skyscrapers towering above me and melt into the soft leather seats.

He drops me off for my audition, and I hold my head high as everyone watches me climb from his shiny new car, his script in my hand. "Goldie Hawn." He smiles. "Al Capp is going to make you a big star."

I giggle and wave good-bye, looking longingly after him as he disappears down the street. Glancing at my watch, I realize I am now horribly late for the bathing suit audition and decide to skip it.

Who wants to be pawed by dirty old men? I tell myself, allowing a little of Bobby's enthusiasm to rub off on me. Any day now, I'll be having an audition for one of the greatest cartoonists in America. And then I can buy Mom wall-to-wall carpeting, just like she always wanted.

Walking down Fifth Avenue, I think about what he said and I start to feel less confident. Do I really want to be a star? That has never been part of my plan. All the stars I've ever read about have screwed-up lives or die tragically young. That's the last thing I want; I just want to dance.

Days grow into weeks, and still there is no call from Bobby as promised. My job as a dancer at the Texas Pavilion of the World's Fair keeps me busy and tired. But I can't help but feel a little sad. Like the cockroach that shares my apartment, my Prince Charming seems to have slipped through the cracks.

The hammering on my door wakes me from a deep sleep. "Goldie! Goldie Hawn?" a voice yells. "Wake up. It's me, Bobby."

Jumping out of bed, I pull a robe around me, tackle the locks and peep out through the gap allowed by the heavy-duty chain. "Bobby? Hang on a minute." I close the door, slide the bolt on the chain and let him in.

"Hi, Goldie," he says, luminous in my shabby apartment in his starched white shirt and pressed pants. I love the way he smells, and I love the way he says my name. I hope Deidre wasn't in the hall when he came up, or the man in the basement apartment.

Blinding me with his smile, Bobby plants himself on my bed and picks up the telephone. "Goldie, I want you to talk to Mr. Capp. I just spoke to him, and he's so excited about meeting you that he wants to talk to you right now. He's out of town, but when he gets back into the city you're first on his list."

"Are you serious?"

"Yes. Now, let me call him. He likes to speak to all of his actresses first."

Before I can stop him, he is dialing Mr. Capp's number. When he gets through, he hands the receiver to me. I freeze. What am I going to say to this world-famous stranger? I don't even know him. I can feel myself perspiring.

"Oh, hello, Mr. Capp, this is Goldie."

"Darling Goldie," Mr. Capp's deep voice bellows his reply. "I can't wait to meet you. Bobby's told me all about you. I'm in Washington, D.C., right now, accepting an honorary doctorate from the American University, but when I get back we'll arrange a meeting and you can read for me." He ends his sentences with a strange little giggle, like a secret afterthought.

Weird. Just weird.

The audition is arranged for the following Friday, and Bobby prepares me for it. "Al Capp is the funniest man alive, and is adored by women all over the world," he says. "He's been like a father figure to me. I want you to be extra nice to him, honey. I don't want to let him down."

I can't hear anything after the word "honey." My heart is hammering under my ribs.

On Friday, rain falls from the sky in sheets, and my hair won't do a damn thing. Staring at myself in the mirror, helplessly trying to fight the ravages of humidity, I tease it higher, spraying it rock-hard and hoping it will stand tall for my big audition. What if Mr. Capp likes me? What if I get the job? What if I end up in Hollywood and become the big star Bobby told me I'd be? What about Mom and Dad? The whole idea scares the hell out of me.

I smear on my last coat of frosted lipstick and slip into my favorite pink crocheted dress. I wrap a string of orange pop beads around my neck, grab an umbrella and dash out of my armored door. Flying down the stairs, I leap over Deidre without a second thought and out into the rain. I open my umbrella but the damn thing breaks. Running through the wet streets, with spokes sticking everywhere and the black cloth flapping round my head like a nun's habit, I finally manage to flag down a cab before my hair is completely ruined. He pulls away at such speed that my head snaps back against the seat.

"Are you here to see Mr. Capp?" the doorman greets me at 400 Park Avenue. "Fourteenth floor." He points to the elevator.

How does he know who I am?

The elevator bounces, settles, then opens. A man dressed as a butler is waiting and ushers me into the apartment with grand formality. "My name is Eric, miss," he says in an impeccable English accent. "Mr. Capp is running a little late, but he will be here shortly. Please take a seat."

Openmouthed, I stand in the middle of this amazing space, admiring the view and the paintings and the objets d'art and the hundreds of books lining the walls. Needing to sit down, I ease myself onto a fluffy white couch that swallows me up in its feathery softness. Struggling to escape, I wish my dad could see me now. We would have shared a good laugh at how absurd this all was.

Suddenly remembering why I am here, I pull my script from my white vinyl bag and apprehensively study my part for the umpteenth time.

The butler waltzes into the room carrying an elaborate silver tea set, which he sets down grandly in front of me. "Mr. Capp likes his women to pour his tea for him," he says with a smirk before leaving as quietly as he came.

His women? But I'm not even a woman yet. I stare at the two-hundred-pound tea service and wonder how best to tackle the teapot, which looks like it weighs more than I do. I stare at it defiantly—my first test. I practice lifting it up and down with both hands over an imaginary cup. I try resting my elbows on the table to take the great weight but realize that pushes my bottom too far into the air. Determined to look elegant, I continue practicing for several minutes until I realize that someone has come into the room and is watching me silently from the doorway.

His bellowing voice startles me. "Goldie! Having trouble with the teapot?"

I stammer and crash it back down to the tray, most inelegantly, as Eric appears to take his boss's damp coat.

Al Capp chuckles. "I'm sorry I'm late, but I'm so happy to finally meet you."

A burly man about six feet tall and in his mid-fifties, he barrels toward me. His body tilts and rolls. Oh my God! He has only one leg. I mean, he has two, but one is false. Bobby never mentioned that. Desperately trying not to notice, I extend my hand and giggle nervously. He giggles back, and wobbles away from me with the words, "I'll be right back."

When he returns, he is dressed in a silk dressing gown.

I can feel every muscle in my body tighten.

He chuckles. "Little Goldie, I hope you don't mind, but I slipped into something more comfortable."

I do mind.

"Now, dear, why don't you pour us both some tea?" I hesitate, staring at the teapot again, and he laughs. "You'll do just fine." His guttural chuckle sends an unpleasant chill up my spine. I now realize it is not a chortle of happiness but a peculiar kind of nervous tic. It makes me even more uneasy.

Beads of sweat roll down my armpits. I feel his gaze inspecting me as I follow his directions and pour tea into paper-thin porcelain cups. His body pitches and rolls around the coffee table to reach the other half of the L-shaped couch. Losing his balance, he falls back into a sea of down.

"Ah, that's better," he says with a sigh.

Suddenly, I can't stop talking. "Mr. Capp, I love your apartment. Bobby has said such wonderful things about you. I just arrived in New York from Maryland. My father plays violin, and my mom is a typical Jewish mother. She wanted me to marry a Jewish dentist, but I really want to dance on Broadway . . ."

He stops me. "Let's not waste any more time. I want to tell you that if this works out today, as I'm sure it will, I will put you with one of David Merrick's finest acting coaches. You know who he is?"

"Oh yes. He's the biggest producer on Broadway."

"You'll have to work very hard. This is a difficult business."

"Mr. Capp, I'm a dancer. Nobody works harder than we do. I know what it's like to pick myself up, dust myself off and start all over again."

"Good, Goldie, that's good. Now stand up and walk to the middle of the room."

I do as I am told. The moment has come to prove my talent, and I am terrified. I read aloud the part of Tenderlief Ericsson. I know it by heart but pretend I don't. Unlike my audition for Juliet, this time I hold on to the script for dear life.

"You don't have to project quite so much," Mr. Capp interrupts. "This is film, not theater, so you can just speak normally."

"Sorry," I say and start again. I begin to trust him more. He is actually teaching me. I take a deep breath, relax a little and go on.

He stops me again. "Goldie, I would now like you to read the part of Daisy Mae. I think you could be very good in that part."

"Daisy Mae?" I am stunned. "But she's the lead. She's beautiful and sexy and large-breasted! Mr. Capp, I really don't think I look like she does."

"Nonsense!" he roars. "I created her!"

He watches me with unblinking eyes that sear right through me. He orders me to go to the back of the room and walk toward him as if he were the camera. "I want to see how you play to the camera," he says. "Look kinda stupid. Like Daisy Mae."

I go with it. Look stupid? Well, okay. He is my coach. Using my beads as a prop, I put them in my mouth and dangle them from my lips, eyes wide. I try to look as vacant as I can, all the while imagining that he is the camera.

"Okay, now go and stand in front of the mirror and let me see your legs."

I look around nervously. I pray for the butler to come back with fresh tea. "Oh, don't you want me to read from the scene?"

"In a minute." Seeing my hesitation, he chides, "Go on, don't be shy. I've seen legs before."

I bet you have, I think. Obeying somewhat reluctantly, I walk to the mirror, turn slowly and lift my dress just above my knee. I tilt my head and giggle.

"Higher."

I raise my dress another inch.

"Higher."

My fingers freeze on the edge of my skirt. I'm beginning to feel that this isn't right. I mean, where is all this getting me? What about the part? Looking up, I say, "Mr. Capp, I'm going to be late for work."

He chuckles again, which only makes me feel worse. I am getting sick of that damn chuckle.

"I have to get all the way out to Long Island," I explain, looking longingly at the elevator door. "I'm afraid I'll miss my train."

"Come over here, Goldie," he says, patting the couch next to him. "You won't miss your train."

My knees lock, and I stand stock-still staring at him for a moment, in an agony of confusion. Part of me wants to run from the room; the other part tells me to do as I'm told. After what seems like forever, I walk over and gingerly sit on the edge of the couch.

Afraid to make eye contact, I stare hard at the driving rain beyond the picture windows, biting my bottom lip.

A dark energy fills the room. A shiver runs up and down my spine. When I let my eyes drift slowly back toward Mr. Capp, I see that my host has parted his silk robe to reveal a flaccid penis resting heavily against his wooden leg.

The breath rushes out of me. All I can hear in my head are Bobby's words: I want you to be extra nice to him, honey. I feel sick to my stomach. Bobby tricked me. Al Capp tricked me. Tears prick my eyes, and I bite my lip until I can taste blood. Finally, summoning up my courage, I speak, my voice quivering in my throat.

"Mr. Capp, I will never, ever get a job like this."

Sneering, he quickly covers himself up.

"Then go back and marry a Jewish dentist!" he spits, waving a hand at me dismissively. "You'll never get anywhere in this business, Goldie Hawn." Pulling himself up on his one good leg, he snarls, "I've had them all, you know, much better-looking than you. Now go on and get the hell out of here!" He throws a twenty-dollar bill at me as I fumble with my purse and umbrella. "You don't want to miss that damn train."

I tear out of that apartment as fast as I can. I rush past the disgusting butler and the tittering doorman, both of whom I now realize are accomplices for this ugly routine. I run out into the pouring rain. I run for several blocks without using my umbrella, hoping to wash the filth of Al Capp and Bobby the Pimp from my memory.

Drenched and exhausted, with his twenty-dollar bill clutched tightly in my hand, I hail a cab. I can't be late for work.

Later that night, when I eventually get home from work, dog tired and still deeply affected by my experience, I find a letter waiting for me in my mailbox. It is from my mother and it is a day late.

"Goldie dear," she wrote. "Daddy and I were very excited to hear about this great opportunity you are having with this cartoonist, Mr. Capp, but I have to tell you something, honey. Please know that while these men may offer you the casting couch, while they may promise to give you your first break, it is your talents and your gifts that will sustain you in the eyes of the public. And it is your inner self that can decide what best to do. Remember that. I love you, Mommy."

There is never a happy ending for people who lose their integrity. Not just in show business but in the fast-paced competitive world we live in as well, where so much energy is put into winning, at the sacrifice of so much.

Knowing your limits, and that there is a limit to getting what you want, comes from a sense of self-respect instilled in you from an early age. It takes guts to stand up in the face of what you really want, but you have to know in your heart that if you make the wrong choice you won't be able to live with yourself for the rest of your life. There is only one person that matters at that point and that's you. If you give in to such pressures, you strip away your self-respect, your personal ethics and your standards—the very things that create the fiber that will hold you together for the rest of your life.

We can instill integrity in our children by teaching them not to be afraid to speak the truth about things they believe and not to be intimidated by someone else's view of what's right and wrong. To be able to stand back and observe clearly. The hope is that children respect their parents enough to want to please them. It mattered so much to me what my mother and father thought because I had so much regard for them. So, the circle continues, and I hope that what I learned from my parents I have passed on.

Once you have decided to hang on to your integrity, you have a much easier path to knowing yourself and what you believe in. Because on that last day of your life, that's all that matters. That's where you find peace in your life, your loved ones and your god.

It was several years before Al Capp's cartoon characters, including Tenderlief Ericsson, were taken up by a network and run on national television. I saw the program listed one night, and I laughed out loud. By now a household name myself, I couldn't resist sending him a telegram.

It said: DEAR MR. CAPP, CONGRATULATIONS ON YOUR SHOW. AS YOU CAN SEE I DIDN'T HAVE TO MARRY A JEWISH DENTIST AFTER ALL. SIGNED GOLDIE HAWN.

to my children

My darlings, the pain of growth can be excruciating, to emerge as a whole person as we thread our way through the fire of enlightenment. The tunnel seems black and foreboding, but the pinpoint of light that appears as an apparition is real. It is the true essence of life, and the manifestation of all the perfection in you. Never to be snuffed out by the negative emotions that mask its perfect illumination. Dressed in our armor, we hack our way through the darkness, blindly trying to escape the void of the unknown. At times, we feel penned in by the events of our journey. Be still, watch and listen. Don't run away from the darkness, for therein lies the answers to untold truths you already know. The light may be there to guide you, but you have to first travel through the dark to discover a more fully illuminated you.

life's purpose

When viewing life from a thousand feet up,
we can see our purpose more clearly.

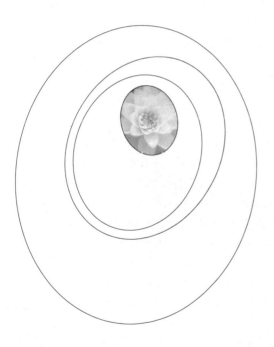

I can hardly hear myself think, let alone speak. My friend Spiro is yelling something in my ear above the music blasting out of the giant speakers in the Peppermint Lounge, but I can't make out what he's saying. Laughing, taking another slug of my scotch on the rocks, I shrug my shoulders and we sit at the bar and carry on watching the go-go dancers.

"Do you want to dance?" Spiro finally yells at me during the momentary break between numbers.

"Sure!" I cry, still energized after a five-hour shift at the World's Fair. I've never worked so hard. I'm about ninety pounds of twisted steel. I spend every night screaming, whooping and hollering, wearing a full cancan costume of red-and-black ruffles, performing high kicks, cartwheels and splits with the rest of the troupe. I have about twenty seconds to change into a black fringed go-go dress before rushing back onstage to dance the pony, the froog or the monkey to the latest hits.

Kicking, spinning, yelling and jumping to the four-four beat, I rush out on cue each night and dance my butt off. Shimmying my fringe in the black-and-white strobe lights, I hardly dare look down. I am twelve feet up, above the bar. Thank God, Spiro has promised to catch me if I fall.

He has brought me to the Peppermint Lounge in Midtown Manhattan tonight after work. Now he leads me up onto the dance floor, where we move and groove to the music, trying to find a space in the crowd. Dressed in a pink top, psychedelic miniskirt and white go-go boots, I lose myself dancing with him, and then spin around to dance with a stranger, before bumping back against Spiro. Then comes my favorite part. As the music blares out of the speakers, the whole club throws their hands into the air and starts to sing as one to "Twist and Shout," laughing together as we launch into the song. What a blast.

When the song's over, Spiro grabs me by the hand and leads me to the bar. "Come on, let's get a drink." A tall, handsome guy in his early twenties nudges between us. "Hey, Johnny, this is Goldie . . . Goldie, this is a friend of mine."

"Hi, nice to meet you," I yell over the crowd.

The bartender plops down two scotches, and Johnny throws down a twenty. "I'm buying," he says. "And another round, please."

"We're having a party now!" I cry.

It's four in the morning and the place is closing up. As usual, I am always the last one to leave. "Hey, guys, need a lift?" Johnny says.

"You have a car? In New York City? Cool!"

"Sure." He laughs. "I'm from Jersey. Of course I have a car!"

"Hang on Sloopy" by the McCoys is blasting out of the car radio when Johnny turns on the engine. I sit on the front seat, sandwiched happily between him and Spiro, two male gods. As we set off the streets are empty except for a few yellow taxis cruising for the last stragglers of the night.

Johnny has what my mother would call "a heavy foot." I'm feeling foggy, but not so foggy that I don't notice that we are reaching speeds of up to sixty miles an hour between stoplights.

Our car bumps and swerves, tossed in and out of the potholes as I bounce around in time to the music. The warm air from the open window tousles my hair. Happy and relaxed, mellowed by the scotch warming my veins, God, I feel good as I sing along at the top of my voice to the chorus of "Hang On Sloopy."

We turn onto the West Side Highway, the fast way uptown. This road is even more pitted, and it curves this way and that. I'm tossed like a rag doll between them.

The car hits one pothole so violently that my head bounces off the roof. The sharp pain jolts me. "Do we have to go quite so fast?" I ask, rubbing my head.

Johnny doesn't answer. I look across at him, but his eyes are glazed. A ripple of fear passes through me.

"Hey, can you please slow down?" I snap the radio off so he can hear me. Gripping the dashboard with both hands, I yell, "Please! Slow down! You're going too fast!"

Johnny hardly slows at all, and I wonder if he's drunk or stoned. I turn to look at Spiro to see if he is as frightened as I am and I can see that he is. Immediately behind us, just a few feet away, I see a yellow taxi heading straight for our car. The driver's head is resting on the back of his seat. He is fast asleep, or worse.

"Hey! Look out!" I cry.

The cab crashes into us at top speed and shoves our car forward violently. Johnny is too out of it to respond. Locked against our fender, the cab pushes us off the side of the road at around fifty miles an hour.

Seeing a lamppost rushing straight toward us through the windshield, I try to slide my body underneath the dashboard to protect myself. Covering my head with my hands, I let out a primal scream.

"Watch out!"

But it is too late.

I s she alive? Can you feel a pulse?" someone is asking the stranger who is bending over my lifeless body, crumpled beneath the dashboard.

"I dunno," comes the worried reply.

I'm floating weightlessly, observing everything from an elevated position, a few feet above his head. "Did somebody call an ambulance?"

In my dreamlike state, I see an ambulance speeding its way down the highway toward us. I hear the siren and I see the pretty lights and I watch the people standing all around. Two paramedics rush from the back to attend to my injuries.

"Is she dead?" one of them yells. "Feel her heart."

I watch, disinterested, as my favorite pink top is snipped clean down the middle.

"She's alive. Help me get her out of here," his colleague replies.

I'm witnessing all of this, but I am not in my body. I'm somewhere else—where, I'm not sure. Maybe it's all just a dream. I can see Spiro and Johnny staggering around in a daze, blood pouring from cuts on their faces. I watch as the paramedics lift my body out of the cramped space under the dashboard. They lay me on a gurney with the greatest of care. As they slam the ambulance doors behind me, my world goes black.

I'm going to throw up."

"Keep your head still!" a nurse barks from somewhere near my feet. A giant X-ray machine clicks and whirrs above me. "I've got to get pictures of your head. I'm almost done."

She forces my head left and right, without any tenderness. Maybe because she can smell the liquor on my breath, she's as unforgiving as the cold table I'm lying on.

"I'm going to be sick."

"Ah, you just have the dry heaves."

As she comes around to the side of my head, I vomit all over her.

"Ah, shit!" she complains. Disgusted, she hands me a rough paper towel and hurries off to clean herself up.

"Mommy!" I wail. "I want my mom."

I can't seem to make sense of anything. I don't even know where I am. Everything feels wrong—upside down. Suddenly, Spiro is at the door. His face is caked in dried blood, and his nose is broken. He's clutching his left arm, which is in a sling.

"Goldie?"

"Uhhhh . . ."

"Goldie, are you okay? I'm so happy to see you. I thought you were . . . well, never mind." He flops onto a nearby chair, his skin waxy.

"Spiro," I ask groggily, "where are we? What happened?"

"We're in the hospital. We had an accident." Standing shakily and walking to my side, he says through clenched teeth, shock vibrating his body, "Nobody can believe we walked out of that car alive. The doctor said we must have an angel watching over us."

I hurt too much to care.

T he school bell from across the street wakes me. My eyes flicker open. The sound of the bell reverberates inside my skull. I'm back in my little one-room apartment. How did I get here? Did the hospital send me home? I don't remember. Sitting up, my head starts to spin. I realize I'm completely alone. Looking across at the telephone on the other side of the room, I stand to negotiate my way toward it. The room tilts around me, and I feel like I could vomit. But I put one foot in front of the other, and dial my mother's number.

"Mom? Mommy?"

"Goldie? What's the matter? What's wrong?"

"I've been in an automobile accident. I'm hurt bad, Mom. I need you."

My mother snaps to it. "Where are you?"

"In my apartment."

"I'm on my way."

The minute I hang up the phone, I rush to the bathroom and throw up.

In no time at all, it seems, she appears at my door in her suit and little high-heeled pointy shoes. Without even going home, she closed up her store, grabbed her purse and jumped on a Greyhound bus to New York.

"The policeman who saw the car after the crash said we must have had an angel looking out for us," I tell her weakly, as she feeds me sweet lemon tea from a spoon. "He said no one should have survived."

"Yes, sweetheart, you do have an angel," she says. "It is Tante Goldie."

"What do you mean?"

"I never told you this," my mother tells me, "but just after you were born in the hospital something extraordinary happened to me. I know that I wasn't sleeping, I was wide awake, but I had a vision. Tante Goldie appeared to me out of thin air."

"Really?"

"She sat on the edge of my bed, put her hand over mine, smiled and said, 'I'm so glad you had a little girl and you named her Goldie. I'll be watching over her.' And then she disappeared."

"She did?"

"Yes. Tante Goldie is your angel. She's watching you."

Life and death live in the flicker of an eye, a flash in a cloud or a bubble in a stream. That's how fragile they can be.

Many years after this experience, I went to see a psychic in Thailand. He didn't know who I was, and he didn't speak a word of English; I had to use a translator. He sat in a room that smelled of incense in a strange little café in the middle of Bangkok. He was a small man with a huge smile that never left his face. He drew illegible scribbles onto paper—strange geometric symbols that made no sense to me.

He sat in silence for a long while, and then he suddenly spoke. "You almost died at the age of nineteen." His interpreter carefully translated.

"No, I don't think so," I replied cautiously, thankful that, to my mind, I'd never had any really close encounters with death.

"Go back in time," he instructed firmly, his doodling becoming ever more furious. "Something happened to you at nineteen. It must have. Think."

"Nineteen?" I said. "No, I don't think so. I was still in New York then, wasn't I?"

"Were you in an accident?" he asked, his brown eyes piercing.

"Oh, yes, of course I was," I said, suddenly remembering. "I was in a car crash."

"Did you leave your body?"

"Well, I don't know. I thought I was dreaming, but, yeah . . . maybe I did," I replied, goose bumps appearing on my skin. "How did you know that?"

"Your life changed drastically after that, didn't it?"

I started thinking about it and nodded my head. "Yes, it did," I said quietly, more afraid now.

"That is because you were not supposed to die. You were sent back because you had something to do. You are here for a reason, and what happened to you then was supposed to happen to you."

A few minutes later, he shut the lids on his smiling eyes. The session was over. The interpreter told me it was time to go.

I could barely stand and leave the room. I thanked him and staggered out into the bright white light of day, completely winded. The truth of how close I had come to dying, and how it was always supposed to happen, shook me to the core.

"So, I have a purpose," I whispered, repeating his words. "I was sent back for a reason? Hmm. I wonder if I'll ever really know what that is."

trusting men

*The uncertainty that darkness brings
can humble even the hardest soul.*

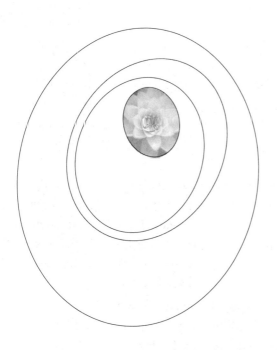

G oldie? Is that Goldie? This is Max down at the Stage Deli. Your dad's been on the telephone again. He said to call you and get you down here and eat some blintzes."

I laugh and climb out of bed, the phone still in my hand. "Okay, Max." I giggle. "I'm on my way. Thanks, honey."

Gee, I love my dad. He seems to know just when to pick me up with a call to Max, or by sending twenty bucks in the mail. This is perfect, because the Stage Deli is around the corner from my new apartment and just down the street from Herman, my newfound go-go agent, whom I have to go and see today.

I take a shower and throw on some jeans and a T-shirt. I run to the Stage Deli for coffee and blintzes. Stuffing my face, I sit there happily contemplating my new life away from Needle Park. I share a great apartment now with four roommates, all of them dancers, in a brand-new building on Eighth Avenue. It is right next to Jilly's Bar, the hangout of Frank Sinatra and his friends, and just around the corner from Broadway. I feel one step closer to my dream just by living there.

"Thanks, Max," I say, kissing him on the cheek and grabbing my dance bag. Running from the deli, I skip up the three flights of stairs to Herman's office and push open the door. Herman is a tall, dark, handsome showbiz agent, and he handles all kinds of third-class acts, everything from the Dancing Waters to the Catskills, and even an act with a singing dog.

Slamming down the telephone and looking up at me, he smiles. "Hey, Goldie, looking good. Come on in and take a seat."

"Herman, you got anything for me?" I say hopefully. "I gotta pay my rent next week."

"No luck on Broadway, little girl?"

"Almost . . . I auditioned for *On a Clear Day* and I got down to the last ten, but I was too short."

"Well, you're not too short for me. Let me see what we got here." Flicking through his Rolodex, he asks, "What about Dudes 'n' Dolls?"

"Herman, I'm working there already. Friday nights. And by the way, the pedestal is so high I get vertigo each time I go up there. Can't you get me something closer to the ground?"

"No problem, honey. Your wish is my command. We've always got the Entre Nous."

"Again? I already did the Entre Nous. I quit because the guy wanted me to have a drink with Huntington Hartford."

"You sure you don't want to go topless?"

"What, with these?" I laugh, pointing at the two fried eggs on my chest. "No, I don't do topless, Herman. I'm a trained dancer."

"You could double your money," he reminds me.

"Top on," I state flatly.

"Okay, okay. How about modeling? I'm a friend of the woman who runs the Candy Jones modeling agency. You should maybe go and get some test shots done for hair commercials, because, you know what, Goldie, you got great hair."

"Yeah, great, Herman, thanks anyway, but I did that already." I sigh, swallowing the memory. I went to that place after my car accident, you know, when I lost my job at the World's Fair. The photographer invited me into the darkroom and attacked me. When I finally pushed him off, he told me I'd never make it anyway because I wasn't pretty enough. "No," I tell him. "No more test photographers . . . So, you don't have anything for me, then?"

"I dunno, kid," he says, shuffling some papers on his desk. "Have you tried out for the Copacabana?"

"Yes. I had to dance in a cage, but they fired me because I was too skinny. That was the night I got molested on a subway by those two guys on the way home and ended up asking a doctor who was on the train to walk off with me."

"Oh, poor kid."

"I know, I know. So, Herman, what do you have? Because all I'm doing at the moment apart from Dudes 'n' Dolls is the supper theater out at Danbury, Connecticut, once a month. I go on between a comedian and a belly dancer."

"Have you ever danced at the Peppermint Box?"

"The Peppermint Box?" I cry, sitting on the edge of my seat. "You mean in Midtown? I was there the night of my accident!"

"Er, no, honey. That's the Peppermint Lounge. The Peppermint Box is in Jersey."

"In Jersey? Oh, come on. How much does it pay?"

"Thirty-five dollars; thirty for you and five for me."

"How am I going to get to Jersey for thirty dollars?"

"You take the Greyhound bus. It stops right outside. It's just across the river on Palisades Highway. And, I'll tell you what. I'll come and pick you up."

"You will?"

"Sure. You're my favorite go-go girl. Consider yourself booked."

I dash home and tip the contents of my dance bag out onto my bed. I sew up the holes in my fishnet stockings. Some of the gold fringe on my trusty go-go dress has come undone, so I spend the next day stitching it back onto the black leotard that comes up high over my hip bones. I double fringe the top of my leotard so it really shimmies. By the time I am done, I am starving. I am always hungry. I lick a spoonful of honey from the jar I carry with me wherever I go so that I can have a quick hit of energy.

The following night, I take the Greyhound across the George Washington Bridge to New Jersey. Befriending the driver, whose name is Sam, I ask him to let me know when to get off. Sitting right behind him, knitting some new leg warmers and chatting away, I try not to notice how bleak the area is getting.

Just when we reach the middle of nowhere, in an area of industrial nothingness, Sam tells me, "Okay, Goldie, this is your stop!"

Disappointment sucks the air from my body. The Peppermint Box is nothing more than a fifth-rate truck stop, slumped by the side of the road like Deidre the junkie. Eight eighteen-wheelers are parked right outside.

As I lug my dance bag off the bus, I hear its doors slam shut behind me as Sam pulls it away. Too late to get back on.

Pushing open the creaky door of the bar with its diamond window, I am hit by a wall of heat, cigarette smoke, sweat and stale beer. "That's Amore" belts out of an old jukebox to my left. The room is dank and dirty, littered with chairs and tables. At the bar stand a few indifferent truckers, in denim and work boots, being served by a butch-looking woman who stares at me as if I have just landed from Mars.

Hitching my dance bag high onto my shoulder, I approach the bar. "Excuse me, my name is Goldie," I say.

"And?" says the woman bartender.

"The go-go dancer."

"Oh, yeah, right."

"I'd like to see the boss."

"Merv!" she yells at a thousand decibels. A fat, middle-aged man with a ruddy face and a cigarette stuck to his bottom lip staggers out from behind the bar.

"The dancer's here."

"Oh. Okay. This way." He shuffles along in front of me, leading me into a back room. I look around nervously, wondering if I should just take off.

I smell the bathrooms before I reach them. They haven't been cleaned in years. "This is where you change," he says, flinging open the peeling door. I stare at the brown-stained toilet bowl and almost retch.

"In here?" I ask, piteously.

"Unless you want to do it in full view of all the guys," he smirks.

Breathing through my mouth, trying not to look too closely at the walls, I wriggle as quickly as I can into my tights and outfit, making sure nothing accidentally touches the floor. Peeping through the door, I step out nervously in my spiked heels, fringed leotard and fishnet stockings. Only a couple of men even bother to look up from their beer.

There is no stage and no clear space on the sticky floor to dance. Spotting the owner at one of the tables, a bottle of scotch and a smeared whisky glass in his hand, I ask, "Excuse me, where do I dance?"

"Pick a table," he says, waving a hand expansively.

"A table?"

Looking around, I try to find one that is less rickety or at least less filthy than the others. Using a chair to get up, I place my leg on a few to test their sturdiness. Several fail the test, and I move on until I find a square, three-legged table that will just about take my weight.

"That's Amore" finishes playing and is followed by "Volare." Then "Everybody Loves Somebody Sometime" comes on. It seems to be on a loop. Great, the only man in the bar who can be bothered to put a quarter in the jukebox is a Dean Martin freak. Perfect. How in the world am I supposed to dance to this? I improvise as best I can. Thirty bucks is thirty bucks, after all. Whenever I take a break, someone yells from the bar, "Hey, put another quarter in and make her dance!"

At last, a regular guy walks in wearing a suit. Relief floods me. I smile across at him and he smiles back. Once he has a beer, he turns around and really stares at me. Being the consummate performer, I really do my stuff for him, despite the appalling soundtrack.

The guy takes a seat at one of the tables and looks up at me with sympathetic eyes. I glance back at him and half smile. I twirl around and do a little move, but when I turn again he has pulled out his penis and is jerking off right in front of me.

Letting out a small cry, my knees buckle from under me. I collapse to the tabletop. This is about all my body and spirit can take. I sit there staring at him incredulously. You too? I want to scream. I can't take any more. Nobody else notices or even cares.

Seeing my reaction, the man quickly puts himself away and scurries out like a weasel. I remain slumped on the table, quivering miserably. Beyond tears, I crawl off, every ounce of air knocked out of me. Grabbing a towel and draping it over my shoulders, I stagger to the bar. Where's Herman? He should be here by now.

"What time is it?" I ask the bartender.

Looking at her watch, she replies, "Almost one."

"One? But I'm waiting for my go-go agent. Oh, shoot! I guess he's not coming. Okay, so now I guess I need to get home. Where's my money?"

"I dunno." She swigs from a beer bottle.

"Well, where's the owner?"

"He passed out hours ago."

"But I haven't been paid!"

She shrugs her shoulders.

I sigh. "Just tell me when the next Greyhound bus is so I can go home."

The woman laughs in my face—a big, wide-open laugh. "There's no Greyhound bus at this time of night, honey."

"No bus? But how will I get home?"

"Take your pick," she says, waving her arm at the handful of truck drivers left in the bar. "Or," she says, leaning over the bar conspiratorially, "if you want to go party, I could close this joint and you could come home with me."

My heart can't sink any lower. I'd rather stick pins in my eyes, I think, recoiling physically. "No thanks," I say. "I'll take my chances with this lot. I just want to go home."

Too afraid to think what might happen to me if I don't get a ride, I walk slowly around the bar, starting my search. Sizing up the unsavory characters propping up the bar, I spot a few who look slightly less like rapists than the others.

"Could you please take me home?" I ask them. "I need to get back to Fifty-second and Eighth Avenue."

Most of them shake their heads, but two drivers, who share the driving, agree. "We'll finish our beer," they grunt, "and then we'll give you a ride."

My heart in my mouth, I pick my way to the restroom and change back into my ordinary clothes, no longer caring how filthy the place is. Sitting back down at the table I was dancing on, my head in my hands, I wait for a signal, half afraid they might change their minds.

"I hope you know what the hell you're doing, Goldie Jeanne," I whisper to myself.

In no time at all, these two big men nod at me and I follow them outside. My blood is pumping so hard around my veins it is making me breathless. Looking around the parking lot, there is one vehicle that dominates it, an eighteen-wheeler Mack truck that is bigger than the Peppermint Box.

"Is that it?" I ask, my mouth open.

"Jump on in."

Before I know it, I'm sitting high up in its enormous cab, bouncing back to Manhattan between these two big men in complete silence. As our giant truck trundles along the highway, we cross the bridge to Manhattan and see New York in all its glory, lit like a stage set. It is the same skyline I entered not so long ago, full of all my hopes and dreams. Now it fills me with a strange sense of foreboding and fear.

You know, Goldie, maybe it's time to chuck in the towel, I tell myself. Go back home. Open a dance school. Get married and be happy. There is no future for you here.

The following morning, a chilly day in November, I am picking up my go-go outfit at the dry cleaner's. As usual, I am chatting away with Eddie, who runs it, Maria from across the street and to a couple of unknown customers. I guess Mom was right—I've never known a stranger.

Waving good-bye to Eddie and backing my way out of the store, I literally run into two people walking by on the sidewalk. I drop my bag, and, after I pick it up, I come face-to-face with two adorable-looking young men.

"Oh, excuse me, I'm sorry," I say.

"That's okay," they reply with a smile, looking me up and down. "What you got in the bag?"

"Oh, some yogurt and my cleaning."

"Well, can we help you carry it?"

"Oh, no thank you. I just live across the street. Right over there. I live on the third floor right up there on 888 Eighth Avenue," I say proudly. "It's a brand-new building. That's my bedroom window."

"Cool."

"So, where are you boys from?" I blush, chattering on.

"Poughkeepsie."

"How long are you staying in town?"

"Not long. We're on a road trip. You know, like Jack Kerouac in *On the Road*. We're starting here and ending up on the West Coast, to find those California girls."

"Very cool."

"Anyway, nice to meet you," they say, smiling and moving on.

I say good-bye and cross the street. Halfway across, I turn. "By the way," I yell, "my name is Goldie. Oh, and don't forget to go up the Empire State Building while you're here. It's much better at night."

"Great. Thanks, Goldie. Bye."

Talking to my mother on the telephone later that night, I am in my kitchen making a piece of toast. "I dunno, Mom," I say, pulling a plate from the cupboard as I rest the telephone in the crook of my neck, "maybe I should just come home. I mean, New York is great and everything, and I love my new apartment, but I think maybe it's time to come home."

Watching the toaster to make sure it doesn't burn the bread, all of a sudden the lights go out and the line goes dead. The toaster glows red but then fades. "Mom? Mom? Mom? Are you there? What happened?"

It is pitch-black. Putting down the telephone, I peer out the window and gasp when I see not a single light in any of the windows across the street. Only the car headlights illuminate the street. Feeling my way to the cupboard under the sink, I retrieve a flashlight and wander through my apartment and into the hallway. All my neighbors are standing around.

"What happened? Why did all the lights go out?"

"We dunno. Do you have lights?"

"No. Is there a fire? Did something happen?"

"Looks like the whole block's out. I can't see a light on anywhere."

"Oh my God, the elevator! Is someone stuck in there? I can hear shouting."

I run downstairs to the lobby and find Ernie the doorman lighting a candle.

"Ernie, what happened?"

"Looks like a blackout. The whole of New York is out. It's inky out there."

"I think someone's stuck in the elevator," I tell him.

"I know. I just called the fire department."

I walk out into the street and look around in wonder. I have never been in a blackout before. Looking up, I realize that the Empire State Building is in darkness, something I have never seen before.

Wandering back into the lobby, I see Ernie has been joined by others from our building. They are listening to a transistor radio. "What's going on?" I ask.

"It's a massive blackout, honey," a woman tells me. "It's affected the whole northeast coast, right up into Canada. They reckon there are thirty million people in the dark."

"Oh no! Do you mean there are people trapped in buildings?"

"Yes, honey, right up in the Empire State Building."

"Oh my God!" I cry, my hand to my mouth. "I told two strangers to go up there tonight."

"And on the subway," Ernie pipes in, his ear to the radio.

"None of the stoplights are working, so the traffic's at a standstill," a man I don't know tells me.

I go out into the street again, craning my neck to look up at all the buildings shrouded in darkness. Everyone seems so calm. The people who live in my building are all talking to each other for the first time. Jilly's is crammed with strangers sitting around candles, talking and sharing and connecting. Nobody can get home, so they have just stopped where they are. It feels like we are on the safest island in the world, and all of man's foibles, all our anxieties, aggressions and fears, have melted away for one night

"Isn't this awesome?" I tell Eddie, the dry cleaner.

"Sure is, Goldie. I've lived here all my life and I ain't seen nothing like this."

"Isn't that old Mrs. Krokovitch?" I say with surprise, pointing to a gray-haired woman standing talking to someone else across the street.

"Oh my God, you're right!" he says. "She hasn't unlocked that front door of her apartment in ten years. Wow, this night is really something!"

I run back up to my apartment to find my roommates drifting in from their auditions or from Phil Black's dance class. They are half giddy and half hysterical.

"Did you see the moon?" asks Anita.

"I know," says Susan. "I've never seen it so big."

"And how about the stars?" says Roberta. "It feels like I've never seen them before."

We run around and light the candles as more and more friends arrive on our doorstep. "Okay, I guess the party's at our house!" I laugh as I bring some glasses in from the kitchen.

"Well, you're the only people we know who live in a three-story walk-up!" Eddie cries, holding up a bottle of scotch as he waltzes in.

We finish lighting the candles, relishing their flickering light. Someone strums on a guitar and another rolls a joint. My front door is wide open, and, suddenly, standing there are the two guys I met in the dry cleaner's earlier this morning.

"Hi, Goldie! Sorry to crash this party," they say in unison.

"Hi! Oh, thank God you're okay! Come on in, this is great. I thought you might be stuck at the Empire State."

"We didn't get there yet," one says. "And 888 Eighth Avenue was the only address we knew in the whole city!"

"Welcome!" I say, and happily fix them a drink.

Other friends and strangers arrive with bottles of liquor or tins of food. People empty their refrigerators, and they bring transistor radios so we can listen to some music. We create our very own nightclub—partying together by the golden glow of candlelight.

I stay up all night, chatting and laughing with my two new friends. Sitting cross-legged on the floor, we share joy and friendship, touching and laughing and telling our secrets. We have no judgment, no history. We are just three people, united in the moment and enjoying the freedom of it. They don't push themselves on me, or try to take advantage. We have a closeness and an honesty that completely restores my faith in men.

At dawn, I eventually crash. I wake to find these two guys I have only just met sleeping on my pillow. My apartment is littered with people still making love or staring out the window, marveling at the tentative first light of morning. Reaching out, I switch off the table lamp, which tells me the power is back on. The blackout is over; the moment has passed. But this beautiful, magical experience, this perfect night, will forever mark my heart.

When we strip away the things that seem important and go back to the basics, we discover that all we really have is each other. I was a naïve out-of-towner who had been in New York less than a year. In that crazy period, everything had happened so quickly. I'd had some powerful, huge experiences, wins and losses, many of which had presented me with great personal dilemma. I had to get myself out of some tricky situations that I would never have even shared with my mom and dad.

I had left my rose-tinted family values behind and somehow come to be regarded as a strange sexual object by people who didn't even know me. I had been leered at and groped almost daily. More than any childhood experience I'd had, even the young man kneeling on my bedroom floor in Takoma Park, the Al Capps and the subway jerks and the seedy bargoers of this city had almost succeeded in breaking my spirit, in making me lose my faith in men.

Then, just when I'd decided I'd had enough, I was going to quit New York and find a healthier path somewhere else, the blackout restored that trust. A sheet of black velvet fell over the moonlit city that night, and, as if by magic, all that was dirty and cheap vanished. This one night became, for me, the epitome of the flower-power, peace-and-love days of the sixties. No one slept. Everybody loved each other; strangers made friends with strangers, and we had the wildest, funniest, most romantic night.

There was no fear in the air, no robbery, no murder. New Yorker helped New Yorker. Volunteers assisted the police and fire service in rescuing those who were trapped, or sent coffee and blankets to the hundreds without food or heat. Even the people stuck in the elevators of the Empire State Building didn't panic. They held hands in the darkness and sang.

That beautiful night of lovemaking and gentleness gave me a respite from the relentless onslaught of the worst, most predatory traits of man. It acted as an antidote and allowed me to lift my head again and decide to keep trying—both with my career and with men.

I have since come to learn a lot about men, about why they behave the way they do. Men had to protect their women and children when we were all out roaming the earth. They were the hunters. They became sexual animals that wanted multiple partners. I am so happy I was born a girl, because I have never had to struggle with that innate need to spread my seed or impregnate a mate.

Instead, I have learned over the years to feel a deep understanding for how difficult it is for men just to be male, to have this hormone raging through their blood like a drug. It makes it difficult to control their behavior. Just going out on the street can be hard for men because the sight of a girl in a short skirt, even if she has a bag over her head, ignites them physically. It goes directly to their sexual energy.

Men fight such impulses every day, especially in their prime years, always having to corral themselves because they have a family, a wife or responsibilities, because they have to be good boys, be part of society and hold down a job. We women can't identify with the frustration that they feel at having to bottle that up. If we could have testosterone shot into us daily and experience what happens to our tempers, our sexual energy and our destructive forces, we would be horrified.

Most important, I no longer blame the male sex. I may not like it when they misbehave or are disrespectful to women; it doesn't feel good, and, in fact, it hurts. But then I try to summon my higher self, the one that gets to observe, and look at the bigger picture. Only then can I see what happened and understand that when they say, "But I love you, honey, it didn't mean anything," the sad part is that for them, it *didn't*.

The man who jerked off in front of me at the Peppermint Box probably went home to his wife and kids. Similarly, the photographer who groped me in the darkroom, or the two thugs on the subway. If I had acted differently, if I had responded to their advances, it wouldn't have made any difference to them. They would merely have satisfied an urge, like scratching an itch, and—as sure as eggs are eggs—the itch would have come back sooner rather than later, with someone else.

What was so wonderful about the night of the blackout and its perfect timing in my life was that it taught me the beauty of a world where people's defenses come down, where primeval urges are set aside and love and understanding prevail. We were all just human beings in the candlelight that night, trying to help each other out. I'd never felt more alive, more a part of everything. Everyone was just living in the moment. It was the most extraordinary revelation and a real awakening for me. Most of all, it allowed me to have hope again.

And with hope, I could pursue my dream.

postcard

Have you ever doubted the existence of God? I have, and I am sure most of you have, for it is a normal thought. But take the time to look around at some of our natural resources: the mountains, the rivers, the deserts, the oceans, the sunrises and sunsets.

All these things were created by God Himself, for man is not capable of making anything so beautiful. Yes, man can reproduce a mountain or a sunset on canvas. Man can make a lake, but never will he capture the true colors and feeling that God has created.

God made man just as beautifully as He constructed these geographical wonders. He has been able to preserve them just as He wished. Man is unable to change them, yet there are so many things man has altered against God's wishes. How beautiful they must have been when they were first made; many have remained as beautiful. Sadly, man has ruined a great deal.

—*Written at age nineteen, as I flew from*
New York to California for the first time

courage

*It is not who we meet along
life's highway that matters;
it is how we treat them.*

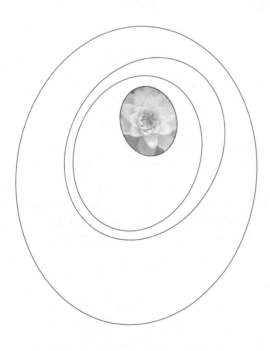

O kay, girls! Let's roll!" yells my friend Sandy as we suck the last of our Orange Julius drinks through straws at Pete's Hotdog stand in West Hollywood, Los Angeles. "Las Vegas, here we come!"

Shrieking with excitement, we five dancers jump into our separate vehicles for the five-hour drive to Vegas. I'm the only one with a traveling companion: Lambchop, a toy poodle I impulsively blew two hundred bucks on in a pet store just before I left New York. It is August 1965.

"The Desert Inn, right?" I ask as we start up our engines and lean out the windows, calling to each other from across the lot. My '59 Chevy convertible with the cool fins and the permanent squeak coughs to life and almost drowns me out.

"That's right, Goldie," Sandy yells from her '58 Cadillac, which, like mine, has seen better days. "Just stay on the 15 Freeway across the desert until you see the pretty lights." She floors her accelerator and races off with a squeal of tires. Horns honking, the others follow close behind, and I hurry to bring up the rear.

I haven't a clue where we are going. I have only been in California a few months, and I still feel like a foreigner amid the flower-power, anti–Vietnam War, hippie culture. I am sharing an apartment with a family near the famous NBC Studios in Burbank and am about to embark on a new adventure.

The sun is shining, the radio is playing "I Got You Babe" by Sonny and Cher, and I am back to being a gypsy in the chorus line again. Sitting in my long, low, sexy Chevy, with Lambchop in the passenger seat, we are off to Vegas. Honking at the girls in front and laughing, I know I made the right move in heading west. Everything feels fresh and bright and new here. It is a place of opportunity, not a city of broken dreams.

Singing along to the music on our radios, our little caravan snakes along Sunset Boulevard, past the Beverly Hills Hotel, Dino's Lodge from *77 Sunset Strip* and Ciro's Restaurant. Waving and whistling at the tanned young men who stop and stare, we felt life couldn't be sweeter.

Rounding a corner at the famous Chateau Marmont Hotel, our cars nearly bump into one another when we come face-to-face with a sharp reminder of reality. Marching down the middle of the street toward us is an antiwar protest denouncing President Johnson for sending a further fifty thousand troops to Vietnam.

DON'T SEND OUR BOYS TO THEIR DEATHS, reads one banner. Long-haired hippies trail past us, handing out single roses with the message "Make love not war." I take a rose and watch them shyly as they march slowly past in their combat jackets and multicolored headbands, not really understanding the politics of their protest or the intensity of their emotions. I was never one for rallies; I missed all that because I was too busy working. Every time I heard that somebody I knew from high school or Takoma Park had died in Vietnam, I would cry. I knew I wanted Americans out of there, but I didn't really know why.

The marchers march past, and I wedge my red rose between the cigarette lighter and the ashtray, as a silent reminder to myself. "Every day I'm going to make myself think about our boys fighting out in Vietnam," I tell myself aloud. "Losing their lives in what seems to be a senseless war."

We head for the California freeway that wends its way through the eastern Mojave Desert, and I watch the scenery shifting all around me. The tall buildings give way to smaller ones; the shops and houses become fewer; and there is gradually more countryside. Soon, I find myself surrounded by rolling hills, parched brown by the summer sun, a few palm trees dotting the horizon. The wind is in my hair, the radio is now playing "Mr. Tambourine Man" by the Byrds, and I feel so free.

Looking around, I realize that this is the extraordinary landscape I flew over when I first came in from the east. This is what inspired me to write about God. These are the undulating mounds of earth and rocks that form voluptuous contours from the air. I've never seen spaces like this before, such vast uninhabited areas colored gold. I have lived a tiny little life on the East Coast where the mountains are so old that they've turned into bald hills. I thought the trees that grew over my house were big. I've never seen barrenness like this, peppered only by cacti or Joshua trees, and I am mystified.

With hardly any other cars on the road, and the late afternoon sun beginning its slow descent over the spectacular mountains that form the horizon, I have rarely seen anything more beautiful.

Passing road signs to places like Sidewinder Mountain, Coyote Lake, Devil's Playground and Ghost Town of Calico, I whoop and holler to Lambchop, who is perched up against the rear window, the wind ruffling his curly brown fur.

Thump, thump, thump.

My car starts to pull violently to the left just past a place called Barstow. A strange vibration beneath my feet shakes the car, and it is accompanied by an even stranger sound.

Thump, thump, thump.

Switching off the radio, I can hear the odd noise at the back as my vehicle weaves right and left. The car becomes increasingly wobbly, and I struggle with the huge steering wheel. Leaning on my horn and flashing my lights, I try to alert the girls in front of me, but they are all too busy singing along to their radios, hair flying.

"Hey! Guys! Help! Help!" I yell, trying to keep up despite the terrible noise my vehicle is now making as bits of rubber fly off the rear tire. "Hey! Please! Wait!" I wave at them frantically out my window, hoping one of them will spot me in her rearview mirror. To my horror, I watch as all four cars disappear over the horizon.

I pull the car over to the soft shoulder in a billowing cloud of dust. There isn't a vehicle or a building as far as the eye can see. As I turn off the engine and step out, I have never heard such silence. I am completely alone in this desolate spot, just Lambchop and me.

Getting out to check the damage, I discover my rear tire in shreds. Damn it! A blowout. Why me?

With just a critical tilt of his head, I can almost hear Lambchop saying, This is a fine fix you got us into, Mom.

Glaring back at him, I say, "Well, I don't know what the hell we're going to do. How are we going to get out of this?"

Lambchop rests his head on his paws and closes his eyes.

I sit dejectedly on the fins at the back of my car, ready to wave down anyone who passes. I am sporting pink hip-hugger capris, a midriff top and orange flip-flops. It is ages before I see anyone, but then a pickup appears on the horizon like a mirage, shimmering in the heat. Jumping up on the trunk of my car in case he doesn't see me, I put both arms in the air and wave dementedly.

"Hey! Hey there!" I yell, "I need help. I have a flat tire!"

The driver of the pickup truck gives me a shrug of his shoulders and speeds on by.

"You horse's ass!" I yell after him, the worst cussword I can think of. I watch as it takes his truck a full ten minutes to become a dot and follow my friends over the horizon.

The sun is sinking fast and the sky is changing to purple. In the lessening light, the landscape takes on a different perspective. It feels gloomier somehow, sinister even. Each new minute brings down another layer of mauve gauze. The wind picks up, and every minute the air seems to be losing its comforting yellow heat. Looking forlornly at my soundly sleeping dog, I start to feel scared.

To my intense relief, another car appears on the horizon twenty minutes later, coming from the direction of Las Vegas. "Perhaps the guy had a change of heart," I tell Lambchop hopefully. "God, I hope he didn't hear me swearing at him." I pause and scratch my head. "Or perhaps he did, and he's come back to rape and murder me, before scattering the pieces of my dismembered body all over the desert!" Scooping Lambchop protectively into my arms, I stand apprehensively at the side of the road.

I only exhale when I realize this is a different car, driven—thank the Lord—by a presentable young man in smart clothes. He slows down and pulls onto the side of the road just beyond my beleaguered vehicle.

"Are you in some kind of trouble, miss?" he asks me, his accent unfamiliar.

"Yes, I am," I reply. "I have a flat, and I'm afraid I don't know how to change it."

Peeling off his jacket, he pulls out some tools from his trunk and brings them back to my car. He rolls up his shirtsleeves and reveals a pair of well-shaped arms. I sigh with relief. After taking off my old tire, he looks up at me and asks, "Do you have a spare?"

"Gee, I don't know," I say. "Where would it be?"

He laughs at me and opens my trunk. "In here," he says, effortlessly lifting out an old spare, getting dirt all over his shirt.

"I'm so sorry about your clothes."

"It's not *that* that I'm bothered about," he says, smiling up at me wistfully. "I'm going on a date with my girlfriend tonight, and now I'm gonna be late."

"Oh no!" I cry, thinking of the poor girl waiting for her handsome young beau in his finest clothes and with his bunch of flowers on the front seat. "I'm so sorry."

My sweet Good Samaritan not only changes my tire, he then offers to follow me back the way he came to a small town called Harvard a few miles farther on, where someone should be able to replace my flat.

"Oh, it's okay, really, you don't have to do that," I say apologetically.

"Yes, ma'am, I do," he replies. "This spare isn't in great shape either, and you could be stuck with another flat just a few miles up the road. Harvard's just up the way a piece."

I feel terrible, and my face must show it because he adds, "Don't worry, I can call my girlfriend from the gas station and explain."

Listening to him making the call, I can tell that his girlfriend isn't happy.

"Oh, hi, honey. Well, I had to stop and help a girl just out of Barstow, she had a flat . . . No, no, not that kind of a girl . . . Well, she was stuck on the freeway . . . I know, I know . . . Listen . . . No, she's not that pretty."

Watching him, my arms crossed, I think, Hmm, but I am interesting-looking.

"You should be all right now," he tells me when he hangs up the phone, his face flushed red.

"I can't thank you enough," I reply, reaching up and pecking him lightly on the cheek. "I hope I didn't get you into too much trouble."

"Aw, no." He grins and his cheeks go the color of watermelon.

"Bye, then." I wave with a smile, and off he goes.

After paying the gas station attendant an exorbitant sum for his labors, I ask, "Which way to Vegas?"

"Straight up the 15 through the bottom end of Death Valley for about a hundred and fifty miles," he says, without humor. "You'll see a sign and you turn off there."

"Wait, wait. Stop. Death Valley? Is that, like, a scary place?"

"Can be," he says, without elaborating.

By the time I get back in my car with Lambchop, it is almost seven o'clock and getting dark. Death Valley? A hundred and fifty miles? Perfect. I trundle along at sixty miles an hour, the road stretching ahead of me relentlessly. The soft hills around me become jagged outcroppings of rock, and the landscape becomes very bleak. The temperature plummets, and I reach round to my suitcase and pull out a sweater I knitted. Soon, there is hardly any light at all, just the pale moon over the mountains, which, silhouetted in black, are eerie and menacing.

I have no concept of how long I have been driving or how far I have to go. It feels like I will be on this solitary road crossing the desert forever, hemmed in by a tunnel of dark shapes looming on either side of me. Only a handful of vehicles pass me or come at me from the other way. Each time one does, I sit rigidly in my seat, checking the rearview mirror to make sure I'm not being followed by an ax murderer.

I am soon desperate to pee, but I don't want to stop by the side of the road in case of snakes or crazy men. Up ahead, I see a truck stop, and I pull in gratefully. Running from my car with Lambchop in my arms, I use the grimy facilities as quickly as I can and run back, locking and then relocking the car door and checking behind me all the while.

Lambchop settles onto my lap to sleep, giving me a welcome sense of calm. I wish I could just stay where I am for a while, in this pool of light from a single bulb swaying in the night breeze. "Maybe if we slid down in our seat, nobody would notice us, and we could wait until morning,"

courage

I whisper into Lambchop's ear. He looks up into my eyes and I look down into his, but I know we have to keep going. Starting the engine, I yank the shift into drive and pull away as Lambchop jumps into the back.

Just a few yards up the road, I falter. Standing by the side of the road is a dark shadow. It is the figure of a man with a duffel bag and some sort of hat on his head. He is lit by the moon. When my headlights fully illuminate him, he turns toward me, raises his arm and sticks out his thumb.

What should I do? Should I pick him up? It would be nice not to be alone. Maybe I shouldn't. Would I be safer with someone else in the car? Or am I asking for trouble? The closer I get, the more I agonize. Getting closer still, I see he is a soldier, and I stand on the brakes.

"Hi there," he says with a smile as he pokes his head through the open passenger window. "Could you give me a lift?" The lights on my dashboard illuminate his face. He is about my age, with an open face and a beautiful smile.

"Yeah, where are you headed?"

"I'm going home," he says.

"Going home, huh? Great. Jump in."

He opens the door and folds his six-foot frame into my car, filling the space with his broad shoulders. I breathe a sigh of relief. A soldier is escorting me through Death Valley.

"So, where's home?"

"Good Springs. It's about sixty miles this side of Vegas."

"Vegas? That's where I'm going. Have you ever been there?"

He laughs. "Yes I have, ma'am. Too many times."

"Uh-oh, what's that supposed to mean?"

"Nothing," he chuckles. "What are you doing in Vegas?"

"I'm a dancer." Seeing his surprise, I add hastily, "Top on."

We both laugh.

"Where are you dancing?"

"The Desert Inn. I'm doing five shows a night for three months. If I ever get there, that is." There is a pause, then I ask him, "Are you on leave or something?"

He nods. "I'm going to surprise my mom. She doesn't know I'm back."

"Back from where?"

"Vietnam."

I stammer my reply. "V-Vietnam? You've been in Vietnam?" I think of all those banners, the grim statistics in the papers about how many people are being killed every day, and how young the U.S. soldiers are—average age, nineteen.

"Yup," he replies without missing a beat. "I'm a Green Beret."

"Wow! That's pretty heavy. You must be, well, God, a Green Beret . . ." I look up at the beret with renewed respect. Seeing me staring, he pulls it from his head to reveal a closely shaved scalp.

"I've got a week's leave," he says. "I didn't tell Mom. It's her fiftieth birthday next week. My name is Stu, by the way."

"Oh, hi, Stu," I reply with a giggle. "I'm Goldie. And this is my dog, Lambchop."

He turns to look at my sleeping poodle and smiles.

"So, what happens at the end of your leave?" I ask.

Staring straight ahead at the empty road winding off into the desert night, he says, in a small voice, "I have to go back."

"Go back?" I gasp, but I stop myself from saying more. We drive in silence for several miles, both lost in our own worlds.

"Are you hungry?" he asks suddenly.

"I'm a dancer." I grin. "We're always hungry."

"Then turn off up ahead. There's a good little diner in a mall just along the next road."

Over an ice-cream sundae that Stu can barely believe I will finish, I tell him about my childhood in Takoma Park, my dream to be happy and a few of my more salutary experiences in New York.

He tucks into a chocolate fudge sundae and listens intently to every word I have to say. "Boy, this is good. I sure miss this," he says, enjoying every mouthful.

"Gee, listen to me chattering on," I say, suddenly embarrassed. "You must think me very shallow compared to what's happening in your life. I mean, you're a real live soldier, in a war and everything."

Stu laughs. "Yeah, but I've never met a real live Vegas showgirl before. Who knows, maybe you'll be a star one day. When I'm back in

Vietnam, I'll think of you dancing your butt off to 'Mustang Sally' in your little fringed costume and it will remind me of home."

I look in his eyes and wonder if he will ever make it home again.

"What's it like in Vietnam?" I ask finally, almost afraid of the answer.

He stares at his big hands for a moment before answering. "Ugly . . . I've lost a lot of good friends."

Reaching out, I take his hand in mine and squeeze it. No words are necessary. Pulling myself together, I tell him proudly, "I have a friend who's a captain in the Army out in Vietnam."

"You do?" he replies, relieved by the shift in mood.

"Yes." I nod. "His name is Michael Waghelstein. He was at Montgomery Blair High School with me in Silver Spring, Maryland, and then they called him up. He is a good Jewish boy and a great student with not a fighting bone in his body. Hey, would you please say hi from little Goldie Hawn if ever you meet him?"

Stu laughs. "Yes, I will." Grabbing his beret, he slides out of our booth. "Come on, now. It's getting late. Time to go."

We travel in silence for the next hour. The landscape is lunar, with just a few little pockets of humanity clustered around the odd truck stop. We pass Baker and Soda Lake, Clark Mountain and Jean. My heart sinks when I see the town sign to Good Springs, and Stu points out where to turn off.

"You can drop me on this corner," he says. "I live just down that street."

Bringing the car to a halt, I peer beyond him into the darkness and see a series of unremarkable low-rise houses flanking a road with nothing else along it.

Stu turns to look at me for a moment, and I think he is going to say something. Maybe he's having second thoughts? Maybe he wants me to drive straight on to Las Vegas and help him go AWOL. Why don't we just run away together and forget all about the things we were supposed to be doing? I can almost hear him say. But whatever he is thinking privately he decides not to share.

Without speaking, he grabs his duffel bag from the back and dumps it on the ground next to him. He pulls on his green beret and smooths down his uniform. I open the driver's door and step out and walk round to where he is standing. Reaching up, stretching on tiptoes, I adjust his beret so that it comes down at a slight angle over his right eye.

"Good-bye, Goldie Hawn," Stu says with a smile, leaning down and kissing me tenderly on the lips.

"Good-bye, Stu," I reply, kissing him back. His lips are soft and taste of vanilla. "And good luck."

Stepping back, he brings his right hand up to his head in a crisp salute before turning sharply on his heel and walking away.

I climb wearily back into my car with Lambchop for the final leg of my long journey. Starting the engine, I pull slowly away from the side of the road as if floating in a dream.

In my rearview mirror I watch for as long as I can until Stu melts into the darkness and disappears from sight. When he is gone, I realize with a heaving sob that wells up from somewhere deep inside me that I will probably never know the fate of my "unknown" soldier.

War. When will we learn?

courage

choices

Doors slide open and shut along life's path.
Roads diverge right and left. The only way
to discover where they lead is to
choose which one to take.

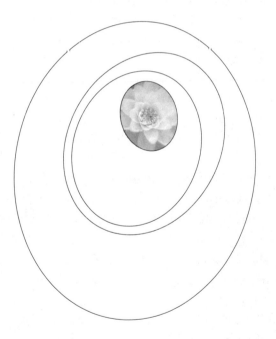

C ome on, Lambchop," I whisper, opening the door to my apartment so he can follow at my heels. "Let's get out of this place!"

It is dawn, and I am fleeing Las Vegas like a thief, slamming the door
on the five shows a night, the vampire hours and the drooling perverts.

The wheels of my car spin dust as I head for the Mojave Desert highway that brought me here three months ago. Three whole months of
sleeping when I can during the day, tinfoil taped to my window to block
the light. Three months of never venturing out in the daylight because of
the ferocious heat. Three months of having to dance in half-empty bars.
I've had enough.

Goldie, I can hear my dad's words of advice ringing in my ears. Go
back to L.A. and see if you can get some work at one of the television studios. Give yourself a set time period, and, if it doesn't work out, then
come on home.

Nine months, I tell myself. I'm giving myself nine months. If I
haven't got a dancing job by then, I'm going to go back to Maryland, and
I'm going to open that dance school.

Escaping now in the middle of the night, Lambchop at my side, I
retrace my journey across the desert toward L.A. The top down, the
wind in my hair, I drive up through the mountains and down the other
side. My road to hell has become my road to freedom. Passing through
Good Springs, I wonder about my unknown soldier and what kind of
hell he is in.

Back in the city, pounding the pavement with a portfolio that is bigger than I am, I try to get work at a studio or in commercials. Time and again, I am turned down. Time and again, I put myself in a place of rejection.

"Oh, thank you, Miss Hawn. That was lovely . . . Next!"

"You're too unusual-looking . . . You can't be pigeonholed . . . We don't know what to do with you." One agent even tells me, "We don't really know where to place you. Go get a job and then come back and we'll see what we can do."

I go through all the usual agonies of wondering what it is about me that the producers and directors don't like. Is it my face? My body? How I look? How I read the line? The scrutiny is intense and only brings more self-scrutiny, feeding on my insecurities.

"I am not going to be one of those sad L.A. girls who grow old here waiting to be discovered," I tell my new roommate, Shawn Randall. She's a dancer too, and we share an apartment in the heart of Hollywood.

Looking up a list of talent agencies, I find one in downtown L.A., on Fourth Street. I take the freeway, the top down, but the smog is so bad that it burns my eyes. Pulling my car over, I wipe the smudged makeup from my eyes in the rearview mirror and carefully reapply it. I try to put my top up, but it won't go. My car, like my life, is falling apart.

Eventually finding the agency, I push open the door and scale a mountain of wooden stairs with paint-chipped walls on either side. I reach the top and a door with a rickety knob. I turn it tentatively and step inside. A big guy sitting behind a desk smiles at me. "Come on in," he says with a wave.

He has a broad smile and a colorful shirt. His name is George, and I like him. The wall behind his desk is plastered with photographs of his clients.

"So, what can you do?" he asks as he pores over my portfolio of publicity shots.

"I'm a dancer."

"Great. How about commercials? Do you have any experience?"

"Well, yes, I did one for a hair product in Vegas. But I had to wear a big red wig and I looked awful."

"I don't know why they didn't let you show your pretty hair."

"George," I ask, looking up at his wall of fame, "tell me, do you represent any white clients?"

George laughs, a big open laugh that reveals a mouth full of teeth. "Well, no, girl," he replies with a chuckle. "You'd be my first. Don't you worry, Goldie, I don't care what color your skin is. I can help you . . . I can definitely help you."

So now I have an agent, only he never asks me to sign anything, and he never seems to call. I continue to spend my life traipsing from one audition to the next, my dance bag slung over my shoulder, sometimes with Shawn, sometimes without, always hungry for work.

One day, we spot an advertisement in the show business rags for *The Andy Griffith Special.*

"Yes!" I cry, excitedly. "This is exactly what Daddy said I should go for."

We drive to the CBS studios in Shawn's Oldsmobile, which looks and sounds like a Sherman tank. Laughing, chatting away, we are as free as birds and looking forward to our audition. Finding the rehearsal hall, we see some familiar faces from other auditions, girls like us who are doing the rounds. Most of them are older, and have been dancing in L.A. for years. They form tight cliques, and know their presence here is perfunctory; they will almost certainly be selected.

"Okay, five, six, seven, eight . . ." the choreographer, Nick Castle, puts us through our paces. We begin in groups of ten, and then he mixes the combinations, watches some of us perform solo, hears a few of us sing, and finally whittles us down to twenty girls.

"All right, now," he says, clapping his hands together and lining us all up in front of him. "You, you and you, thanks so much, but not this time. You and you, you're in." He was pointing at Shawn and me.

"Really?" I cry, looking excitedly at Shawn. "We're in?"

"The pay is four hundred and fifty bucks for the week," Mr. Castle's assistant tells us. "There'll be four days of rehearsals and three days' shooting. You'll be doing some singing as well as dancing."

"Four hundred and fifty dollars?" I reply, my eyes wide. "God! I was only making one-eighty in Vegas!" I am so excited, I can't wait to call Mom and Dad.

"I'm going to be dancing on an Andy Griffith special for Nick Castle, Mom," I tell her later that night from somewhere above cloud nine. "Nick's a god to the dancers in Hollywood. If he likes me, then I'm made."

"Oh, Andy Griffith is my favorite, doll," she says, in her gruff voice. "Goldie, this is going to be so much fun. Rut! Rut! Come and speak to Goldie. She has some good news."

"Way to go, Kink!" Dad says. "We'll be watching. Wear something red so we can see you among the spear throwers." It gives me a thrill to imagine him watching me with his TV tray and his socks half off.

I arrive on set the first day, and Tennessee Ernie Ford, the statuesque country-and-western singer who shares the show with Andy Griffith, stares down at my old dancing shoes, which have holes in them. My eyes follow his.

"So, what's with the shoes?" he asks. "You going for extra ventilation?"

"These are my lucky shoes." I giggle.

"Hmm." He smiles and walks away.

Later that day, he stops the rehearsal in front of the whole cast to make an announcement. "Everyone chipped in," he tells me with a grin, presenting me with a brand-new pair of shoes.

I am so overwhelmed I almost cry. Happily, I pull them on, and they feel great as we do some new routines. A short while later, Nick Castle pulls me to one side. "You've got it, Goldie girl!" he tells me. "From now on, you're going to be in all of my shows." As he walks away, I stare down at my new shoes. Wait a minute, I think. Maybe *these* are my lucky shoes!

That night, I glue glitter on them so that it spells out THANK on one shoe and YOU on the other.

I t is the first day of shooting, and now I know why I'm being paid so much. Nick is a wonderful choreographer, but we sweat and pant our way through the grueling routines we have to learn in just a few days. The constant repetition to get the shot just right is exhausting.

Twelve of the older girls are up front, singing and doing their thing, and Shawn and I are in the background, high-kicking and trying to synchronize our movements and singing all at once. It isn't easy.

"Okay, everyone," Nick yells, clapping his hands together, "take a break, and then we'll go again. Five minutes, everyone."

Leaning up against the back wall, swigging thirstily from a bottle of water, I spot a handsome young man walking straight toward me with a big smile on his face. "Uh-huh," I say to Shawn, with a nudge, "here we go."

"Let's hear his line, at least," she says.

"Excuse me," he begins, extending a hand, "my name is Art Simon. I work for the William Morris Agency, and I'm servicing the show."

I look at him like he has six heads. William Morris? I don't think so.

"Tell me, are you represented?"

"Not really," I say, thinking guiltily of dear George, who hasn't called me in weeks.

"Well, can you come to my office next Wednesday so we can talk?" he asks, handing me his card. "Say, at eleven o'clock?"

"Uh-huh," I reply, coolly.

"Okay, everyone! Places!"

I can hardly believe my five-minute break is over. I take the man's card and stuff it down the front of my leotard without another thought.

The following Wednesday morning, the telephone rings in my apartment just as I am halfway through a piece of Sara Lee vanilla cake, the kind my dad loves.

"Miss Hawn? This is Art Simon's secretary at the William Morris Agency. We got your number from CBS. Mr. Simon's waiting for you here, and we just wondered if you were coming for your eleven o'clock appointment?"

"Oh my God!" I cry, spitting crumbs from my mouth. "He really is an agent for William Morris? Okay, I'll be right there."

Scampering around the apartment in a blind panic, I grab an orange jersey dress with a bold psychedelic design, tousle my hair and smear some lipstick across my lips. Slipping on some sandals, I rush out the door and jump into my trusty Chevy, which is now really falling apart on me. The passenger's-side door won't latch, and each time I make a right-hand turn it flies open and exposes me and any passenger to the street. Driving with one hand, I have to lean across the front seat and pull it closed. Left-hand turns are no problem—but, then, they never have been.

Looking like something out of *The Beverly Hillbillies*, I find the agency on El Camino Drive, in a smart area I don't usually frequent. Parking my car illegally, I run into the building and ask a receptionist where to go. Rushing upstairs, I say to anyone I see, "Art Simon? Where's Art Simon's office?" Several people point or give me directions, and I barrel through his door.

"I'm so sorry I'm late," I say, breathlessly.

Art is sitting behind a long desk, flanked by six other men, all dressed in identical suits and ties. They all stare back at me.

"Hello, Goldie," Art says. "Good of you to join us."

"Hi," I say, catching my breath and sitting down. "I really didn't think you were serious."

"It's okay," Art interrupts. "You're here now. Well, guys?"

I sit on my hands, fidgeting as seven pairs of eyes give me the once-over.

One of the agents looks down at his notes and speaks to Art as if I am not even in the room. "Well, what can she do?"

"She can sing."

"Actually, I'm really a dancer," I chip in, but no one looks my way.

"She can dance."

"Anything else?"

"She has something about her, don't you think?"

They all look up at me with blank faces.

I stare back at them. Gee, what should I do? Maybe I should break into a soft-shoe shuffle.

A man on the left asks Art, "What were you thinking of sending her up for?"

"*Good Morning World.* That new CBS comedy sitcom by Persky and Danoff."

"But she's too young for that character."

"I know, but I thought Persky and Danoff should meet her."

Good Morning World? Persky and Danoff? What in the world are they talking about? I wish someone would cue me in.

"Okay," one of the men says, standing up. The others follow him toward the door. "Do what you want. Go ahead. Sign her." They leave the room without as much as a good-bye.

Art looks across at me and gives me a conspiratorial wink.

I read the few pages of the script Art gave me and then go to my meeting with Bill Persky and Sam Danoff, who, it turns out, are the biggest TV producers in town. The story revolves around two radio disc jockeys who are friends and neighbors, one married and one single. I'm supposed to play the wife. I arrive lugging a huge shopping bag that clanks as I heave it into the room.

"Come on in, Miss Hawn," one of them says. "Well, now, what have you got in there?"

"Props," I say, putting down the bag and pulling out a Corning Ware teapot, cup, saucer and plate, as well as spoons, knives, forks and napkins. "The script says I have to make some tea."

They start to laugh.

"Did I do something wrong?" I giggle.

"No, it's just that we're not used to actresses bringing in their own props."

"Oh, really?" What an ass, I think to myself. Could I be any dumber?

"Anyway, dear, that's very clever of you to think of it, so why don't you go ahead and get it all out and then you can read your lines?"

I am so nervous that when I open my mouth to speak, I am shocked by my own voice. What comes out is eight octaves higher than my own. I can't wait to finish. I know I'm completely wrong for this part.

"Thank you so much, Goldie," they tell me when I'm done, nodding and smiling.

"No thank you, guys," I say, embarrassed. "This was really a lot of fun." They watch me as I repack my bag of tricks, excuse myself with a bow and run down the stairs. Boy, well, I really screwed that up, I think to myself.

Back in my apartment, I call Art Simon immediately.

"Hi, Art, it's Goldie."

"Hi, Goldie. Listen, you didn't get the part . . ."

"Oh, I know, and I really thank you so much for believing in me, Art. But, you know what? If you don't want to represent me anymore, that's fine too, because I sort of have an agent downtown, and I think that maybe I should really go back with him."

"No, Goldie, you don't understand," Art replies. "You didn't get *that* part."

"What do you mean?"

"They wrote in a new part for you."

"Wait a minute, you mean I didn't get *that* part, but they wrote another part for me with *that* character?"

"No. They liked you so much they created a whole new character just for you."

"They did?" I slump back into a chair, all the wind knocked out of me.

"Goldie? Did you hear what I said? You've got the job. You're going to be an actress on television. This is just the beginning."

A rt Simon believed in me. He discovered me in a chorus line and had the fearlessness to stand up and put his instincts on the line. He became my trusted agent, and then manager, for many years to come. If I hadn't chosen this show to do, I would never have met him, and who knows what my life would look like today. I still question that thing called destiny. The choices we make in life and the roads we choose to travel take us to places we may only dream about.

The choices we make can change the course of our lives. It is not the course of our lives that changes us. The road doesn't come to you; you go to the road. I chose to leave Vegas and try for a career in television. I chose to go to that audition, and I chose to follow the path that Art

Simon set for me. The choices I made set in motion a series of events that were now completely out of my control.

Sometimes the choices we make are good, and sometimes they are bad. Sometimes the fear of making a bad choice prevents us from making any choice at all. It is a question of doors opening and shutting in front of us along the way. Should we go through this door, or that one? Should we wait? Or move forward to the next door? Luck certainly plays a part in fate, but what gets us to that lucky place in the first place is a direct consequence of our own decisions.

In my case, I met someone pivotal in my life—Art Simon—who was to become my manager, confidant, laughing partner and guru. He helped me make the right choices along the way. He believed in me and guided me with dignity. He protected me as one would protect a precious jewel. That is rare in Hollywood. I cherish him to this day.

Sometimes we make choices that turn out to be bad, but, if we do, we shouldn't dwell on it. Instead, we should really stop and think about what happened. Only then can we uncover the hidden lesson, the golden nugget of truth that previously we may not have seen. Mistakes are good, because in illuminating the wrong path they remind us not to go that way again.

Change is the key. Whatever our choices, good or bad, we must learn from them, we must change, and we must move on.

success

Success is just a word, a relative concept.
It's how we handle success that matters.

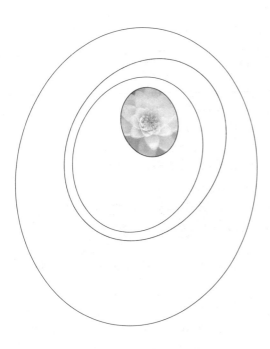

Entering the elevator of the Hilton Hotel on Sixth Avenue in New York, I hear the doors slide shut behind me and stare at my reflection in the smoked-glass interior.

I barely recognize myself. My hair has been coiffed, my clothes are new, and I have just walked out of the luxurious thirtieth-floor, three-room suite that CBS has provided for me.

I am two blocks from 888 Eighth Avenue, where, just over a year ago, I was sharing a three-room apartment with five other dancers. Now I am a guest at this brand-new hotel I could never previously afford, near the Stage Deli, where I used to sit with Max eating blintzes.

The doors slide open when the elevator reaches the lobby, and I am faced with a wall of people I have never met.

"Goldie Hawn! Miss Hawn! Over here!" Cameras flash, and strangers press in on me, thrusting pens and pieces of paper into my hand. "Can I please have your autograph?" they ask.

"I can't wait to see your new show, Miss Hawn," someone tells me, squeezing my arm a little too tightly.

"Thanks," I reply shyly, trying to find enough elbow room to write my name. All the while, I'm thinking, Who are these people? How do they know me? The CBS publicity people did warn me that there had been a lot of hype about this new show in New York, and that the press would jump all over us, but this is crazy. I haven't shot a single scene of *Good Morning World,* and nothing has been aired yet.

Pushing my way out through the crowd and into the vast lobby, I try to look for the public relations woman who has organized this parade of new fall shows for the CBS affiliates meeting at which I am an honored guest. I want to ask her if this is normal. But she is nowhere to be seen among the milling throng of journalists and invited viewers. Nor are any of my costars—Joby Baker, Ronnie Schell, Julie Parrish—whom I haven't even met yet.

"Miss Hawn? Miss Hawn? This way, please."

Another photographer. Another flash. I am left blinking into the glare.

"How does it feel to be one of CBS's rising stars?" a pushy young reporter asks me.

"Well, gee, I don't know," I reply, trying to smile.

"Your promotional material says the writers created a character especially for you," a woman tells me. "Has anything like this ever happened to you before?"

"Oh God no! I only just started really. I left New York a year ago with just fifty dollars in my pocket."

"Fifty dollars? That's great, thanks." She disappears.

The elevator doors *ping* open behind me. Spotting an escape route, I slip through the doors impulsively, getting out while I still can. Hurrying to my suite, I open the door and slip in, pressing my back against the door once it is closed. The momentary peace is shattered by the sound of the telephone, which sits on a polished mahogany table laden with bowls of fruit and vases of flowers.

"Miss Hawn?"

"Yes."

"Could you please come down to the lobby immediately? We need you for a photo call."

Replacing the receiver, I take a deep breath and head once again for the door.

T he yellow taxi turns into my dead-end street and I finally exhale. Cleveland Avenue, Takoma Park. My childhood home. The Holy Grail of my mind. I feel the car bump over the potholes that still haven't been fixed, and I sigh with relief.

This'll be great, I tell myself. Mom's matzo ball soup. Dad's crazy jokes. They'll love to hear all the stories. I can hardly wait to sleep in my old bed, between Mom's crisp white sheets.

Paying the driver, I grab my bag and hurry toward my parents' red-brick duplex, savoring every step closer to home. In one bound, I am up on the front porch where dear Nixi always used to wait for me and through the door that is never locked.

"Mom? Daddy? I'm home," I call, rushing into the hallway and dropping my bag at the foot of the stairs. I can't wait to see them, to run into their arms and just be held. "It's Goldie. Are you home?"

Silence greets me. I wander into the living room and no one is there. Glancing at my watch, I realize with dismay that they must still be at work. Walking into the kitchen, I take stock and look around. Was this room always so small? Have they done something different? Did Mom really bathe me in this sink as a child?

I open the door to the basement and peer down at the tiny space where Jean Lynn and I played house, where David Fisher helped my father with some of his inventions. Daddy's workbench is still there, littered with watch parts, strange objects and tools.

In the living room, the stuffed pheasant is no longer on the mantelpiece. Searching for it, I find it in a cupboard in the back room, its feathers moth-eaten. Stepping lightly on the unfamiliar wall-to-wall carpeting I just sent my mother the money for, I revisit all the rooms of my childhood, as if I am seeing them for the first time. There is the piano I learned to sing on. There is the mohair armchair Daddy sits in to drink his scotch and sniff his sauces.

Climbing the stairs, past the balusters I used to peer between at the Christmas tree, I see that my parents now have separate bedrooms. With me gone, there is no longer any need for pretense. I walk into my little green bedroom and sit on the bed. Outside are the oak trees that no longer seem as tall. I wonder if the descendants of the squirrels I fed as a child still live inside their trunks.

I want to feel happy. I want to feel comforted. I want to feel safe. But, for some reason, I don't. Outside, I hear the sound of a car's wheels on gravel. Jumping up and looking out, I see my parents walking wearily from the car toward the house. Throwing open the window, I lean out and say hello.

"Hi, Mom! Hi, Daddy! I'm back!" I wave excitedly.

My father's face lights up. "Hi, Go!" he says, beaming. He gives me his little glide-step and dances around my mother as she bats him away with her hands.

Running downstairs, I meet them in the hallway and allow them to enfold me in their arms. "I'm home," I tell them. "Oh, Mom, Dad, it feels so good to be here."

"Okay, Kink," Daddy says, uncomfortable as ever with physical contact. "Let's get a cup of coffee and sit down. I want to hear everything."

Dad looks just the same, but Mom seems a little fuller-figured, a little quieter. She makes the coffee, and I sit at the dining-room table, answering a thousand questions from Dad about how I feel and what my trip to New York was like.

"I flew over the Grand Canyon on the way back, Daddy," I tell him. "You really must come out and see it someday."

"Aw, no," he says, dismissing this great wonder of the world with a wave of his hand. "Once you've seen one ditch, you've seen them all."

"Oh, Rut, shut up," Mom growls. "So, Goldie, how was the Hilton Hotel?"

"Well, kinda busy. I was really there for the affiliates meeting."

"The affiliates meeting?" Dad interrupts. "That's where everyone goes to promote their shows, isn't it?" His eyes are on fire; this is nectar to him, someone to talk show business with. This is his world.

"Oh, for Christ's sake, Rut," Mom interrupts, "let her finish." Bustling around the kitchen making cheese blintzes with sour cream—I can hear them crackling in the butter on the stove—she brings me in a plateful when they're done and says, "Here, honey, eat." Sitting next to me, her head in her hands, she watches until I finish every bite. This is her world.

While Dad grills me on and on about every detail, my mother puts her two cents in. "You see, Goldie, you studied, you went to dancing school, you got the audition, and then you had the goods to back it up. See, I told you, Rut. I knew this was how it would happen. This is the way you do it."

Dad jumps in. "Laura, I was the one who got it right. I told you. First, she'll act, then she'll sing, then she'll dance." Turning to me, he adds, "You got a lucky break, kid."

"Oh, for God's sake, Rut," Mom spits, lighting a cigarette.

"Well, I was right about it! I knew how it would go. Laura, you don't know how this business works."

"What do you mean I don't know how this business works? It's not about the business; it's about talent. You either have it or you don't have it. Goldie has talent; she has it!"

They are so busy bickering over who is most responsible for my success, so excited about my lucky break, that I can't possibly tell them how I am really feeling—which is out of sorts with all that is happening so fast. I feel ashamed of my feelings; I wonder if there's something wrong with me, because everyone else seems so happy. Apart from my parents, that is. They aren't happy together. I can see that now.

Watching them, I realize that all these two people ever did was bicker. I realize how far apart they've grown. I have probably been the only thing keeping them together. Patti is grown and married with a child and another on the way, and I am all they have left.

I want to tell my parents the truth. I want to say, Hey, guys, stop! I'm not feeling that great inside. I know you're excited and everything, but I feel really scared and unprepared. Everyone's asking me for my autograph, and I know that sounds cool to you, but I don't even know who I am yet.

Instead, I sit sadly between them as they move on to the subject of what's best for me. All I can think of is how awful it must have been for them to be left alone in this house with each other.

Patti walks in and says hello, her son holding her hand. I am happy to see her. I always feel so guilty that all the attention is on me. She works so hard, such long hours, as a social worker and being a mom at the same time. I want to tell her, and my mom and dad, Hey, this isn't a fait accompli. I might fail yet, you know. Anyway, if this doesn't work out, I'll just go back to being a dancer. And, you know what? Right now, that would be fine with me.

Aunt Sarah and Uncle Charlie turn up, along with some of my other relatives. Word soon gets out that I'm home, and half the neighborhood is suddenly milling around the house, walking in unannounced, congratulating me, asking me one question after another about my life.

"Hey, Goldie, you're on television now!" Uncle Charlie grins. "Oh boy, you're going to be a big star. You better give me some of those fancy-schmancy pictures of you so I can show them to my clients. Boy, I guess you're a big schmear. Gee, how am I supposed to treat you now?"

"Just the same, Uncle Charlie," I say with pleading eyes, desperate to hold on to my fantasy of still being the baby. "I'm still Goldie. I'm just the same."

Nothing has changed, I want to say. Only your perception of me. I thought going home would be nectar to my soul, but it isn't. Instead, I am caught between two worlds. I can't go back, and I don't want to move forward. The fear is choking me.

I fall asleep on the plane, and don't know I've arrived back in L.A. until the stewardess wakes me up. Walking the long concourse at the airport, carrying my small suitcase in my hand, I feel as if I am in a metaphorical birth canal, about to be reborn into a new life.

My boyfriend picks me up at the airport. Sitting in the car on the freeway headed home, I feel so strange. I am not in my own skin. Staring out the window at the same Sunset Strip that filled me with joy not so long ago, I can't understand why I feel like curling up in a ball and hiding from the world.

I push the palm fronds away from the front door of my new, three-bedroom apartment in the Hollywood Hills. I put my key in the lock, and my boyfriend follows me in.

"Why don't I pour us some wine?" I say. Putting on an act, I pretend that I am completely happy with the turn of events in my life. Walking in my little kitchenette, I get some glasses.

He puts *Sgt. Pepper's Lonely Hearts Club Band* on the record player and settles down on the couch in front of the low coffee table. Out of the corner of my eye, I watch him rolling a joint. I'm not much of a pot smoker; I've tried it a few times and never much liked it. Gee, I'm not sure I'm in the mood for a party tonight, I tell myself with a sigh. But—once again—I hold my tongue.

Reaching for the stereo, he turns the music up loud, and I think, Okay, well, looks like the party's on. I slide onto the couch next to him and hand him his wine.

He asks about my trip, and I lie some more. "My parents were over the moon"—I smile—"which was really great. Oh, and it was amazing to be at the Hilton Hotel with all those celebrities and fans." It is not worth telling my version of the truth at this point. After all, why ruin the moment?

I sip my wine, and he hands me a joint. What the heck. Maybe it'll help me relax. I don't want to say no because I'm afraid he might leave if I do, and I really don't feel like being alone tonight.

I don't inhale much at first because I don't like the way it feels as it travels to my lungs. Even though I smoke cigarettes, pot scratches my throat and makes me cough. He laughs and I smile. "I don't do this very often," I say, handing it back. "I'm not much good at this." I drink a little more of my wine to soothe my throat, and I guess I loosen up a little because, before long, I am taking another puff.

The music seems to get louder and louder. John Lennon seems to be right there in the room with us, singing "Lucy in the Sky With Diamonds" about the girl with kaleidoscope eyes. The sound surrounds me. It is all I can hear. I feel my legs turn to liquid and my heart pounding in my chest. My friend puts his arm around me to pull me close and I feel the room spin.

"No! Something's wrong," I say, pushing him away. Sliding off the couch and onto the floor, I am breathless. "What's in this? Is this just pot? I don't feel so good."

The music is inside me now, thumping away deep in my chest cavity, making my heart jump restlessly. I close my eyes and feel as if I am floating in black space, completely alone, with no reality to hold on to, where no one knows or understands me.

My friend kneels on the floor next to me. "What are you feeling?" he asks.

"I don't know," I cry. "I don't know what I'm feeling." My entire body starts to shake uncontrollably. I can't get a grip. My heart is thumping in my throat; the room is spinning; the noise is deafening. I feel sick to my stomach.

He starts to stroke my hair, to caress my arm, my breast.

"No, no! Don't touch me! I don't feel well. There's something wrong; there's something very wrong." I crawl across the floor to the bathroom and throw my guts up. My friend just sits there watching me, in his own drug-induced style.

I want him to do something, to save me. I want him to tell me what's wrong with me. I lie back on the floor and images of my mother and my father flash before me. I see Mom's face, and then Dad's. What is this? Is this guilt because I'm doing something wrong? What is happening? I don't know.

I open my eyes and I can still see them. Then I begin to hallucinate big-time, my parents' faces swirling and melding into shafts of color, of yellows and blues so bright they hurt my eyes. I am no longer in my body. I am no longer somewhere safe. I am somewhere else, somewhere strange and frightening and lonely that scares me half to death.

Where have I gone? Where is Goldie? The happy girl? The joyful creature who loves to laugh and everyone thinks is so silly? Who embraces life with no questions? Who thinks she has all the answers? No one can answer me. No one can help me.

Shivering uncontrollably from the top of my head to the tips of my toes, I crawl to the bed. I'm shaking so violently that my teeth chatter. It is as if it's thirty degrees below zero.

I watch my friend walk across the moonlit bedroom and sit down in a chair next to my bed. I squeeze his hand and tell him again, "There's something terribly wrong with me."

success

"What do you want me to do?" he says, wincing under the grip of my fingers. "I don't know what to do."

His admission only makes me feel worse, for I was sure he would. Seeing my eyes darting right and left around the room, he takes me by the shoulders and speaks into my face.

"Tell me what you're seeing, Goldie. Talk to me!"

"It's—like—there—are—no—walls—around—me," I tell him, my throat closing as I hyperventilate. "I can't hold on to anything anymore."

He stands up for a moment and steps away from the bed with a look of horror.

"Please don't leave me, please don't go," I tell him. "I can't be alone tonight."

My friend holds me in his arms and strokes my hair as I lie there crying, more afraid than I have ever been in my entire life. Every cell in my body feels poisoned, and my body shakes uncontrollably all night long. My eyes never close—they dare not—and despite the minutes ticking away into hours, I sense no improvement or respite. The night is relentlessly, miserably without end.

I stare at the window, waiting for the dawn, willing it to come. When it eventually arrives, its cold gray light pushing through the windows, I am horrified to find that I don't feel any better. That scares me even more.

"I'm sick," I whisper hoarsely to my friend as he stirs from his awkward slumber. "I'm sick and I'm scared. I need a doctor."

Smoking that one joint triggered something in me psychologically that took me to the brink of a deep abyss. Thus began one of the scariest periods of my life. A time that still makes me shiver to think about it.

Every morning I had to force myself to get out of bed, take a shower, get dressed and go to work. Arriving at the studio each day, I put on a face and an appropriately upbeat voice and did exactly as I was told. Between takes, I hurried to my dressing room, where I lay in a nauseated faint, holding on to the sofa with both hands, afraid of falling off. No one knew what I was going through, and no one guessed. Until I eventually found my doctor, a man who would begin to lead me through the untapped passages of my mind, I was alone and scared in the big wide world called Hollywood.

It has always been my primary goal to be as happy as I can be. Like most of us, I believed that fame and fortune would make that elusive cocktail of happiness, giving me the elixir I sought. But I have learned that success does not always translate into personal happiness. Fame and fortune do not automatically grant you joy or even inner contentment. Some of the unhappiest people I know are some of the most successful.

I think I had to become successful to understand what success really means. I was supposed to be happy about it, but I wasn't. Instead, I felt bereaved—mourning the life I wanted, the life I had striven for—that of a chorus girl. Having more money than I knew what to do with, having more opportunities, a new apartment, a new car—all these things brought me down instead of lifting me up. It was such a shock to feel so much guilt about my success.

Success isn't a bad thing, but sometimes we put too much emphasis on the things that appear to be the outward signs of success. The real success is how you handle your success. How generous you are with it. I believe that success only enhances who you are. It confronts you with the truth about yourself. People who are nasty become nastier. People who are happy become happier. People who are mean hoard their money and live in fear for the rest of their lives that they will lose it. People who are generous use their gifts to help people and try to make the world a better place.

My father always said, "Expectation is greater than realization," and he was right. Success is something worth striving for, but be careful what you wish for. It may not be all that you expect it to be.

163

success

altered states

*Exploration of the mind is
the most powerful frontier of all.*

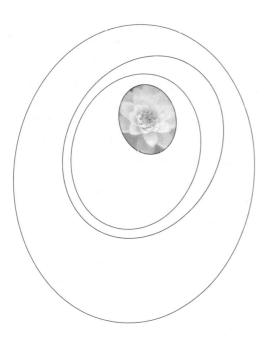

L ie down, Goldie, and tell me what you're feeling."
My analyst's voice mellows me, and I breathe a deep sigh of relief. I have found my doctor.

"I don't know what's happening to me," I tell him, lying on his soft leather couch. "I am so scared, and there is so much going on in my life. My whole life is changing, and I feel like my friends are changing around me, and my world just doesn't look the same as it did. I'm always happy but . . . but now I'm not happy anymore. I really want to go home, I just want to go back to where I was before, because I'm scared . . . and yet I don't know what in the world I'm scared of. And yet when I went home, that had all changed too, so now there's nowhere I can go that feels safe anymore. I don't know what to do . . ."

"Okay, now, Goldie, why don't we slow everything down and start at the beginning?" he says, patting my arm. And so we do.

Having been given his number by a friend, I dialed it more than fifty times before I got through. Like an addict who needed a fix, I needed him to mend my head. When I finally spoke to him, he sounded to me like the voice of God.

Until I walked into his office in Century City, I was like an automaton, barely able to place one foot in front of the other. I'd had two full days on the set of *Good Morning World*, where, for the first time in my life, I had to force a smile. I could barely speak. I was still sleepwalking through a living nightmare. Between each shot I ran to the bathroom to throw up.

Dr. Grearson is my ticket out of this kind of hell. When I set eyes on his open, smiling, wonderful face for the first time, I know I've found the right man. I am so relieved to finally have someone I can talk to, some professional who can try to figure out what is wrong with me.

"Now, Goldie, tell me all your thoughts as they come into your head. It's called 'free association.' Don't be afraid, and just relax."

With his help, I have just enrolled in the University of Goldie Hawn, the best college I ever attended. Gently, he leads me on the long journey down into myself. Tenderly, he teaches me about anger and fear. Tactfully, he makes me accept and understand my uncertainty about stretching the umbilical cord to leave all that I've ever known. Under his close guidance, I major in my own psyche, taking his enlightening tutorials as often as four times a week. I live for every session. I become his most devoted student.

Day after day in those early months of my time on *Good Morning World,* I turn up for work, do what I have to do and lie down in my dressing room in between takes. Anxiety attacks, depression and overwhelming nausea are my constant companions. Maintaining the cover that I am feeling happier than I am is a hundred times harder than the acting I had to do before; so is trying to be funny when I am going through the most devastating period of my life to date.

I can't remain in the apartment where I first felt I was losing my mind, so I move to a different one, a place that isn't so isolated, an apartment block built around a swimming pool where I can look out the big picture window and see people, night and day.

Despite dozens of offers to go to parties or out to clubs and restaurants, I become a recluse. At the end of my working day, I hurry home and cloister myself away in my big blue fuzzy chair, drinking tea or trying to read *The Art of Loving* by Erich Fromm. It is the only thing that brings me peace.

Severed from the world, I find that my only other trips out are to Dr. Grearson to spend an hour or so lying on his couch. Even with his almost

altered states

daily sessions blunting the edge of my pain, I suffer anxiety attacks at all times of the day and night, when I least expect them. I lose my appetite, and my weight drops below ninety pounds.

"Tell me about your father," Dr. Grearson asks softly, and I think of Daddy with his glide-step and his hee-haw laugh. "And your mother." I can see my mom in her pointy heels and pencil skirt. "Tell me everything."

This episode was probably one of the most important of my life. It presented me with a pure and simple opportunity for growth. These events forced me to go inside myself and examine what was wrong. My analyst provided me with the help I needed to do that.

I'm not saying that a psychologist is always the answer; I'm not married to psychology. It could be a faith, Buddhism, a wise man, a friend. It doesn't matter how you do it, but it is very important to understand the workings of your own mind and to unlock your own truth fearlessly.

I have come to believe that the decade between the ages of twenty and thirty is the most difficult of our lives. We individuate from our parents, and questions arise like, Who am I? What am I going to be? We don't know where we're going, or if we'll be successful when we get there. But before we even address those questions, we should take the time to find out who we really are. What do we believe? And how do our relationships inform what we believe? Because if we don't figure out who we are in our twenties, the question is going to hit us hard later. We can't sail through life's difficult passages until we have first dealt with the child in us, the place in us where we feel like being young will just take care of everything, because it doesn't.

With Dr. Grearson's help, I was able to carefully peel away the layers of my own being and examine what was underneath. I worked harder at my therapy than almost anything else. I became intimate with my fears and my insecurities and my lack of self-esteem, and I was able to dissect these deficits and see what they were made up of, and how much of it stemmed from my mother's control issues and my father's physical aloofness. Despite regular anxiety attacks, agoraphobia and the frequent need to go to the bathroom to heave, I persisted.

Only when I really started examining my life and my relationships honestly, without painting them rosy pink, did I truly begin to understand. My self-image was changing; the image others had of me was changing; my relationship to my parents was changing. Finally, I was able to forgive and come to love fully, deeply and honestly.

I remember one day in my analysis when I was crying and crying because I realized that however much I loved my father, however much I cherished his free spirit, he was a man who couldn't nurture others. He couldn't nurture my mother; he couldn't nurture me. I was the one who took everything from my father; I took what I needed at any cost.

As I was lying on my back on the couch and crying about Daddy, I suddenly realized that I was playing with my toes just as I did when I was in the crib. I could suddenly remember everything about that perfect yellow day when I was a tiny baby. I could remember the warm water and the baby oil and the powder and my mother's love, and I realized that I could go back there whenever I wanted and feel safe. It was such a wonderful feeling.

Dr. Grearson also helped me deal with my success. He helped me understand that the adoration or unkind criticism wasn't mine to own. That it was all about how other people perceived me to be, not how I really was. I needed to take no responsibility other than just being a Rorschach test, an inkblot that others interpreted whichever way they needed to.

The key is to learn to respect and honor the complications of other people's lives. It allows me to not identify personally with others' perceptions, or to become wrapped up in my own defenses against them. If someone tells me "I love you," it should carry no more weight than if they say "I hate you." I give them back their joy; I give them back their anger. My truth is detached from theirs.

Consequently, I became infinitely more self-aware, more enlightened and more connected with my own mind. I was able to see that my parents' relationship wasn't perfect; I was able to forgive them for the things that they couldn't do, things that people never do in a lifetime. I was able to redirect the music of my brain and take a look at the beauty of my life instead of its ugliness.

The joy of all this was that I started so young. I was just twenty-one, such a malleable age, with my childhood still so fresh for psychological excavation. Digging around in the mud of my psyche was the most important thing I could ever have done. It helped me be a better mother ultimately, a better mate; it helped me become tolerant in the face of intolerance. It helped me become, in the long run, more balanced in my failure as well as my success.

It took dedication, and great tenacity, and it would be nine long years before I graduated from my own personal college, but, when I did, I felt safe in my own arms.

I remember the day I went in to see Dr. Grearson not realizing it was to be our last session. He didn't ask me to lie down. Instead, he took my hand, sat me on the couch and said, "Goldie, I am so proud of you. There is nothing else I can do to help you. You are on your way. You don't need me anymore."

Looking up at him, I couldn't believe what he was saying. "But . . ."

"No buts!" he interrupted, shaking his head at me. "It is time for you to fly."

postcard

I rejoice in the spaces between thoughts.

A beautiful woman leads me into a quiet room. The warm California breeze drifts through the open window, gently billowing the curtains and lifting my hair.

Dominating the room is an altar, adorned by a pretty pink-and-gold cloth. On it is an exquisite rose in a glass vase and a single lit candle. A picture of Maharishi Maharesh Yogi hangs on the wall above.

There is a lone chair in the room. She offers me the seat and whispers a secret mantra in my ear. Just before she leaves the room, she says, "Repeat this in your mind, over and over again." She closes the door behind her, leaving just me and my secret mantra.

I have always been drawn to unseen powers, to the mystical and the magical in life. With her help, I am about to discover the power of my own mind.

Closing my eyes, I feel the breeze lightly brushing my skin, while in my mind I dutifully repeat my mantra. I can smell incense burning in the room and the rose petals scattered all about me. This is my first experience of attempting to quiet my mind.

I chuckle to myself at first. What a cliché I am, sitting here in this room, in the seventies, with flower power at its peak, the latest celebrity to join the Transcendental Meditation bandwagon.

Whoops! That's a thought. Shhh. I have to go back to my mantra. She said thoughts would come in and out of my mind. "Just witness them," she whispered. "Don't judge them or give them any credence. Let them drift away, and then go back to your mantra."

It is not so easy to do.

But the more I repeat the mantra, over and over, the more I feel my body relax. My breathing falls away to an almost imperceptible rate. My heart beats more slowly, and the blood it pumps through my veins lessens its pressure.

Thoughts roll into my busy mind again—people I must call, places I must go—and I push them away, hoping for a longer period of calm before the next wave of thoughts.

Listening to my mind saying the words of my mantra, sensing their rhythm and primordial sounds in my head, an inexplicable feeling begins to wash over me.

Deep inside, I feel I am going down and reconnecting to something I know, like an old friend, that deep place that is ever constant, ever joyous, ever alive with creativity. It is the deeper part of me that knows something. It is such a great connection, and fills me with such joy, that I feel like giggling.

Pushing the temptation aside, I carry on, wanting to feel it again. The more I repeat my mantra over and over, the more I let go. As my thoughts flow in and out, I become quieter and quieter in my mind.

My consciousness feels like a teabag being dipped into a glass of hot water and lifted out again. I can feel it becoming slowly saturated with nothingness. When I say nothingness, it is sort of a space in time in which no thought takes place.

Each time I repeat the mantra, the phenomenon becomes stronger, and the teabag becomes heavier and heavier, sinking deeper and deeper, its rich essences seeping into the water.

After a while—I can't say how long—I lose my sense of place. I can visualize the clear glass full of the rich goodness that is my life. I feel like I am merging my spirit with something that is very familiar to me, very safe, and it tickles my joy center.

I am filled with a sense of such purity, such clarity, like I have never experienced before. There is no ego, no self, no thought. I am just here. Nothing matters. I am coming back to the purest state of being. I feel unadulterated bliss.

laughter

Comedy breaks down walls.
It frees us for just a moment
from the ugliness of this world.

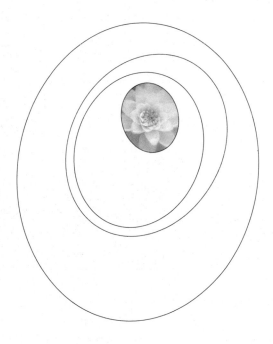

G ood morning, Miss Hawn," the security guard greets me cheer-
ily as I pull in to the NBC parking lot for the last time.

"Morning, Jim," I reply with a smile that doesn't quite reach my eyes.

Steering my maroon Chevrolet Corvette into the slot, marked by a sign on the wall that reads LAUGH-IN: GOLDIE HAWN, I head with a heavy heart for the door I have opened every working day for the last three years, in beautiful downtown Burbank.

As I walk down that long, long corridor to the studio, passing people I have come to know and love, I can hardly believe I am leaving the show today. Peering in through every doorway, I am wistfully aware of how much I have taken everything for granted. Five days a week, I have walked this corridor without thinking. Now I really look at the stages, the rehearsal halls I've worked in, the room where my bikini-clad body was painted with words and symbols, the newsroom.

Past Hank, the funny makeup man, the one I joked with all the time about the double chin he insists I don't have, I wave and giggle. Past Tom Brokaw, the new NBC anchor, who greets me each morning with a smile and a bright hello. I must admit, I have a bit of a crush on him.

Looking into one rehearsal hall, I remember the day I danced there in a tight red sweater jumpsuit. Glancing up, I could hardly believe my eyes. Elvis Presley had wandered in to watch us rehearsing.

I stop, soaking up the memory now, and still taste how it felt to see the King standing there, emitting such incredible sexual energy. I thought I was going to swoon just being in the same room. That man and his music made my teenage hormones rage. Despite my promises to my father to listen to only classical music, I lived head to toe for rock and roll.

Elvis was introduced and walked over to me, reached out and touched my tousled hair. "Why, Goldie," he said, smiling that crooked smile of his. "No wonder you're so funny. You look like a chicken that's just been hatched."

Walking on down the corridor, I remember the time we all chased George Schlatter, the producer and director of *Laugh-In*, when he had us working on a sketch until three in the morning. Dick Martin, Dan Rowan, Ruth Buzzi and I were dressed in overalls, supposedly to paint a wall, but it was so late and we were so tired and none of us wanted to get covered in paint. With one look, we yelled, "Get George!" instead. We chased him down this hallway with rollers dripping paint until he ran upstairs and locked himself in his booth.

Turning down a side corridor into the *Laugh-In* hallway, the place where our little family gathers every week, I step into my dressing room that looks just the same as it always has. There is the old telephone, the bowl of fresh fruit, the makeup table and the ugly brown couches. Only now they don't look so ugly anymore.

Usually from here, I can hear George's voice bellowing down the hallway. Usually, he pops his head around each dressing-room door. "How are my crazy inmates?" His large physique fills the doorway, as do his big blue eyes. He is a man who laughs easily and with all his heart. He looks like a big strong bear on the outside, but, boy, is he soft and mushy on the inside.

But George doesn't come this morning. Everything is quiet. I know why.

Nobody knows me better than George. He sees my soul. He gets the way my brain works and the way my heart feels. He always used to say, "Goldie is as dumb as a fox." He knows me so well. I can't fool him, nor would I ever try. He is one of the great loves of my life.

The first time I met him, he came onto the set of *Good Morning World* and stood there, staring at me disconcertingly. I was summoned to his office at NBC a few days later and sank to the bottom of his big red leather wing chair.

"Now, what do you do?" George asked, looking down at me and laughing.

"Well, I dance."

"No. I mean, what do you do, Goldie Hawn?"

I hesitated. "Wh-what do you mean?"

"Well, tell me about yourself."

"Er, I did a bit of acting on *Good Morning World,* but that didn't work out, and, really, I'm a dancer. I mean, is that what you want to know?"

He laughed deep and loud. "Well, can you sing?"

"Yes."

"Can you tell a joke?"

"No. Not to save my life!"

"And where are you from, Goldie Hawn?"

The interview went on. I told him all about myself, but I still didn't know what I was being interviewed for. At the end he said, "I'll tell you what, would you like to be on *Laugh-In?*"

"I don't know. I can't tell a joke, and I can't be funny like that," I said. "I've never done a review or anything, so I'm not sure what I would do on the show."

George laughed again. "Well, I don't know what you're going to do on the show either, so why don't we give it a try? Three shows and we'll see if it works out. What do you say?"

"Well, okay. Thanks."

I left his office thinking, Wow, what was that all about? This is crazy. I just got three shows from a man who doesn't even know what he wants me to do!

The first time I arrived at the Burbank Studios, I got lost and had to ask someone the way. I walked into the rehearsal hall and found the cast standing around a piano, singing songs and laughing. There seemed to be a cacophony of creative indulgence.

Gee, this sure looks like fun, I thought, hugely relieved.

Cher, an icon of the time, was standing with them, rehearsing for the show as that week's special guest. She was the epitome of the sixties and looked like a million dollars with her long black hair and her platform boots and her beautiful white Mongolian lamb coat.

"So, you're Goldie Hawn," she said in her unique voice, looking me up and down. "We've been waiting for you. We wanted to see what you looked like. We thought you were a myth."

I was so intimidated. I couldn't find the words, so I giggled. Ruth Buzzi beckoned me to the piano. "We're just running through some stuff with Billy." She pointed to Billy Barnes, the musical director. "Just watch the others and fall in when you can."

I stood there with the whole cast as they sang, "What's the news across the nation? I have got the information . . ." and as I joined in, Cher put an arm around me. I melted and started to feel safe again. Yes, yes, yes, I am back, I am back, I am back in the chorus again!

Next came a read-through of the script, sitting around a table, each of us reading our lines in turn. This was my newfound family—Ruth Buzzi and Arte Johnson and Jo Anne Worley. I liked all of them. But staring at my lines, I couldn't see what was funny about them. They seemed to be straight introductions: "Here's Dick and Dan with the news of the future!" or "Okay, now over to Ruth." My lines just weren't funny like everyone else's.

Oh boy, this is going to be so frigging boring, I told myself on the way home, wondering what Art Simon had gotten me into.

The day of the shoot, I was all ready, if a little nervous. "Okay, Goldie, you're up!" I rushed out of my dressing room, wearing a pillbox hat, skimpy top, bangles and a turquoise Pucci miniskirt. Taking my place at the podium, the studio was in darkness and silent. There were three cameras, little lights shining all around me and someone holding up cue cards. I'd never seen cue cards before and I squinted at them anxiously.

"Okay, Goldie," George said from his booth somewhere high up in the darkness above me, "all you have to do is read the words off the cards when the red light goes on."

But what George didn't know—and I didn't tell him—is that I am mildly dyslexic and sometimes mix up words when I read. So when the red light flashed and the cue cards began rapidly flipping over and over, instead of reading, "Dick and Dan, Ladies and Gentlemen, *Laugh-In* is proud to bring you the News of the Future," I read: "Dan and Dick . . . I mean, Dick and Dan is . . . I mean, are . . . Oh."

I started to laugh because I felt so stupid. I mean, how simple could this be and I screwed up? The more nervous I got, the more I giggled. The more I laughed, the more we all laughed.

Holding my hand up against the bright lights to see if I could see George, I called up to the booth. "Wherever you are, George, can I please do this again? I screwed up. George? Where are you, George?"

His deep voice boomed out across the studio through the speakerphone. "No, Goldie. That will do just fine."

"No, but please, George, give me another chance."

"We like you just the way you are, Goldie," came the reply. "Keep the cameras rolling, fellas."

"No!" I protested, still giggling at myself and thinking of my father, who always told me never to take myself too seriously.

"That's right, Goldie," he said, "it was just perfect. Next time I want you to do it again just like that."

And so a career was born.

By being a little bit absentminded and accidentally inverting my words, being nervous and then laughing at myself, a character emerged. I guess part of her was me. I guess this part of me had popped up in the high school play when I kept fainting like Olive Oyl; it was there when Ronnie Morgan slammed a plate into my face; it was onstage when I inadvertently made the audience laugh as Juliet. I was even called the "giggly girl" in a Disney movie I'd done called *The One and Only, Genuine, Original Family Band,* with Buddy Ebsen and Lesley Ann Warren. It also starred a popular child actor of the time named Kurt Russell.

Suddenly, I was the Ditzy Ding-a-ling, the Dumb Blonde, the Bubblehead. Some sections of the press accused me of setting back the Women's Liberation Movement. My answer to one reporter from *Good Housekeeping* was, "But I am already liberated." One time, a reporter asked me if I felt any responsibility for the Women's Liberation Move-

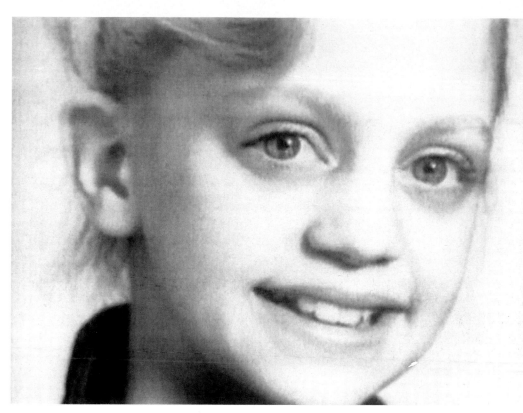

My ears were too big, my nose was too flat and my mouth was too wide. As a little girl, the only thing I liked about myself was my hair.

(AUTHOR'S COLLECTION)

From as far back as I remember, all I ever wanted was to be happy.

(AUTHOR'S COLLECTION)

My four best friends in Takoma Park, May 1951: my first boyfriend, David Fisher (*front left*), with his older brother, Jimmy, behind him, and Jean Lynn Srour (*front right*), standing with her big brother, Joey.

David Fisher, aged eight. He had two sets of front teeth, so I acted as his interpreter until he got them fixed.

My beloved Nixi, the pet Dalmatian who waited for me on the front porch every night after school. (COURTESY OF JIM FISHER)

Eleven years old and wearing my first bra, in June 1956, flanked by Jean Lynn (*on the right*) and her little sister, Lyla (*on the left*). Boy, was Jean Lynn jealous!

(COURTESY OF JIM FISHER)

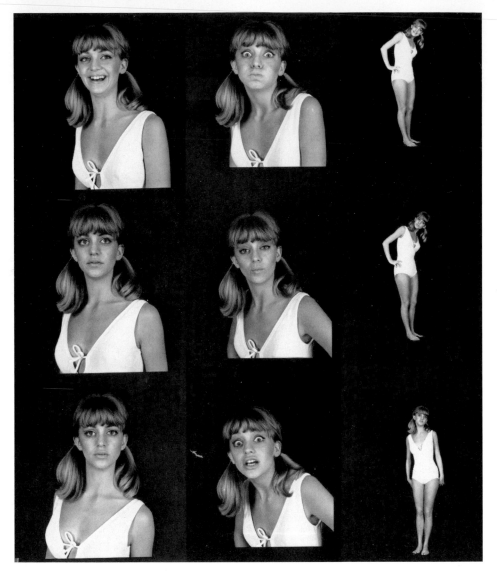

Sweet sixteen, and posing for a modeling agency, but still unhappy with my looks!
(AUTHOR'S COLLECTION)

My beloved dad and
mom on a beach outing
in Ocean City, Maryland,
in 1957.

A comedic publicity shot
from the 1960s.
(AUTHOR'S COLLECTION)

Art Simon is the man who discovered me and became my first manager.
"There's something about her, don't you think?" he told his colleagues at
the William Morris Agency. (AUTHOR'S COLLECTION)

A publicity photograph for *Good Morning World,* my first TV series.

(CBS/LANDOV)

With Ingrid Bergman at the premiere of *Cactus Flower.* Dear Ingrid taught me so much about the vagaries of Hollywood.

(©1969, RENEWED 1997 COLUMBIA PICTURES INDUSTRIES, INC.)

Publicity photographs taken around the time of my big break, the *Good Morning World* TV series. (CBS/LANDOV)

Dad and me all dressed up and nowhere to go, on the set of *The Duchess and the Dirtwater Fox* in the wilds of Colorado.

(© TWENTIETH CENTURY FOX)

Dad jamming with my costar George Segal on the set of *The Duchess and the Dirtwater Fox*. (© TWENTIETH CENTURY FOX)

Stan Kamen was my beloved agent for fifteen years, and the reason I made my first trip to Jerusalem.
(FROM THE ESTATE OF STAN KAMEN)

Between takes—and between hospital visits to Daddy—with Kate and my costar Burt Reynolds, on the set of *Best Friends*. (© 1982 WARNER BROS. INC.)

The moment I met my new costar for the movie *Swing Shift,* I knew I was in trouble. Kurt Russell stole my heart. (© 1984 WARNER BROS. INC.)

At last, I'd met someone who could love my kids as much as I did. Kurt with me, Katie and Oliver on the set of *Swing Shift.* (© 1984 WARNER BROS. INC.)

The inimitable Laura Hawn, my mother, in her cameo role as a landlady on *Swing Shift*. Her single line took dozens of takes.

(© 1984 WARNER BROS. INC.)

Ma and me taking a break on the factory set on *Swing Shift*.

(© 1984 WARNER BROS. INC.)

Kissing Jonathan Demme, the director, on the final day of shooting *Swing Shift*, before everything started to go so wrong. (© 1984 WARNER BROS. INC.)

Patti, me, Dad and Mom at the premiere of *Sugarland Express*.

Feeding Kate between takes on the set of *Private Benjamin.*

Dressed up for a wedding on the set of *Private Benjamin,* with my "husband," actor Albert Brooks, and members of my real-life extended family. My mother is second from the left.

life's rewards

True rewards come from the intention
of living an honorable life.

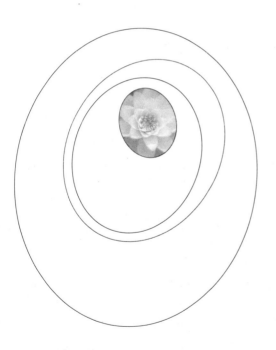

S omewhere deep in my dream there is a bell. It is ringing incessantly. Oh God, I don't want to wake up yet. It can't be time. There must be a couple more hours before I have to get up.

My hand reaches for the telephone in the dark. "H-hello?"

"Goldie? You got it."

"I got what? Who is this?"

"This is Alan from Columbia."

"Oh, oh. Hi, Alan. How are you?"

"You got it."

Half asleep, I pull myself up, rubbing my eyes. Staring at the clock, I see that it is four in the morning. "I got what? What are you talking about?"

"You got the Academy Award."

Sitting up in bed, I shake my head of sleep. "I what? I got the Academy Award? You mean, I won?"

"You won the Oscar, Goldie. They just made the announcement. You got Best Supporting Actress."

I hear the words, but they don't make any sense. I feel them reverberating inside my brain, ricocheting off the walls of my skull. Oscar? Best Supporting Actress? I knew I'd been nominated, but I never thought in a million years that I would actually win. When the words finally sink in, I jump up and switch on the light.

"I did what?" I yell, pacing back and forth beside the bed. "Say that again. I won what?"

"The Oscar, Goldie!" Alan laughs. "You won the Oscar for your first movie. It's amazing!"

"I won? B-but how is that possible? You mean for *Cactus Flower*? Oh my God! I totally forgot it was last night."

"I want to be the first to congratulate you, honey. I'm backstage here at the awards ceremony, and everyone is just so pleased for you. The studio asked me to call and let you know."

I can't wait to get him off the phone, to call my mom and dad. It all feels so unreal. Sitting on the edge of my bed, in the middle of an unseasonably cold London night, I begin to shiver as I dial my parents' number.

"Mom? It's Goldie! I won, I won the Academy Award! I'm in my hotel bedroom in London, Mom, and I just heard. I mean, I don't understand. I won, Mom!"

What I can hear in the receiver isn't so much understandable English as a series of high-pitched syllables. She is crying, I'm crying—both of us sobbing into the telephone. "Goldie, Goldie, my Goldie," is all she can repeat through her tears.

"Oh, Mom," I cry, "this feels so weird. This is all happening so fast. I mean, I'm not even there to pick it up."

Daddy comes on the extension, and I can't tell if he is laughing or crying. Breathlessly, he tells me how he and Mom sat and watched it together on TV with some friends and neighbors. "I wish you'd been there, Kink! It was incredible."

"But who picked it up for me?"

"Raquel Welch," Mom chimes in.

"Raquel Welch?"

"Yes, honey. I didn't know you knew her."

"I don't know Raquel Welch!"

My mother begins to cry again. "Oh, Goldie, honey. You made it. I'm so proud of you. We both are. Aren't we, Rut? Rut? You there?"

I hear a strange choking sound and know my father is crying. "Yes, honey," he says. "So proud."

"Thanks, Daddy," I reply, tugging shyly at my T-shirt. For a moment, I am unable to say anything more, thinking of them sitting in their living room, watching the ceremony on television. I can feel their joy. I made them proud.

The telephone never stops ringing for the rest of the night. My producer and father figure Mike Frankovich screams into the telephone at me, "I can't believe you did this, kid! I can't believe you pulled this off."

Telegrams arrive at the hotel and are brought up to my suite on a silver tray, most of them from people I have never even met. One of them is from my childhood hero, Fred Astaire. "CONGRATULATIONS ON YOUR OSCAR, GOLDIE HAWN" is all it says. I hold it in my hands as if it is the most precious jewel on earth.

After taking a shower and pulling on some clothes, I float down into the lobby to wait for my wonderful driver, whom I love. A round-faced Cockney with a broad smile, he is early and ushers me into what I call my "Princess Coach"—the Daimler I literally walk into, it being as big as a living room.

"Congratulations, Miss Hawn, this must be so exciting for you," he says, handing me a beautiful bouquet of flowers.

"Oh, thank you, Harry." I smile, burying my nose in their scent.

Sitting in the backseat on my way to Shepperton Studios as my car finds its way across central London, I sip my coffee and look at my flowers and can't help but feel how hollow it all seems. What would it have felt like to get all dressed up and go to the ceremony with Mom and Dad? To walk the red carpet? To smile and wave and do all the things I used to watch the big movie stars do when I was a child? Once again, I am on the outside looking in.

More than that, this award scares me a little. There is so much inside me that I still want to do, to stretch myself and to do some real drama. I sense that it will probably be a long, long time before I ever experience anything like this again.

Crossing a bridge over the River Thames, I let my mind drift back to my experiences on *Cactus Flower*. It really wasn't that hard, I remind myself. It was a very light role, and it was easy for me. Walter Matthau was supposed to be my love interest, but he was more like a father, or a Jewish uncle. "Goldala, my Goldala," he used to call me affectionately, shortly before spraying the room and himself with disinfectant so he didn't catch any of my germs.

Walter was strange and wonderful and interesting, but he wasn't the easiest person to work with. When I couldn't rehearse with him one day because of a magazine interview I had to do, he punished me. Giving me a withering look when I returned, he put me under such pressure, not trusting that I knew my lines, that he sabotaged me and made me flub them for the first time.

Ingrid Bergman couldn't have been kinder. She became a mother figure to me, caring for me when I had a cold and worrying about me constantly. She was such an icon, a grande dame of movies. I had always imagined her being delicate and angelic and soft, like Ilsa in *Casablanca*. I was surprised to find that she was incredibly powerful—a tower of female energy.

But despite that strength, she was also extremely nervous about her return to movies after an eighteen-year hiatus. She had led a very singular life, and had been exiled from Hollywood for a controversial love affair. I couldn't help but think how difficult that must have been for her, and how our industry can be so cruel. She was always cordial and lovely to me, but there was something very lonely about her. She kept to herself, retreating alone to her dressing room every night.

During an intimate scene in the movie where we had to share a listening booth in a music store, Ingrid turned to me and whispered, "Tell me, how do you do it, Goldie? You look like you've been doing this for a thousand years. I am so petrified I can hardly speak."

"I don't know," I replied, shocked by her honesty. "I guess my family brought me up to be pretty unflappable. And, let's face it, this is hardly Juliet."

"Is this really your first picture?" she asked, wringing her hands.

When I nodded, she said, "Then I think I need to take some tips from you, my dear." I looked at her askance. All my illusions about her faded.

Underneath it all, she was a frightened and vulnerable human being, just like the rest of us.

Now here I am a year later, halfway through my second movie, *There's a Girl in My Soup,* and suddenly, at the age of twenty-three, I have an Oscar. Arriving for a regular working day, my driver sweeps me through the big front gates at Shepperton and up the long drive, and I make my way across the set.

"Congratulations, Miss Hawn!" yells one of the cameramen.

"Thank you, Joe."

"Well done, Goldie!" My director, Roy Boulting, hugs me.

"Thanks so much, Roy."

"Wonderful news, darling." Tony Britton, one of my costars, kisses my hand.

"Why, thank you, Tony."

"Thirty minutes, Miss Hawn."

"Okay, Charlie."

I reach the old property at the heart of the lot that has housed some of the greatest actors of all time. I close the door to the dressing room they tell me was once occupied by Vivien Leigh. I throw open my French doors and inhale the fresh English air. Gazing out on the sweeping lawns, with their big cedar trees, I listen to the songs of the birds.

Here in the sanctuary of my room, I don't have to put up a front anymore. I don't have to pretend. I can feel it all—the joy and the disappointment and the fear. Holding my head in my hands, I bawl and bawl.

Pulling myself together, I put on my costume and apply makeup. I brush out my hair and wander back out onto the set. Peter Sellers, my costar, opens his arms wide to greet me.

"Goldie, my dear, sweet girl, my warmest congratulations, this is wonderful news," he says effusively, enveloping me in his flamboyant velvet jacket.

"Thank you, Peter," I say, with a smile.

Every day with Peter is like a balancing act. At any one time, he can be manically depressed, ecstatically overjoyed or just plain mad. He is always tender with me, but it could so easily have gone the other way.

For my first day on the set, I agonized for an hour over what I should wear. It was cold and damp, but I wanted to look my best. I finally selected an outfit I loved—purple bell-bottom trousers, a purple sweater and a long purple cardigan vest, all worn with purple platform boots. I thought I looked *très chic*.

As I walked onto the set, the wardrobe lady looked at me and shook her head. "Oh dear," she said, before hurrying off without saying anything more.

Looking down at my clothes, suddenly worried, I saw a woman rushing over to me, aghast. It was Peter Sellers's assistant.

"Oh no!" she said, looking me up and down.

"What? What's wrong?"

"Peter can't stand purple!" she said. "He doesn't let anyone around him wear it."

Oh no, I thought. How crazy is this man I've heard so much about really going to be? "Why on earth not?" I asked her.

"Well, he died of a heart attack once on the operating table and came back to life. But, you know, all he saw when he was dead was purple. You should have been told."

I wanted to rip the clothes off my body as fast as I possibly could. "Have you got anything that I can wear?" I asked, panicking and plucking at them uncomfortably. But then Peter walked in and headed straight for me with that devilish smile on his face.

"Oh my God, Goldie," he shouted from across the room, "but you're lovely."

It was a line straight from the script. I looked into his burning eyes and thought, Oh my God, he's already in character.

"Oh, thank you, Peter," I said, coyly. "But, listen, I'm so sorry I'm wearing purple."

"Why should you be, darling?" He grinned, waving his hand dismissively at his assistant. "It is one of my favorite colors."

But when Peter laughs the world laughs too. He can't stop, I can't stop, no one on the set can stop, and we have to turn off the cameras and break for lunch. We break for lunch a lot.

A few days after I won my Oscar, we were given a day off. "I'll pick you up at ten," Peter told me. "I want you to meet some friends of mine." He arrived in his Rolls-Royce convertible and drove me to Windsor Safari Park. There, we were formally introduced to the owners, who were at one time members of the circus. They were all little people, not more than four and a half feet tall. It was more than a little strange to me.

He swept us through the high security gates into the wild animal compound, and, within minutes, we were surrounded by dozens of baboons with big red bottoms. As I squealed, they clambered all over his beautiful Rolls-Royce and began playing with the windshield wipers.

"These are the friends I wanted you to meet," he said, smiling.

We watched, laughing, as the baboons groomed each other on the hood of his Rolls. Babies clung to mothers with tiny little hands. Fathers strutted around, naked rumps in the air, tails held high.

The largest male suddenly jumped up onto the soft roof of the car with such a thump that I screamed. Above us, I could see the imprint of his huge body. Sliding down the windshield, he picked up a wiper and snapped it clean off, glaring at Peter threateningly through the glass. I glanced over at Peter furtively, taking in his slightly manic behavior. As much as all this was absurdly funny, his reaction seemed a bit extreme to me.

The two of us sat there helplessly, his Rolls-Royce being destroyed all around us.

"Peter, what are we going to do?"

Looking across from me, his eyes full of mischief, he replied, "Nothing. Absolutely nothing."

We laughed so much it hurt.

It was never my ambition to win an Oscar. The only competition I was ever in was with myself. I never wanted to be number one, and I never aspired to be a movie star, rich or famous. While I am proud of winning the Oscar, and delighted to have it, the whole experience was so surreal that it sometimes feels like it never really happened.

It wasn't that long before I won it that I had been dancing on a three-legged table at the Peppermint Box. Since then, I'd been transformed into a star of television, had gone into analysis, and married my first husband, someone I believed I was going to spend the rest of my life with. I was halfway through my four-movie deal with Columbia, so there was no major hike in my salary, no change in the studio's perception of me, just a couple new words at the beginning of my name on the credits. They now said "Oscar winner" Goldie Hawn.

Although these new words were now attached to me, I never considered them part of my definition of me. At this stage in my life, I was still trying to figure that out for myself. Instead, I came to the conclusion that these kinds of iconic things are just what they are: icons. They shouldn't hold any other power. They shouldn't become a symbol of anything other than that special moment in time. My father taught me that it is important to remember that no matter how wonderful applause is, it is just noise.

The important thing in life is what we are doing today. What we are doing tomorrow. Not what we did yesterday. Through my long journey of self-discovery, I have come to understand that my Oscar is not who I am. I am not my success; I am not my model; I am not my fame.

I was right about my Oscar. It was a long time before I was ever nominated again, and I haven't won an Oscar since. I can't say that it hasn't been lovely having my gilded statue sitting in the various places that I have put it over the years. But getting awards is not what I work for; it is not what any of us should work for. Such motivation, for your art, is misguided.

Decide what your clear intention is in your chosen field. If it is to win an award, then you may or may not win, but it won't change the reality around you. It's nice to have; it's a good thing. But to set more importance on it than it deserves means you are overestimating its power. An award is just a little icing on the cake, a fun night, but it can never fully define you or be the declarative sentence that describes your genius, because it doesn't.

We play a game at home. Who won the Academy Award last year? Who won it two years ago? In my book, only the geniuses remember that.

The next time I came in contact with Ingrid Bergman was entirely unexpected. Shortly after my marriage to Gus sadly ended, I went on a journey across Europe with a Swedish actor I had met. I took a left-hand turn.

Almost strangers, the two of us traveled across Europe before arriving in Norway, en route to his home. It felt like we had landed in fairyland with all its little houses and heart-embossed shutters. One day, I promised myself, I would build a house like that.

My friend took me on an old fishing boat out into the North Sea to meet a friend of his called Lars, who owned a house on an island. Crossing the oily dark water, we finally reached our destination: a small island on which sat a house built out of the rock. Lars and his girlfriend, a beautiful young model, were waiting for us on the dock. They were charming and hospitable, and as the boat disappeared off into the mist I felt as if I had landed in one of Grimm's fairy tales. Inside their beautiful home, they had prepared for us a delicious dinner of gravlax and salads, meatballs and herrings. I watched the love and reverence with which they prepared the food and was in awe. Outside, through the window, I could see the waves crashing dramatically on the shore.

Tired but elated, we retired that night with full and happy hearts. They showed us our room, which was dominated by a most beautiful wooden chest. Painted across it was a single name: INGRID.

"Who's Ingrid?" I asked innocently.

"That's Ingrid Bergman," my friend replied.

"Why, is this Ingrid Bergman's house?" I asked.

"Yes, it is." He nodded.

Thrilled to be in the home of someone I considered a friend, I looked around with renewed interest at all her lovely things, the way she had decorated the rooms with hearts and flowers and candles. I could feel her presence in this house, sense her remarkable spirit. I was suddenly filled with joy. Turning back to my friend, I asked curiously, "Then who is Lars?"

"Her husband."

I slumped onto the bed, winded. Looking up at him in horror, I whispered, "Does she know?" There was a lump in my throat. "Does she know he has a lover?"

"Oh yes," came the casual reply. "A long time ago. It is just one of those things."

I slipped between the sheets that night unhappily. I wanted to be far away from this place.

Is this my future too? I asked myself sadly. Is this how it ends? Marriage after marriage after marriage before settling for whatever you can get, even if it means knowing there are other people? Is this my fate? Is this the fate of all successful women in Hollywood?

I had already seen the loneliness of the female movie star. It is a cross borne by every successful woman in Hollywood. When you are famous, no matter how much you try to include your partner, whenever you walk into a room people look only at you. You end up being endlessly apologetic, trying to introduce him, make him feel less excluded. There are very few men who can live with a woman who is, or is perceived to be, more powerful than they are.

That is what destroyed my marriage to Gus—and that alone. There was never a lack of love or comfort. Stardom and the baggage that came with it is what drove a wedge between us. And because there was so much love, neither of us wanted our relationship to die an ugly death. He wanted to see me succeed. I wanted to see him thrive, to feel like a man in his relationship. And so we had to end it. We both knew it. We let each other go, fully mindful of the reasons why.

I shed silent tears for dear Ingrid that night. She didn't deserve this. She was beautiful and powerful and loving, and she so deserved to be loved in return. Like me, she had won her first Oscar very young, when she was still in her twenties. She went on to win two more. But, more than that, she had tended to me and cared for me and shown me such kindness. I wanted her to have all the rewards she deserved for a life well lived. I felt that I was betraying her in some way by even being in the same house as her husband and his lover. I felt complicit. I knew I couldn't stay.

We left the following day. Thanking our hosts for their hospitality, I turned my back on Ingrid's beautiful house of hearts forever.

sisters

*Rediscovering the fun you had
in childhood when you were
sisters is one of the great
joys of growing up.*

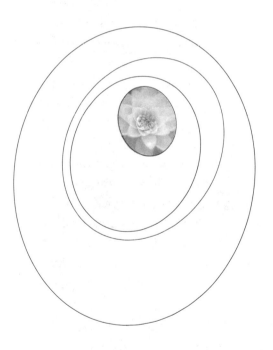

My father is laughing, rocking back in his chair, his eyes squeezed shut. My sister and I are sitting opposite him and Mom around Patti's kitchen table. There is a barbecue going outside, there are cream puffs in the oven, but we are too busy telling our parents of our great adventure to Italy together.

Dad is all ears while Patti and I roll over each other as we speak, finishing each other's sentences with our sisterly syncopation. We can hardly talk because we are laughing so hard at all the things that happened to us in Europe.

Mother, sitting with her legs crossed, flicks her cigarette absent-mindedly on the tablecloth while beaming proudly from ear to ear.

Daddy says, "Laura, your ash is going all over the table."

In her raspy voice, my mother snaps, "Oh, Rut, for Christ's sake, listen to the kids already."

Patti and I glance at each other and smile. I am home at last. It feels so good. Little has changed, and I feel like Patti's little sister again, my favorite role of all.

Daddy takes his trusty tape recorder out of his pocket and hides it behind the milk carton, recording our every word. Yeah, like we can't see it. He is always up to something.

"So," he says, baiting us, "start from the beginning." He hee-haws in his high-pitched way and starts firing silly questions at us, just to keep us going.

Patti begins, "It was so hot . . ."

"Yeah, it was really hot. We wanted to jump into the . . ."

"How hot?" Daddy asks.

"Oh, I dunno, eighty-two . . ."

"No," I cut in, "maybe eighty-five."

"Rut, let them finish, honey," Mom cuts in. "Who cares how hot it was? Come on, let's go. Go on, girls."

We continue like this for hours—Dad taping the whole story, making us repeat things just in case the recorder isn't working; Mom trying to keep things on track, knowing it doesn't really matter. It is the most beautiful day. Here we are, just the four of us, our entire family, rolling with laughter. This is what I miss the most—just hearing the harmony of our joy.

My sissy is so beautiful, I think, as she reaches up and places her bag in the overhead compartment of our plane. She is the true flower-power girl. Everything, including her big straw hat, is adorned with flowers. I notice her hourglass figure, the one I didn't get. Small waist, beautiful breasts, and a shock of red hair falling down to her shoulders from beneath her hat. She loves hats. She loves to party. She loves a good time. And that's just what we are going to have in Italy.

It is 1970, and I have been awarded the coveted David di Donatello Award, Italy's equivalent to the Academy Award, for *Cactus Flower*. Goody, goody, I finally get to receive an award for that movie in person. Maybe this will make up for the time I wasn't able to be there. Only I'm a year late in picking it up, because I've been filming *There's a Girl in My Soup*. With all expenses paid, Rome is a place I have never been, and I have an extra ticket. My sister is the only person I want to go with. It is time for us to play.

Our lives up to this point have been badly out of sync. She moved out of the house when she was nineteen, leaving me like an only child. She moved to the suburbs and had babies and had the life I once imagined myself having with Willy Hicks. Only I didn't have the babies, or Willy

Hicks either. I became a movie star instead, and wasn't home enough to bridge the gap to our grown-up years.

This is time for us, just us. Not Mom or Dad. Not husbands or children. Not the growing responsibilities of our daily lives. Patti can dress up every day in a new outfit, and so can I. We can go wherever we want to go—the best hotels, great restaurants, in chauffeur-driven cars that can make left-hand turns.

We fly over Rome, peering down at all the buildings and the rolling green hills threaded by the mighty River Tiber. When we land in Rome, we are whisked by limousine to our hotel, which is on a hill. The weather is glorious for June, and as we stare in openmouthed wonder as we pass the Coliseum and the Vatican—which is like nothing either of us has ever seen—the laughter just pours out of us.

"Okay, what do you want to do first?" I ask as we unpack in the suite we have decided to share.

"Drink a cappuccino by the Trevi Fountain!" she announces.

Our feet barely touch the ground for the rest of the trip. We walk the streets as if we own them. In our floaty frocks and big hats, we make quite the pair. The Italian men flirt outrageously with us, and we flirt right back. We feel sexy and sassy. My sister. I don't want this feeling to end.

My sister has such big energy; she is so alive. She walks quickly; she talks quickly; she is always on the go. She loves to sing; she laughs big; she is very feminine, and there is a lot of sexuality about her, the flaming redhead. Best of all, she has so many of the childlike qualities that I do.

Over the course of the next few days, I watch Patti be as happy as anyone I could possibly imagine. And it doesn't take a lot to make her happy. A chance to go somewhere new, a new hat that looks fabulous— these things can make her day. I wish I could give her a new hat every day.

On the night of the Di Donatello Awards, we get dolled up to the nines in our suite like two best girlfriends, drying each other's hair, sharing makeup, zipping each other into our clothes. She looks gorgeous in a beautiful green silk gown. I choose something simple, a sparkly little dress that I wear with some perilously high-heeled shoes.

The limousine collects us and drives us to the ancient Baths of Caracalla, built by the Romans in the third century A.D. It is an amazing setting for the awards, open to the sky, surrounded by redbrick walls and deep sunken baths in which emperors once bathed.

"*Prego, signorine.* This way," someone urges as they usher us past the waiting paparazzi and into the main arena. Patti and I blink into the flashlights popping wildly all around us and do as we are told. The evening has been organized with great pomp and circumstance, with a grand procession to the stage, but also with the Italians rushing about and speaking so fast and so expressively that it all seems a little chaotic.

"*Mamma mia!* Where is the stage director?" someone shouts.

"*Bellissime.* This way. *Prego!*"

The organizers seem so disorganized, and everything looks like a Fellini movie, it is so over the top. I start to giggle, and then Patti starts to giggle, and we both know that we are treading on very dangerous ground. When the organizers try to separate us, sending Patti to the auditorium with the other VIP guests and me up toward the stage to wait for my award, we almost lose it completely, and they have to leave us for a moment and come back.

"Okay, now, stop it," I plead, wiping tears from my eyes and checking my makeup in her mirror, "we've got to pull ourselves together. I know Dad instilled a healthy disrespect for this industry in us, but in a few minutes I have to go up and make a speech."

Nodding, pursing her lips, yet with her eyes full of mischief, Patti allows me to compose myself before kissing me good-bye and wishing me luck.

A handsome young Italian in a tuxedo leads me backstage and introduces me to my fellow awardees. There is Bernardo Bertolucci, and Franco Zeffirelli, the famous film directors, and all these other *ucci*s and *elli*s whose names I can't remember. With only one syllable to my surname, I feel like an impostor.

Oh well, I think to myself. At least I get to take home one of these gorgeous eighteen-karat-gold replicas of the statue of David by Donatello. He'll look just perfect next to Oscar.

Ryan O'Neal arrives backstage, and the chaos rises to a new level. Everyone fusses around him, wanting his autograph or his photo. He is here with Ali MacGraw to accept an award for *Love Story*.

"Stand here, Signor O'Neal. Wait there, Signor. Smile into this camera, Ryan." They say the name Ryan so that it sounds like "Orion." I can't help but giggle.

Ryan and Ali are at the peak of their careers. They seem unstoppable. Robert Evans is there too in his capacity as Ali's husband, but he is a big producer at Paramount and really happening in Hollywood. I stand to one side, watching these big players being shoved this way and that with increasing pandemonium, and feel completely out of place.

Ali MacGraw sweeps in, wearing the most amazing gaucho outfit, with a black hat and silver studs, looking absolutely gorgeous. She strides across that stage—which I now notice with alarm is raked dangerously downhill toward the audience—and accepts her beautiful golden statue with a flourish. Not only does she look fabulous but, to my horror, she speaks fluent Italian both to the presenter and to all the people watching.

"*Grazie tante*," she concludes, as the crowd applauds enthusiastically. "*Mia tutte*. I love you all."

Perfect, I mouth to myself. How in the world do I follow that?

"And now," the presenter announces, "for Best Supporting Actress for her role in *Cactus Flower*, Signorina Goldie Hawn."

A ripple of polite applause goes up, and I teeter with little baby steps down the stage toward the presenter. The closer I get to the microphone, the more I imagine what I must look like after Ali, and the more I begin to laugh.

Hardly able to walk as I negotiate the raked stage, I can see myself flying off and straight down into the Baths of Caracalla. Worst of all, I know that Patti is out there somewhere. Catching a glimpse of her at the front, I dare not look at her.

Reaching my spot with enormous relief, I turn to the presenter and try to pull myself together. Turning to his assistant for my award, he takes not the beautiful gold statue of David worth thousands of dollars but a strange and rather ugly lump of green rock with a gold-embossed plaque. He plops it in my hands, and it is so damn heavy that it almost throws me off balance and straight into the orchestra pit.

"Oh. Oh, thank you." I smile, looking longingly at the other gold statues.

"I'm sorry," he explains, "we don't give those to people who come a year late."

Finding the whole situation more and more absurd, holding on to my lump of green rock with both hands, I approach the microphone and open my mouth to speak. But just as I begin with "*Signore* and *Signori* . . ." the orchestra cuts in and my time is up.

Catching my sister's eye and abandoning all attempts to control myself, I give myself over completely to the sheer release of laughing. My mascara bleeding and desperately trying not to blow snot from my nostrils, I climb to the back of the stage, knees bent, steadily making the ascent clutching my rock, while the orchestra drowns out my howls of mirth.

My award being the last, suddenly everyone else is brought back onstage, and I find myself standing next to Sophia Loren, who is proudly flaunting her beautiful gold statue. With a long drumroll, the presenter announces that the 1970 David di Donatello ceremony has come to an end. As the orchestra strikes up, he pulls on a red cord and fifty white doves are released from a box into the warm night air above us, flicking feathers and droppings all over us.

Well, that just about finishes me off. I am now laughing so hard that I actually pee my pants, right then and there, next to some of the most illustrious movie stars in Europe.

Goldie Hawn, I hear a voice say in my head, you might as well just pack it up and go straight back to where you came from, girl, because you sure as hell don't belong here. My knees clamped together, doubled over, I know that I shall almost certainly never be asked again.

A nd then . . . and then Goldie was holding this thing that was so heavy she could hardly move!" Patti is squealing into Daddy's tape. "My sister—your daughter—was standing there, laughing so hard,

I just knew she'd wet herself . . . I thought she was going to roll down that stage, right into my lap."

My father is laughing. So is my mom.

"Honestly, Daddy, I felt like I had my finger up my hiney! I didn't know where to go. I didn't feel like I belonged."

My father laughs. "Oh, you two hippies. You so don't belong up on that stage!"

"I know!" I agree.

"Oh, but then we went to Capri," Patti continues, her eyes bright, her skin golden from the Italian sun. "Ryan O'Neal invited us to a party at Valentino's house! It was amazing. Right by the sea . . ."

"And everything was in zebra," I chip in. "Even the bathroom!"

"Zebra?" Dad repeats.

"In the bathroom?" Mom scowls.

We giggle some more, and Dad moves the microphone closer to capture every precious drop.

"We hired a little motorboat, driven by this gorgeous Italian," I continue, "and he took us to the Blue Grotto."

"We had to crouch down to go in, and, when we did, it was unbelievable. Electric blue. Oh, Mom, you should have seen this place . . ."

"Then there was the Green Grotto," I exclaim. "We couldn't believe the color . . ."

"I can still see it in my mind's eye," Patti adds. "Emerald. It was so cool."

An image flashes across my mind. My sister's red hair, streaked from the sun, blowing away from her face as we blast across the sea, sitting on the bow of a speedboat, heading for the Green Grotto.

"But we haven't even told you about when we went back to Rome," Patti cries, bringing me back to the present. "We got to the hotel, and they were on strike!"

"They were on strike?" my father interrupts, checking that his machine is still recording. "Everybody's always on strike in Italy."

"I know, Daddy, it was so funny. There were no rooms."

"But where the hell did you sleep?" Mom asks.

"On the couches in the lobby."

"On the couches in the lobby? Oh, that's great." She throws her head back and laughs like hell.

Patti and I catch each other's eye and begin to laugh from a place deep within us that only we really understand. Our special time together is drawing to a close, and soon we shall be back on different sides of the country. But as we cling to each other, we both know that we have amassed a precious store of memories to feed on for the rest of our lives.

Sometimes a jewel can be right under your nose and you don't appreciate it. Then, one day you suddenly realize that it was there all along. Because of the history Patti and I share as siblings, sometimes we feel we don't have to work at our relationship. It is so easy to overlook each other because each assumes the other is always going to be there.

The trip to Italy allowed Patti and me to discover each other as women, not just as sisters, because the sister thing can sometimes really get in the way. Here we were, away from Mom and Dad, away from sibling rivalry and all its attendant issues, just being a sister's sister. And guess what we discovered? That sister or no sister, isn't she a blast?

I was never supposed to be the successful one. This wasn't meant to be. I was just a fluke of nature. Patti was the smart one. In the space of a few years, she must have gone from wondering if I was even going to get through school to being amazed that I was a regular on a popular television show and everybody knew my name.

Siblings don't need much to feel threatened by each other; that's a force of nature in itself. Then when success gets in the way, the ripples start to spread. There must have been times when all anyone ever wanted to ask her about was me. I mean, how many times do you want to answer the question "What's Goldie really like?" or questions about whichever male movie star I was working with at the time.

I am sure she must have wanted to scream, "Yeah, Goldie's okay, but you know what really ticks me off about her is . . ." and list my most annoying traits. So, at times she must have felt as isolated from me as I did from her.

No matter how hard you try, success promotes guilt in the person who is successful—especially when you know that deep down, it can't be making others feel all that good. It is a very tough thing to look at someone else's good fortune and say, "Oh, I'm so happy for you." Somewhere inside there has to be a voice screaming, "What about me? Why was I dealt this hand and you dealt that hand?"

What was important for me about taking this extraordinary journey with Patti was that I learned I couldn't fool her. I couldn't be who I was not. I couldn't fake it. She knew me better than anyone. It didn't matter what I looked like with Patti. I could go without makeup, or even tie my hair back off my face, and it didn't matter. A lot of people arm themselves with who they think they should be so that they can become individuals and break away from what they have been in the past. But until you can be completely raw with someone—as happy as you want to be, as loving as you want to be, as mean, as helpless, as bereaved, as scared, as lost—then you can never really feel comfortable in your own skin. I can be that honest with Patti.

As life goes on, you realize that as siblings, you are the only people in the world who can reference your lives from a similar perspective. No one else has that ability; no one else lived inside those walls, knew your parents as people and is able to laugh or cry at the same things in the same way.

There will always be something about siblings that irritates or annoys you, but, as with any other relationship, in order to sustain it you have to learn to show tolerance for whatever they are going through. Just because there is a threatening situation or maybe anger bubbling beneath the surface, don't overreact. There are ways to handle it. You might sometimes see your sibling acting out and you may not like it, but you have to know when it matters and when it doesn't.

The relationship between siblings is about as deep as you can go. As your parents die and fall away from this earth, the bond becomes deeper, and, if you have honed it, massaged it, nurtured it, then on the day you both become orphans you will be able to seek solace in each other and know that you are all each other has.

No one on the planet will ever know you better than your sibling. They know the good parts, the bad parts, and the secrets. It is a very powerful and valuable relationship. Don't let it slip through your fingers. It is like going home in your heart.

wonder

Wonder shows in the light of our eyes.
Without it, they become dull and old.

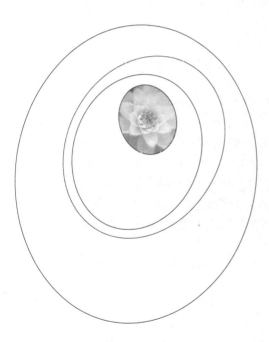

B ut I don't look Russian!" I protest to Richard Zanuck and David Brown, who are sitting in my trailer on a film set somewhere deep in the heart of Texas.

"Oh yes you do!" they sing back in unison, perched on the edge of my couch. "Do you think we would offer you this part if we didn't think you were perfect for it?"

Zanuck and Brown are the beloved producers of my fifth movie, *The Sugarland Express,* directed by Steven Spielberg. They look like Mutt and Jeff: Dick Zanuck, with his jaw sticking out, and David Brown, with his round teddy-bear appearance, always sporting a cigar. I'm crazy about these guys; they are the most dedicated producers, devoted to their films, to their actors, to their directors and to the goal we're all trying to achieve. They defend their films with their lives, and they are a dying breed.

The rain beats down on the tin roof, drowning them out, as I continue to argue my case.

"People just won't buy me as a Russian. I mean, I'll have to speak with a Russian accent, and who on earth will believe me? I mean, really."

They are trying to persuade me to accept the role of Oktyabrina, a Russian ballet dancer, in a new movie called *The Girl from Petrovka.* Based on the book by George Feifer, it is the true story of a young girl who falls in love with an American reporter before being banished to Siberia.

"Goldie, don't underestimate your own talent," they tell me. "Of course you could do this."

"All right, guys." I smile. "You're wearing me down. I'll tell you what. Let me go to Moscow and meet some Russians for myself and then I'll see if I even look Russian."

"Great idea!" they respond in unison.

It is October 1973 when I land with a *thud* on the tarmac of Moscow's Domodedovo Airport. I am flying Aeroflot, which has the worst safety record in the world. The Cold War is in full bloom.

As I walk through the drafty immigration hall, I look right and left at the gun-toting soldiers standing guard, all buttoned up to the neck and as stiff as boards. It is the first time I have ever witnessed a military presence at an airport, and the sight chills me.

When I finally get through the endless process of checking my papers, I am met by the *Los Angeles Times* correspondent in Moscow, Murray Seeger, who has promised to help me. He reaches his hand out to me eagerly and introduces himself.

"Oh, great, great," I say, taking his hand. "It's good to finally put a face to your name." He is open, friendly and warm.

Chatting to him as we make our way out of the airport, I find him something of a curiosity, for I have long wondered why anyone would ever choose to live in Russia. I frequently read his articles about Brezhnev and the cast of Cold War characters, and Russia didn't seem like a fun place to live.

Outside, the gray air cuts my throat. The opening line in *The Girl from Petrovka* says the cold of a Russian winter can kill even a memory. I am beginning to understand.

Murray drives me down the wide-open boulevards of Moscow, lined with trees that are just about to lose their leaves. We pass grand architecture, great domed churches and opulent halls, beautiful onion-domed buildings erected during the reign of the csars and csarinas. I can smell Moscow's pungent history.

"Have you ever read *The Girl from Petrovka?*" I ask brightly.

"Shhh," Murray hushes me. Whispering, he adds, "The car's bugged. Let's talk about it later." Seeing my expression, he laughs.

I am in shock. This isn't part of any world that I have ever known. I can't imagine not having the freedom to say what I feel. I dare not speak another word.

We pull up outside a building that is enormous and hideously ugly, a big cement block that sits in stark contrast to the older buildings around it. I get out of the car and stand staring up at it, thinking about communism and Trotsky and his band of brothers who really believed that they had all the answers.

"Is this my hotel?" I ask.

"I'm afraid so," Murray says, fetching my bag from the trunk. "It's okay, we can talk now. Everything's bugged. It's the way of life here. It's funny, we talk about it quite openly. As soon as a new correspondent arrives, his vehicle is taken away to be 'serviced,' but everyone knows what's really happening."

He leaves me with a wave and promises to collect me later. I walk up the steps to my monstrous hotel, which looks like a Second World War bunker. Sad is one way to describe it. Devoid of spirit is another.

L ater that night, Murray drives me to his run-down apartment block, where all the foreign correspondents live. It is a veritable village of antipropaganda. The building is very utilitarian, in a style I now know to be typical of communist architecture. Sitting in the lobby on a bench are three old women, chatting away among themselves. They remind me of my aunt Sarah and her friends chewing the fat.

"*Privyet.* Hello," I say with a smile, but they don't respond.

Murray takes my elbow and leads me away. "Those, my dear, are called informants."

"What do you mean?"

"Well, they report when you come in and when you go out; who comes to visit you and what time they leave. They're tattletales. They all work for the KGB."

Upstairs, in a rather drab apartment, I am introduced to some of his colleagues. There is a British reporter who works for the *Daily Telegraph*, a Frenchman who works for *Le Figaro* and a rather dashing correspondent who writes for *Time* magazine. He is very cool and speaks candidly on the complex political relationship between Russia and the United States.

They smile and say hello and carry on with their earnest, intelligent conversations about the state of the Politburo and life in the Soviet Union. I join them, sitting around an oval table, eating a simple dinner cooked by Murray's wife. Sipping vodka and drinking in the atmosphere, I listen as they share their experiences laughingly and speak of their strange lives as strangers in a strange land. Sometimes when they talk, they don't make a sound, they just move their mouths and the rest of us have to lip-read. When I look quizzically at Murray, he laughs and points to the ceiling, and I realize that his apartment is bugged too.

"We have to be careful what we say," he whispers in my ear. "They are always listening."

I am endlessly fascinated by his guests' stories and how they cope with living under KGB rule and dealing with a repressive government that doesn't allow truth. They speak of the corruption of the Communist Party and how difficult it is to get information. I am in awe, and more than a little stimulated, in this place that is nothing like home, or anyplace I've ever been in my entire life. This is an interesting table, full of smart people, intellectuals involved in reporting world affairs. It is a million miles away from show business.

"Does anyone here ever see movies?" I ask, wanting to contribute.

"A select few," comes the reply.

"Well, only the elite in the party," another laughs. "And then only the films they choose."

I have started them off talking about Hollywood, the subject that interests me the least. Some tell me they have seen *The Exorcist* on recent trips home, the hot film of the year. They ask me who I know.

"Has anyone here read *The Girl from Petrovka?*" I chime in softly, eager to change the subject.

The *Time* correspondent says, "Yes, I know the writer."

"You do? Oh, I'd love to meet him."

"George? Well, I'm sure that can be arranged. I'm not sure which country he's living in right now, but I could make some calls."

"And is it all true?" I ask. "Has the story been embellished at all?"

"Yes, it's true. The girl was sent away to Siberia because they thought she was a spy when in fact her only crime was to fall in love with him. But, of course, the newspapers accused her of writing subversive material against the party. They said that was the reason."

"Yeah, another lie. Poor girl."

"Poor George. That was a hard time for him."

"Oh, this might be interesting. I'm an actress, and I've been asked to play the girl," I tell them. "But I don't think I look like a Russian."

The British reporter throws back his head and laughs. "I think you do, my darling," he says as the rest of them nod in agreement.

"Have you been out on the streets yet?" the *Time* man asks.

"Not yet."

"Well, have I got a day for you, girl." He grins. "I'm going to take you out and show you a bit of Moscow you'll never otherwise see."

It is he who drives me back to my hotel later, and, as we are driving along, I notice a nondescript black car following us closely. I look round and then at the reporter, and he checks his rearview mirror.

"Don't worry," he says. "That's just the KGB. They follow me everywhere. I don't know what in the world they think I'll be doing. They're probably more interested in you than me tonight. *The Girl from Petrovka* is banned here."

Safe inside my hotel, I pass through the cavernous lobby with hardly a stick of furniture in it and take the elevator to my floor. Facing me, sitting behind a desk, is an old woman who stares at me intently, logging in the exact time I returned. My own personal watchdog. A bit eerie. Closing my door behind me, I have a strange feeling. I wonder what she knows about me already.

The next morning, the *Time* correspondent collects me as promised and takes me into downtown Moscow. I am shown all the usual tourist sights—the Kremlin and Red Square, the Archangel Cathedral and

Lenin's Mausoleum—and some of the not-so-usual ones, such as KGB headquarters and the state-owned GUM department store. I quickly learn to tell a Russian by his shoes—they are old and worn and far from stylish.

I am surprised to see the windows of the stores full of clothes and appliances.

"Don't take any notice," my friend tells me. "It's all for display. There's nothing inside."

Dressed in a T-shirt and embroidered bell-bottom jeans under my heavy coat, I am completely out of place. What was I thinking? American jeans are very hot on the black market.

The journalist takes me to the house of a friend of his. "She'll give you a sense of what life is like here as a young woman," he says as we pull into the parking lot of her apartment building. "She's not dissimilar from the girl you're going to be playing, actually."

"Really?" I say as we pass another trio of old ladies sitting on a bench. I wink at my friend and giggle.

As we climb the stairs, he tells me, "I've arranged for you to spend the day with her. It's okay. She speaks English. Her sister just defected to the West, so she is alone."

A woman opens the door. I am shocked. She is breathtakingly beautiful. She has jet-black hair and green eyes, a devastating combination. I take note. Uh-oh, I look nothing like her.

She thrusts her hand forward. "Hello, my name Kristina." She smiles and welcomes me in. As I step into her tiny, one-room apartment, a two-year-old boy I assume to be her son dashes from the corner and hugs her tight around the legs.

My friend and I walk in, and Kristina turns to him and says, "They stole the book you lent me. *The Girl from Petrovka.*"

"You're kidding me."

"No, they came when I was out. When I come back, it finished." She shrugs her shoulders and laughs. "So, that's living in Russia."

Kristina is a single parent with no sign of any man in her life. As my friend departs and she turns back to the room, she sees that I am shivering and runs for a sweater that she places over my head and insistently pulls down over me. She puts the kettle on, and the two of us sit on either side of her son by the stove in the corner of the room.

"I'm sorry," she says. "It is cold. But the heating in the building isn't turned on until . . ."

Her final words are drowned out by a sudden terrible sound. What little light there is in the room is blotted out. I can see her lips moving but can't hear her voice, and her apartment shakes violently. Instinctively, she reaches out and places both hands over a pile of dinner plates. Through the small window behind her, I see a freight train rush past so close I can almost reach out and touch it. All around me, the building shudders and jolts. The cracks in the peeling walls appear to be opening farther with each tremor. Then, just as soon as it began, the noise stops. The light returns through the window and all is calm.

"November one," she says, finishing her sentence as if nothing at all has interrupted it.

Kristina is a true girlfriend's girlfriend. I feel instantly connected to her. Hunched by her stove, we nibble cubes of chocolate from a small, flat bar she has bought specially for me. There is little else in her kitchen, and I am humbled by her hospitality.

"You have beautiful hair," she tells me, staring at my now shoulder-length locks. "Like your name. Golden."

Embarrassed, I run my hands through it and tell her, "Oh, it's not looking its best right now. It needs a good wash."

She jumps up like a child. "Please. I will wash for you."

"Oh, no, no, that's okay."

"Please," she says quietly, pressing her hand on mine. "I want. I used to wash my sister's hair."

So, there in her warm kitchen, with her son playing with his wooden blocks, she positions my head over her deep ceramic sink and washes my hair gently with shampoo that smells like Palmolive soap.

"Yes, my sister left. She is in New York. She is now model."

I look up. "You could be a model too."

She laughs. "No." She pauses. "I will never see my sister again."

"Why didn't you defect with her?" I ask.

"My heart is in Russia," she replies simply, her gaze steady.

I am beginning to understand. There is still something steeped in the walls of these old buildings that speaks of this nation's great history, of its poetry and its art.

When Kristina has finished rinsing my hair, she turns on the oven, opens the oven door and leads me to a chair in front of it. She sits me down and pushes my head upside down. Without saying a word, she runs her hands through my hair, fluffing it dry, so tenderly. I feel like we've been friends for years. She must have loved her sister very much.

"Now, how beautiful," she chirps, preening and fluffing the last few strands of my hair. "Now you will meet my friends."

With her child on her shoulders, Kristina and I skip down the stairs, past the suspicious watchdogs and out onto the streets of Moscow.

"I hate those old women," she mutters under her breath.

"Please, first I'd like to buy some treats for your friends," I tell her. "Where can we go?"

"Oh, yes, the bakery. Come."

We walk through the chill air along a grand Russian boulevard lined with baroque buildings and dart into the doorway of one that looks like a royal palace. It is now a bread hall.

I am amazed by all the customers inside, who have formed at least three different lines. Dour-faced men and women in heavy hats with gray scarves wrapped around their faces are lining up to choose what they want to buy from a glass-fronted display case.

I stand in line. A woman in a drab utilitarian uniform puts my pastry choices in a bag and hands me a ticket. I watch as my bag is taken away by another staff member in a uniform and a funny hat.

Kristina leads me to a second line, where I hand someone my ticket and pay for my pastries. Then a man gives me another ticket and points me to a third line, where I now have to wait to collect my goods.

The bread hall is my first glimpse of everyday life in Russia. They had a good idea: that everyone be employed and treated the same. I already know from listening to my journalist friends that the reality is quite different. The results are in plain sight. The human spirit is being crushed, and apathy has set in.

"My God. This is insane!" I tell Kristina. "What a screwed-up system! This whole process has taken almost an hour. It would have taken five minutes back home."

She laughs out loud, hoists her son back up on her shoulders and off we go, down the narrow streets, continuing on our journey through life under Moscow's communist rule.

With my hard-earned bag of pastries, I walk with Kristina and her son in the October morning and down some streets that grow narrower and narrower until the walls are only a few feet apart. I am on an epic journey into Russia's past. I soak up everything I see—the architecture and the faces, the sounds and the smells of this great city, so full of history. There are very few cars, and many people are walking the streets. No one smiles very much. No one looks very happy. And no one looks me in the eye.

We reach a four-story building, and Kristina leads me inside. We are faced with the challenge of climbing the old wrought-iron staircase, whose steps are rusted out in the middle. Placing a foot carefully on each side of the step, being careful not to fall through the middle, we pick our way up and up and up to the top floor.

Kristina knocks on a heavy wooden door, and it is thrown open almost immediately. Facing us are dozens of smiling faces, all welcoming us in enthusiastically. Hands reaching out to us, they draw me into their large apartment with its floor-to-ceiling windows.

"My, what a large family!" I cry.

"This isn't one family." Kristina laughs. "This is three. They share three rooms. Everyone has own private corner. My friends live in this room."

I pass by a small kitchen. On the stove a huge pot of something is bubbling.

Kristina's friends have a beautiful blond child, aged about ten, called Sofia. She has a big, open face, and her hair is pulled into tight little plaited knobs of gold on either side of her ears. She could be my daughter. I hand her the bag of pastries. She gently takes it, smiles and says, "Spasibo," before rushing off to the kitchen.

The light through the high bank of windows on one wall shines a kind of a golden southern glow onto the table we are invited to sit at. It is beautiful. Along each windowsill sit prized tomato plants laden with dozens of cherry tomatoes, a rare gastronomic treat. The father plucks one and offers it to me. I take it and eat it with reverence. He is so proud of his garden. Fruit and vegetables are not easy to come by in Russia, I learn.

We are served steaming bowls of broth with fresh-baked bread and then the treats I have brought. The adults chatter away in Russian while Sofia sits staring at me, and her father throws his head back and laughs uproariously. Everyone else laughs along. I'm laughing too. I just don't know why.

Kristina explains. "He said that Sofia went to school today with poem she wrote about nature and what God means to her. The schoolmaster summoned the father and tells him, 'Your daughter must learn about the party, not art. Not God. Not allowed.' He thinks this crazy."

The family are still laughing, and I laugh along with them. Surely these are not members of the Communist Party.

Suddenly, Sofia tugs on my arm and gestures for me to go with her to her corner of the room. Secretively, she rummages under her bed and pulls out a little red change purse.

"You want to show me something?" I ask, picking up her thoughts. I have no idea what it is but I can tell it means a great deal to her, so I hold my breath, make my eyes big and look excited.

"What can it be?" I gasp as she giggles.

Reaching into the purse, she pulls out a collection of delicate seashells.

Kristina explains from across the room that Sofia collected them on a rare trip to the coast once. They are her prize possessions, and she handles them like rare jewels.

"They're beautiful, honey, really beautiful," I say, taking the time to touch each one and turn it over and examine it as she watches.

Sofia's eyes are round and rich and full. I can feel her dreaminess, her wonder, her bohemian free will rolling around inside her. I am afraid it will be crushed by the system according to her birthright, or no right. I feel intense sadness at the thought that when she grows up, that look of

wonder

wonder in her eyes will almost certainly be replaced by the deadening gaze of the women I have already seen—people whose spirit has been squashed.

Cradling her shells in my hand, I continue to squeal with delight. "Oh, look at this little yellow one. Oh, and that pink one, with the big swirls on its shell. How lovely, Sofia. Thank you so much for showing them to me."

Sofia takes my hand and opens it, dropping the seashells into my palm one by one. Then she closes my fingers around them. "Goooldie." She speaks my name softly.

"No, no, no!" I shake my head vehemently. "I can't possibly take them, my darling. But thank you so much for offering them to me."

"Da." She nods, her big eyes confused. I can tell she is thinking that if I like them so much, then why don't I want them?

"No. Nyet," I say firmly, placing them back in her hands and closing my hands around hers. "You must keep them, Sofia." Staring deeply into her eyes, I add: "These are yours to hold and yours to dream with. Keep them forever, never stop looking at them, and I will always remember you and your shells in a special place in my heart."

She finally understands, and, with what seems like relief, puts the shells away under her bed. She offers me a hug instead. All I have to give in return is my love and my bag of pastries.

I leave that remarkable home reluctantly. They gave me so much— charm, hospitality, potato soup, laughter and love. I am left with the even stronger belief that family is the key to happiness.

Heading back to my hotel, I know that soon I will have to say good-bye to Kristina and return to a world that she may never see. I want to thank her for all she has done for me. I unclip the gold necklace from around my neck, the one my mother gave me for my birthday, and start to hand it to her.

"Here, I want you to have this."

Kristina's eyes register surprise and then alarm. "Nyet!" she hisses. "Not here. Your hotel. We go to your room."

Her nervousness clear, we walk past the matron, who eyes her suspiciously. Only when we are safely in my room does Kristina graciously accept my gift, after placing her finger on my lips to make sure I don't say anything that can be overheard. I try to put it around her neck, but she whispers, "*Nyet.* I put in pocket," and secretes it away.

We hug then, both of us close to tears. She takes off down the corridor, past the watchful old woman, and back to a world I have only had a glimpse of. From the window of my room, I watch her walk down the street with her son—she is a great human being making the most of a tough life.

Despite what seem like insurmountable differences, I can feel myself falling in love with the Russian people, with their passion, their longing, their energy. I feel I understand them so much better now than I ever would have from reading articles or seeing films.

That night—my last—Murray takes me to a nightclub where I can observe young women of my own age. I had always imagined Russian women having high cheekbones and dark hair, like Kristina, all the features I was born without. But all I can see around me are round faces and big eyes. Dressed in their black-market clothes, they wear masses of eye makeup and bright red lipstick. The music is so loud I can hardly hear myself think. Everyone is dancing and drinking vodka and smoking cigarettes as if there were no tomorrow. Trying to keep a party alive inside of them. Living excessively, I guess, to make up for the lack of excess in everything else. There is great spirit here, a tremendous zest for life. It is all the more poignant for its apparent absence elsewhere in this city.

I sit down and observe with the zeal of a paleontologist who has just wandered into the Lost World. My God, I almost completely forgot why I came here in the first place. I do look like these women after all! They give me insight into my character. There is so much to work with here: my wardrobe, my makeup. Somehow it all seems so superficial.

Driving back to the airport the following morning, I ponder how much I have learned from this trip. I feel sad. I realize that I will never see Kristina and her son, or Sofia and her family, again. By the time

I reach the airport, I am in such a haze of nostalgia for the wonders of this proud nation that I barely notice the armed guards, with their stiff suits and cardboard attitudes, as I hand them my papers.

"*Nyet*," an immigration officer tells me.

"*Nyet?*" My attention snaps sharply back. "What do you mean, *Nyet?* These are my papers."

"*Nyet.*" They take my papers away.

My heart stops for a minute. I shift from a feeling of grand Russian romance and wishing I could stay here a little longer to a sense of blind panic.

Okay, wait a minute, I say to myself. I've got to get out of here. My heart palpitates as I see my Aeroflot plane revving up its engines out on the runway. I seriously consider making a run for it.

My voice a few octaves higher, I ask a guard, "Excuse me, is there a problem?" He doesn't answer me.

Desperate for a cigarette, I reach into my purse and my fingers close around a bundle of pens that Murray advised me to bring as sweeteners but which I completely forgot about. Accepting them with a twisted smile, an official waves me through. "You are pleased to go." He hands me my papers in exchange. Before he can change his mind, I dash past him out onto the tarmac and mount the stairs of my plane.

On the plane, I sit back in my seat, staring down at the lights of Moscow as we fly back west. Yes, I can play a Russian, but I could never be one. I understand their need to overcome obstacles, to make the best of their lives. I now know that their passion, love and art can never be extinguished, for it burns deep inside them. No matter what our political party, we are all individuals striving for happiness, just like Oktyabrina.

Something extraordinary happened to me during shooting of the final scene of *The Girl from Petrovka*. The guards were about to take Oktyabrina away to Siberia for a life of hard labor, but they allowed her just a few moments to say farewell to her boyfriend, Joe Merrick, played by Hal Holbrook.

As an actress, you never know if the emotion you need to draw on is going to come, or even where it comes from, but it was truly there that day. Standing there handcuffed in a snowy courtyard in the middle of Vienna, I began to speak my lines when suddenly I was completely overcome.

"If only I hadn't been so stupid," I said, barely able to get the words from the script out. "We could have loved long ago. Then there would have been so much more to remember."

Inside, I was holding back a primordial wail at the injustice and the pain of my character's suffering. I felt such incredible sadness that this light spirit I identified with so deeply had her life so tragically ruined. I could see this beautiful light being snuffed out, as I suspected little Sofia's would be snuffed out one day.

Those moments in an actor's life are magical, and you can never retrieve them. They are a gift. It doesn't take away from the fact that we all worked hard at re-creating the reality, but those instances of real emotion come from somewhere else, somewhere deep within us.

I learned so much in Russia. I learned about humanity, about the importance of family, about religious and spiritual repression. I witnessed what people truly value—the tomatoes grown on a windowsill were worth more than almost anything to them. It is so important to get a different perspective in life, to see what other people have or don't have and what they consider to be valuable. Possessions ultimately do not make us happy, nor does the obsession with acquiring more and more material wealth. How much is enough?

The Russians I met gave me a sense of humility and taught me about resilience in the face of what was, from my perspective, a very difficult life. They had so little. Yet some of those I met seemed to be just as satisfied and connected to their lives as those of us who have so much more.

This paradox has now been proved through research into the science of optimism and hope and the level of satisfaction in people's lives. People in countries with greater poverty and deprivation often have a very high sense of well-being and satisfaction, while those in Westernized societies such as our own are—believe it or not—way down the scale.

Some wonder how people can be so happy when they have nothing.

But in Russia, and for the first time, I saw that what one has or doesn't have is an entirely relative concept. The joy of having my hair washed, the taste of a sweet cherry tomato—that is not "nothing." For the first time in my life, I began to see that material wealth really doesn't automatically bring a sense of well-being or contentment.

Most of all, I learned from a ten-year-old girl that no matter what your situation, you can always have your special place in your special corner of your room or your heart where you can still dream your dreams and feel wonder over something as simple as a seashell.

postcard

My mother steps out of the limousine at the Dorothy Chandler Pavilion and shoots me a wicked grin. Taking her hand and leading her inside, I am seriously beginning to question my decision to invite her along.

I have been voted one of five Women of the Year by the readers of the *Los Angeles Times*. A grand luncheon is being held in our honor in this impressive arena. Looking around, I see that Mom and I are the only ones not wearing hats.

Beneath the hundreds of brims surrounding us lurk blue-rinsed, blue-blooded dames buttoned up to their necks in designer suits with matching purses.

I feel like a freak in my blood-orange minidress, red shoes and false eyelashes. Looking around nervously, I feel like I've been plunked in the middle of an episode of *The Mary Tyler Moore Show.*

I'm even more nervous about what my mom might say to these women. This is someone who never minces words. At the party for *Cactus Flower* held at "21," she walked up to Walter Matthau's wife, Carol, who always wore powder-white makeup that nobody ever commented on, and asked her, "Why is your face so white?"

At another Hollywood party, she had a few too many to drink and not enough to eat and began being rude about all the women strutting about. "What the hell's with these people?" she growled. "No wonder they're so thin: they never serve any food." Deciding to leave early, we were sneaking out through the kitchen when Mom turned and went back inside. "Wait a minute," she said, just as I almost got her out. She walked back into the party and sang, at the top of her voice, "Bored!"

Now I have brought her to this event and I am already reconsidering my decision. But I really need Mom with me in this strange environment that is so *not* my peer group. I'll just have to make sure she doesn't drink any of the free wine.

Inside, the place is full of tinkling crystal glasses and bone china and women with pokers up their asses. It is a big festival of coiffure.

I introduce Mom to a few people, and she says, "Helloooo" in the affected English voice she puts on when she meets people. It is the only time I ever see her not being herself.

"Just say hello normally, Mom. It's okay," I tell her under my breath. She doesn't listen and carries on with her false hellos until it is time for us to take our places in this theater of the absurd.

Surrounded by all these well-dressed, conservative women in hats, Mom and I sit, watch and listen as the awards begin. One by one, these women make their way to the podium and make their oh-so-earnest speeches. Gloved applause ripples round the room. I feel even more out of place.

One of the recipients, a socialite who looks about 105 years old and with a face whiter than Mrs. Matthau's, totters up to accept her award. Taking the whole thing terribly seriously, she stands before a hushed and reverential audience, leans toward the microphone in her hat and her pearls and opens her powder-caked mouth.

"One kind word," she says, with the utmost deliberation, "will keep me warm all winter."

That's it. That's all she says, and there is a long, awkward silence. It is broken only by the sound of me vomiting a laugh from deep within my belly. The noise erupts from my nose and mouth, and there is nothing I can do about it.

Trying to hold myself together, I go into a paroxysm, physically convulsing and snorting snot out of my nostrils.

Mom looks over at me with eyes that say, What the hell do you think you're doing?, but that only makes me laugh even harder.

She curls her hand up into a ball and, from across the table, gives me the fist, something she does when she wants me to behave. Looking at me with the blackest of looks that says, Shut the hell up right now!, I laugh more than ever. And then I catch her eye, which is a bad thing, because now she starts to laugh too.

Knowing that at least she must try to control herself in present company, she screws her face up into a really mean expression that makes her look like she's bitten down on a wasp. This change only makes me laugh more.

Tears are now rolling down both our cheeks. She clenches her hand into an even tighter fist and brings it up in a way that promises to come across and punch me in the jaw any minute if I don't stop. Finally caving in, she puts her head down on her chest and makes a strange laughing-wheezing noise.

"Don't look at me, just don't look at me!" she hisses.

"I'm not looking at you, Mom! I'm not. I'm really not!" I cry, completely out of my mind, but when I do I can see her shoulders shaking uncontrollably.

The other women attending the lunch are beginning to stare. A sea of hats turns 180 degrees to see where the strange choking sounds are coming from. I don't know what to do. Looking around, I see that they don't yet realize that I am laughing.

Mom sees it too. "Pretend you're crying," she hisses through her tears. "Make like you're overcome."

So I go with it. I mean, I truly deserved my award for those next few minutes alone. Looking up, and dabbing the side of my eyes with my napkin, I whisper to a few of the women closest to me, "I'm sorry, but this is so moving."

By which time my mother is on the floor, giving in to all pretense of holding herself together. I sob facedown into my napkin for all I am worth.

"Mom, stop it!" I plead. "I have to go to the bathroom."

Her mascara streaking down her face, she looks up at me and wails, "I already did!"

To my horror, I hear the presenter call my name: "And now, our final Woman of the Year, Miss Goldie Hawn."

Mom pulls herself together and suddenly makes a very serious face. Holding herself in with every inch of her life, she says, "All right, now, just get out of here. Go up there, get your goddamn award and let's go."

Standing up in front of all these hats, knowing my mom is out there hiding somewhere, I am barely able to hold it together as I reach the podium. Starting to laugh, I have to think quickly of something to laugh at.

"Gee, thank you so much for this Woman of the Year Award," I say, giggling freely now. "But I didn't know I was a woman yet!"

Everyone laughs, and I scan the room to try to find my mom. I can't see her face, but a little gloved hand suddenly shoots up above the sea of hats and gives me the thumbs-up.

Fleeing that place, desperate to get away from the whole crazy scene before someone finds us out, just as we are getting into our limo, a woman comes up to us and grabs my arm.

Pulling off her hat to reveal a lustrous head of hair, she says, "I just wanted to say how much I envy you, Goldie."

"You do?" I ask, intrigued. "Why?"

Her eyes sad, she squeezes my arm and says, "Because I could never, ever laugh with my mother like that in a million years."

fathers and daughters

Our fathers are the first loves of our lives.
Take heed, for it sets the patterns
for our future relationships.

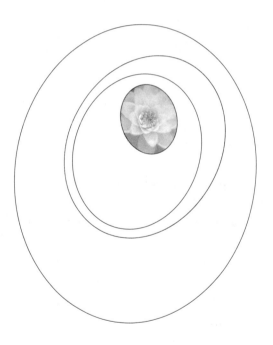

T he little yellow Bug chugs its way up the mountainous curves of Colorado, working its way to see me, my father at the wheel. It is 1975, and I'm doing a film with George Segal, called *The Duchess and the Dirtwater Fox,* and I have got Daddy a seat in the orchestra that plays beneath the stage on which my character, Bluebird, performs.

I can't wait for him to arrive. My dad and I have done several shows together already. He was in my first TV special, *Pure Goldie,* for NBC. He played his fiddle while I danced. We even did a comedy routine on that show, proving that he was funny even when that little red light came on beneath the camera.

Nor could I resist putting him in my one and only nightclub act at the Hilton Hotel in Las Vegas. We stayed in Elvis's suite and had a blast. I love nothing more than being on the stage with my dad, and here we are again.

I spot his car driving up the pass to the location. He is looking for me through the windshield, hands draped loosely over the steering wheel as always, eyes eager with anticipation. I run out into the street that has been turned into a town from the 1800s. I am in my barmaid's costume, which is high-cut, low-slung and with fake plums hanging all over it. My hair is piled high atop my head and adorned with a feather bluebird. I forget what I look like as I run to him.

"Daddy!" I yell as I dart in front of his car. I watch him start to smile, drop his head between his arms and then peek up as I rush to his window.

"Go, you must be kidding. Is this how you look these days?"

He loves all of it: the work that I am doing, the business of acting. I can see how proud he is through his joking bright blue eyes.

"Come out, Daddy," I say, opening his door and grabbing his arm. "Come out and meet everybody."

"Where should I park?"

"Just leave it there. Don't worry. Just come inside the saloon; I want you to meet the crew."

He saunters out of the car, Fred Astaire–style, and glides beside me in his one-step, two-step dance. Inside we go. I am proud to show off my father. I tickle inside when either of my parents shows up on one of my sets. It is so much fun for me, and so grounding.

Someone whisks him into the makeup trailer and transforms him into a man from the Gold Rush days. With his hair parted down the middle and his baggy trousers and shirt, he steps out looking like Alfalfa from *Little Rascals.*

"Oh, Daddy! I wish Mom could see you now."

He gives his high-pitched laugh as he slinks down the street, grinning from ear to ear. Beaming, I follow him into the saloon.

"Places, everyone!" yells the first assistant. "Let's get this shot before lunch."

I take my place behind the curtain on the stage. Daddy, sitting in the orchestra pit, takes his fiddle out of his case, and we are off. The music starts, the curtains open and I stand center stage, gyrating my hips, shaking what assets I have and beckoning men seductively. Throwing myself across a table, I begin to sing, "You can eat my cherry, cherry, cherries, but please don't eat my plums. You can taste my berry, berry, berries, but please . . ."

Halfway through my act, halfway through trying to play a desirable sexual animal, I glance down at my father. He is looking up at me in horror, his face half frozen in a smile. Oh my God! I think, suddenly embarrassed. He's never seen me like this before. All the while I can hear his thoughts. What is she singing? What is my daughter doing now?

Rut Hawn was a Southern gentleman from Little Rock, Arkansas, with values straight out of the Victorian era. His mother had four boys and no girls, all of whom treated her like a queen. My father was always uncomfortable discussing sex or anything having to do with it, much less joking about it.

When I was young and feeling the hormone wave envelop me, I started dressing differently and putting on my pink frosted lipstick and black eyeliner. Daddy was the last person I wanted to see me walk out the door. In fact, I would race past the back room where he was reading a paper or watching TV so that he wouldn't.

"Wipe off that lipstick!" he'd yell, his nose all wrinkled up as if he smelled something stinky. He really didn't want me to grow up and be like the other girls.

I remember when I snuck out of the house once to go to a sock hop at the Armory in Silver Spring, Maryland, telling my folks I was going to a friend's for the night. There were about a hundred and fifty kids there from all the other schools, and it was dance, dance, dance, the music blaring, arms flying.

In midjump, Jean Lynn hissed, "Goldie! Your dad's here!"

I froze.

I looked up and saw my father, his limp hands dangling from the sleeves of his full-length brown gabardine coat. His eyes searching madly for yours truly. He spotted me. His pursed lips meant business. A man of few words, he said, "Get in the car, Goldie." We drove home in silence. He was more hurt than angry. I had lied to him. How could I do that? I thought, the guilt eating me up inside. There were no harsh words spoken, no curfews. Disappointing my father was punishment enough.

I finish my song, "So please don't eat my plums . . . ," shooting my father a guilty look and rolling my eyes. He shrugs his shoulders and he mouths, That's show business!

Daddy and I wave at the entire crew as they drive back down to Denver to nestle in their comfy hotel rooms at the end of each working day. They leave Central City the ghost town it really is, with just a few crazy locals and us left. Not for us the five-star hotels. We are braving it out in a ramshackle Victorian house with no heating and bad plumbing I have rented on a dirt road. Each night, we walk up the road toward our castle in the crisp night air, nine thousand feet up, nearer heaven than I have ever been.

Feeling chilly, I wrap my arm in his. The crew has scattered sawdust all over the set streets, and it crunches beneath our feet. There is still a smell of horses in the air. Along the way, we stop and look in the windows of the perfectly preserved stores. Walking past the Helen Hayes Theater Company, I say, "Daddy, just imagine what it would be like if we really lived here and this was our home. Wouldn't it be neat if life was this simple and every morning we could wake up in the mountains?"

"Yeah," Dad replies wistfully, "gotta stop and smell those roses, Go," as we turn onto our little dirt road.

Back at the house, my father hands me a steaming cup of freshly brewed coffee.

"Thanks, Dad," I say, warming my hands around the cup.

He pulls up a rocking chair and sits down next to mine on our front porch. Cocooned up to our noses in layers of sweaters, we sit side by side and watch the sun dip below the horizon.

"Go, I want you to hear me out," Daddy begins, and I know that I am in for a long haul.

"If they drilled a hole in the Santa Monica Mountains, it would create a vacuum that would empty out the whole damn basin of the smog," he tells me. "See, it would create a suction that would vent out in the desert."

"But then the desert would have smog, Dad."

"Yeah, well, let them worry about it."

I laugh. I have heard the story a hundred times, and I never tire of it. I know he's half serious, if only someone would put his crazy idea into action. And then he talks about other things, about how he wishes my sister didn't have to work so hard and how he wishes my mom would get out more instead of sitting around the kitchen table drinking coffee, smoking and gossiping with her relatives. He tells me of his ideas for movies he wants to write. He repeats stories about his travels. How, as a young boy in the thirties, he hocked his violin on the way to the Cincinnati Conservatory of Music, where he had been offered a scholarship, to buy a saxophone. How he taught himself how to play and got a gig with a band.

"Did I tell you about the time I was on my way back home to Las Vegas and my car broke down in Death Valley?"

"I don't remember," I lie, eager to hear the story again.

"Some guy picked me up in his Maserati . . ."

I cut him off. "His name wasn't Stu, was it, Daddy?"

He laughs. "What the hell are you talking about?"

"Well, my car broke down in Death Valley too, you know, except I gave someone a ride. I never told you that story."

"Oh, anyway, as I said, Go, hear me out."

I let him go on telling me about this man who picked him up, and how he told him he was Goldie Hawn's father. How he tried to prove it by pulling a picture of me out of his wallet. Trouble was, I was only three years old.

"And what did he say, Daddy?" I ask again, prompting him.

"I couldn't get him to believe me!" He laughs. "He thought I was crazy. He floored the Maserati and never spoke another word."

We sit in silence for a while, drinking our coffee. Tilting back on his rocker, Daddy points to the derelict wooden house opposite ours. The shutters hang off their frames like the broken wings of birds. The wooden picket fence has collapsed onto itself like a set of old dominoes.

Mists of steam rising from his lips as he speaks, Daddy says, "People throw things away before their time. Look at that fence over there. You know, that fence was made from an old tree that once stood somewhere on the earth. Even though they cut the tree down, they made a fence out of it, so that it is still alive and useful."

I look at Daddy and can't help but wonder if he is talking about himself.

He goes on. "Things can always be recycled and used in other ways."

"Well, I think that fence could definitely be recycled, Daddy!"

He laughs, his eyes twinkling. "I'll get right on it tomorrow."

We sit in silence for a while longer, rocking in squeaky syncopation.

"I guess it's time to turn in," Daddy says, getting up.

I kiss him good night and go to my room. Through the walls, I can hear his radio playing. The comfort of knowing he is lying there, listening to his talk shows, sends me off to sleep.

D addy isn't required every day on the set, or in every shot, and when he's not needed he disappears into the frozen countryside, like the will-o'-the-wisp he is.

"Where did Daddy go?" I ask the crew. "Hey, did anyone see Daddy?"

"Well, I saw him walking down Main Street about an hour ago, Goldie, holding some stick with a weird thing on the end of it."

"Oh God, not his metal detector!" I cry. He carries that crazy metal detector wherever he goes, hoping to find some old piece of junk someone has dropped along the way. Then, with a hammer or a bit of wire and some nails, he'll make something out of what he has found. It might be an ashtray fashioned from a rusty old carburetor—his "nicotine art"—or a recycled scrap made into a plant pot for the garden. Every evening when I get home, he shows me what he has come across with childlike wonder.

I think of all the crazy things Dad has invented in the past, like his home heating system utilizing Mom's vacuum cleaner. Or the alarm he concocted that blasts Tchaikovsky's *1812 Overture* every time somebody turns the front doorknob. Or his homemade air-conditioning unit for his car, a huge cylinder strapped to the window that blows water-cooled air only when he reaches 47.5 mph.

My father is a gentle man, a philosopher and a dreamer; he is as light as air and just as refreshing. With his blue, blue eyes and the looks of a forties crooner, he is terrible at business and hopeless at being a husband, but he is great fun to be around. People regard him as eccentric, and, I guess, weak, because my mother is so domineering. He has always seemed more vulnerable and more perishable, but in many ways he is the stronger of the two: a survivor. He tells people with self-effacing honesty, "I'm not eccentric. I am just an unusual man who does unusual things."

Not long after I first left home, Daddy left home too, after almost thirty years of marriage. It was as if he was secretly waiting for the right moment. His departure was masked as a decision to go west for work, but he never really came back. Instead, he became the gypsy fiddler, feigning to look for work, roaming the country in his Volkswagen Bug, recording his encounters with strangers, playing golf and dropping in on us from time to time.

He was happy enough, and endlessly self-entertaining, but my poor mother was left home alone with no children, no husband and the bitterness of never having lived the life she dreamed of. There was a continent of regret and guilt between them.

When I look at my relationships with my parents, I think it was a gift, or maybe just survival, to be able to see them separately, because to see them as one would have been a very dangerous illusion.

I hurry home from the set, hoping to find Daddy on the front porch waiting for me. As I round the corner, I smile with relief. There he is.

"Hey, Go!" he yells. "Slow down. You might miss something."

I steady my pace, and he yells, "How was your day? On a scale of one to ten?"

"A ten," I yell as I skip happily toward him. A big, fat ten.

That night, sitting on the porch, watching the sun disappear behind the old house, we sit in silence, our chairs creaking in some sort of mismatched harmony. Staring out at the bitter Colorado landscape, I rock back and forth until it becomes like a meditation to me, just being by his side. A lot of the time, my father just sits there next to me, silently thinking. When he opens his mouth to speak, I turn to him in anticipation of each nugget of wisdom he shares with me, the little nuggets I am stringing into a priceless necklace.

"Kink," he says finally, turning to me, his eyes locking with mine, "you understand me, don't you?"

"Yes," I whisper. "Yes, I do."

Rocking back in his chair, looking out at the landscape, he says, "Go?"

"Yeah, Dad?"

"Never forget how good a glass of water tastes."

"I won't, Daddy. I promise."

. . .

Some people have wonderful relationships with their fathers; others don't. I was lucky. Daddy was my first love, and it was he who shaped me. There was no other man that I ever loved more than him. He was the one for me, for better or worse. One look could have crushed me. One pat on the back could have made me feel like the most beautiful girl in the world. He had that power, as all men do with their little girls.

That is why it is so vital that men understand their value and what effect they can have on their little girls. How they shape their lives is the singular most important thing that they will ever do. How our fathers define us becomes how we see ourselves, or how we don't see ourselves; how we feel sexually, how we don't feel sexually. They inform so much of how we view ourselves as females and how we view men—not only as providers, lovers or givers of the seeds of life but also as friends.

My father wasn't perfect. He hurt my mother badly, and I don't think she ever fully recovered. There were things he didn't do for me too, never snuggling or offering cuddles. I never heard him say, "Hey, Go, come and sit in my lap." I just did because I needed to.

This treasured sojourn in Colorado was the last time we were able to spend this sort of quality time together. I was embarking on a new relationship, which was to lead to a new marriage and parenthood for the first time. I always planned to go on a cross-country trip with Daddy one day in his little Volkswagen Bug, but somehow life got in the way.

We wonder who we take after. We wonder if we are more like our fathers or our mothers. The truth is, we are never like just one of them, but are a conglomeration of the two. It was certainly the sweetest of luck to have them both in my life. Everything that I am is thanks to the great love they gave me. My father's gypsy spirit lives on in me, as does my mother's need to nurture. I am both the genetic fruit of their loins and the product of the environment they created for me, good and bad. What happened to their marriage, sadly, was also a great reminder of how important it is to stay truthful to your feelings.

I think if I were to answer the question honestly, I'd have to say I'm

fathers and daughters

more like my father. I am just the same gypsy he was—traveling, questing, learning and constantly inventing new ways to make life funnier. And, thanks to him, I never forget what that glass of water tastes like.

The following Christmas morning, Daddy couldn't wait to give me my present. He handed me the strange-shaped package, gift-wrapped as usual in old newspaper (always the funny papers), and laughed as he watched me unwrap its jangling contents.

The first thing I saw was a laminated picture of Central City, welded into some rusty old frame. Beneath it, suspended on nails, were eight metal railroad bolts, undoubtedly some of the ones he had found with his metal detector in Colorado.

Lifting the strange contraption out of its wrapping, he held it up and struck each of the bolts in turn. Each bolt was perfectly in tune; each one had been painstakingly chosen for its tone.

As I sat there in openmouthed wonder, my daddy played me his own special rendition of the song he felt best summed up our time together in Colorado. He played "I've Been Working on the Railroad." It was one of the greatest moments of my life.

prayer

*Never doubt the magic of miracles.
Just because we can't see them, taste
them, touch them or smell them
doesn't mean they don't exist.*

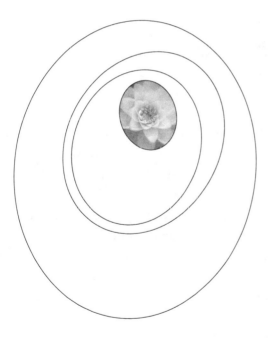

This is my first baby. I am three weeks overdue and feel like I am spawning a whale. My feet are a distant memory. Just getting out of a chair requires assistance. This fifty pounds of love is an adjunct to my belly.

To say I have eaten my way through pregnancy would be an understatement. Vichyssoise and coconut cake are my dietary staples, and my mother—who seems ever-present—makes my every culinary wish her command.

But the days of eating for two are coming to an end—or so I hope. This baby doesn't seem in any hurry to present himself. Or maybe he just likes it in there. I take long walks, hoping to coax him into the world, pointing out its beauties. But he seems attached to his amniotic bliss.

It is 5:30 A.M. Outside, birds sing. Through the window, the sun shines early-morning hues on my bed. Lying next to me, fast asleep, is my new husband of less than a month, Bill Hudson, a singer in a band. This time, my wedding was arranged by my mother, down to the last detail. Determined to take charge of this one, she left no stone unturned. The backyard where I grew up, at number 9 Cleveland Avenue, was transformed into a Garden of Eden.

I was eight months pregnant in a silk cream-colored jersey dress with ruffles around the shoulders. I looked like a great white whale. I had to strap my belly button down so it wouldn't show through my wedding dress.

My prudish father, dressed in a blue suit, looked like one tall drink of water, hips thrust forward. He swaggered down the steps of the back porch, me holding on to his arm for dear life as I negotiated the stairs in heels. Walking down the aisle, my heels sinking into the soft grass, I was having a real wedding at last. Our family and friends all flew in. Waiting for us were a priest and a rabbi, to keep both sides of the family happy.

Standing there in my backyard, the place where I had always imagined getting married, I looked around at everybody from my past—Jean Lynn, David and Jimmy Fisher, my aunt Sarah and uncle Charlie—and grinned. This is what I'd longed for when I put crinolines on my head as a child and pretended to be a bride. Here I was—me, my father and my belly full of baby Oliver.

Now, a month later, September 7, 1976, Oliver's big day arrives with a bang. Pain. Yes, pain. My long-awaited, longed-for baby is on its way. I slip out of bed, calm and in control. I pull some things together, pack them in a bag, take a shower and wake Daddy Bill to tell him it is time.

"Time?" he cries, popping out of bed like a firecracker. I assure him there is nothing to worry about. My mother appears at our bedroom door, dressed in her long white cotton nightgown, making me feel all is right with the world.

"Is it time, kids?" she asks in her warm, gravelly voice. "I'll get a ride to the hospital. Don't worry. You get going."

We fly down the empty streets of Beverly Hills with the excitement of young children on Christmas morning. As I gaze out the window, I can hear my mother's words of warning: "Goldie, dear, you know when you have a baby, your life will change. You will have to say good-bye to your much-cherished alone time." She is right. But, at thirty-one years old, it isn't just my alone time that will change. It will be my faith in God and the miracles that life can bring. Little do I know what I am about to face.

They bind a fetal monitor tight around my belly. I can see the heartbeat of this new life I have come to know so intimately. I think of all the times I sat by the fire and talked to him while he gently rolled around inside me. I told him I could feel his kindness and his poetry. I promised him I would be the best mother I could be, and his most trusted friend. I shared with him my most intimate thoughts about the universe, how connected we are to nature. Together, we were doing our job of making more good humans to grace the earth.

But now the cold, green walls of the labor room are beginning to close in on me. There is not much pain, not much change. Morning seems to morph into afternoon, and the baby still isn't moving down that narrow passage into the world.

"He's going to take his time," I announce with a grin. "He's showing us who's boss already."

No one laughs.

My doctor, Fred Pasternak, a beloved and trusted friend, examines me again with a seriousness that makes me uneasy. Then a brigade of unfamiliar interns marches into my room and examines me, one at a time. I study their expressions as they poke and probe inside me.

The nurse says, "She's only dilated one centimeter. I don't think the baby's coming out." She walks away mumbling something about meconium.

"'Meconium'?"

The doctor shows me. It looks like caramel, or sap, a golden brown goo—not at all what I expect to come out of my body.

The atmosphere changes. Bill stops telling jokes.

"Is something wrong?" I ask, but no one answers me. The fetal monitor begins to make discordant beeps. "What's that?"

"Fetal distress," one of the interns replies.

"What do you mean?" My heart races. Is my baby choking? Is the cord wrapped around his neck? I begin to shake.

"Prepare for surgery," Dr. Pasternak snaps. "I'm taking this baby."

"Taking my baby?" I repeat senselessly.

They jam a needle in my arm before masked strangers lift me onto a gurney and fly me down a series of long corridors. Daddy Bill, who, moments before, was making everyone laugh, looks petrified. He lays his cold, clammy hand in mine as he runs alongside, trying to reassure me. The automatic door to the operating room flies open, and that is the last I see of him. The rest is up to me, my baby and my doctor.

The room feels like a meat locker, cold and unwelcoming. I haven't seen an operating room since I was seven and had my tonsils out. I wish I were seven again because my mother always made everything safe. I know she is outside somewhere, but I want her with me, telling me I'll be fine, just as she did when I was afraid to get a shot, or I feared the Russians were going to bomb us. Or the time that I thought I'd caught cerebral palsy in my sleep and she stroked my head and told me it was only a dream.

But I am no longer a child who can call for her mommy anymore. I have to do this alone.

"Is everything going to be all right?" I ask.

Again, no answer. They are too busy trying to save a life, and it isn't mine.

I am numb from the waist down. Nothing but a white sheet lies between me and my as-yet-unborn child. The epidural makes me shake uncontrollably. Chattering through my teeth, I try to keep it light.

"Hey, you guys behind the curtain? Can you see his head yet?"

"Not yet," comes the reply. "I'm just cutting the last layer. In about two minutes, you'll see your baby."

I look at the big round clock on the wall: 8:25 P.M. My God, where has the day gone? Suddenly, I feel a strong tug, like a tooth being pulled.

"It's a boy!" An explosion of joy erupts beyond the white curtain.

I shriek along with them. "I knew it was a boy, I just knew it!" I want to jump up, scream, kiss my doctor and the nurses. I want to thank the whole world for this moment. But I am paralyzed—a piece of meat on a slab. I can't get to my baby.

Grinning like a half-wit and craning my neck, I try to catch a glimpse of his face as they clean him up and suction the mucus from his nostrils and mouth. The sound is horrible. What a way to start life, with a cold probe going down your nose and throat. He coughs and spews. It doesn't sound quite right to me, but, then, what do I know? I chalk it up to my first experience as a nervous mother.

I can't wait to hold him. They swaddle him in a blanket and present him to me like a prize. His beautiful face is rosy, round and perfect. I lean over and kiss his little pink lips. The floodgates open and I begin to sob.

"I've waited so long for you, little Oliver Hudson . . ."

They whisk him away before I can finish my sentence. Where are they taking him? Why can't he stay next to me? I want to bring him to my breast and give him his first taste of life. I've been abandoned. The doctor is busy sewing me back together. Nausea overcomes me.

"I feel sick," I say, and begin to heave uncontrollably.

The doctor orders the anesthesiologist to give me something to put me out. Next thing I know, the room is filled with soft clouds. As I start to float off on one of them, I hear a distant voice say, "He's in ICU."

In spite of the fog in my head, I ask, "Are you talking about my baby?"

The anesthesiologist strokes my brow and tells me that everything is going to be all right. I drop into oblivion, a safe place that shields me from reality and the truth. But not for long.

I awake in Recovery, sucking my thumb. My belly hurts. I am exhausted and thirsty. I look up to see Bill standing over me. I am almost too weak to speak. "Where's our baby?"

Bill looks like a young deer caught in the headlights. He touches my forehead. "Goldie, our baby is very sick. He is in the neonatal unit. He might not make it."

My doctor appears through the mist in my eyes and takes my hand. "They are doing everything in their power. I promise you, Goldie, he will be all right." But I can see fear in his eyes. I close mine and slip back to the void, where it is safer.

The slow ride to my hospital room feels like traveling through the catacombs of hell. My belly is empty of life. My baby is dying, and my mother is nowhere to be seen. My world has changed. What seemed to be a blessed life, radiant with love and joy, has evaporated.

Sun floods through the window, just as it did the day before, when I was so happy. Yesterday, I waited for a new life. Now I anticipate death. My body contracts every time the door opens. I hold my breath with each update, afraid they will tell me that they have done all they can. There is no release from the agony. I can't even cry. My chest will explode if I do, I feel sure. I will bleed to death from a broken heart.

Dr. Pasternak comes with a wheelchair to take me to see my son. The journey to the seventh floor is interminable. Butterflies flutter in my empty belly. What if he dies? What if he looks up at me and brands me his for life? I will melt at the sight of him and love will cement us forever. I can't handle having that and then losing it. For the first time in my life, I am afraid of falling in love.

Bill is beside me, cracking jokes. I will forever be grateful for that comfort. As I travel that long hallway, I glance into other rooms. Flowers. Balloons. Teddy bears. Healthy babies being fawned over by jubilant parents and grandparents. I have no flowers. No mother or father. No bouncing baby boy.

As I enter the elevator, a revelation comes to me. My mother lost her firstborn, also a boy. She named him Edward Rutledge, after my father. It was against Jewish law to name a child after someone still living, but she wanted to keep this fine American name alive. It was her gift to my dad.

She found her baby dead in his crib when she went to his room for his 6:00 A.M. feeding. I now recall her voice in my head, "Honey, please don't name your baby after Daddy." I assured her that I would only use Rutledge as a middle name, and that it was all superstition anyway. But was it? Was I suffering the same fate as my mother? Was God punishing me too? The thought is too much to bear.

The elevator doors open, and they wheel me into another world. A world of uncertainty and fear, of beginnings and endings. A discordant cacophony of buzzes and beeps fills the room. I look frantically for Oliver. I begin to tremble in anticipation of seeing him again.

I spot my baby right away. No mistaking him. He looks exactly like my father. His tiny, sedated body lies passive on a metal slab. Heat lamps warm him as his little chest mechanically inflates and deflates, a breathing tube pumping oxygen into his lungs. Other tubes sprout from his head and his feet. The nurses hover near him, pushing chemical cocktails through the narrow lifelines. But it suddenly occurs to me that the only true lifeline isn't connected. That of a mother's love. My love.

Reaching out, I touch his chest. I kiss his face and watch the beat of his heart flutter methodically across the monitor. The nurses tell me it is too slow. I feel so helpless. Where is our God? The God I prayed to as a little girl with Jean Lynn when we were frightened of the bomb? Who brought me peace before I fell asleep with Nixi? The Almighty Who'd answer my prayers, if only I asked?

Rising from my wheelchair, as if airlifted to my baby's side, I lean over and whisper in his ear. "Oliver Rutledge Hudson, you are going to live." And, with that, I place my right hand on his torturously heaving chest. "Please, dear God, make me the conduit of Your healing. Send

prayer

Your healing power to my child that he might recover and be strong enough to fight for the life he has chosen here on earth. I know he will be gentle and kind, a true gift to humanity. I will mother him with the laws of nature, so he will be a living mirror of Your kind heart."

Suddenly, a warm blue sensation courses through my veins. I become intensely calm. A wonderful aura of unconditional love permeates the space around us. I look up at the monitor and watch it show definite signs of change.

Oliver's tiny heart begins to beat faster and faster, its rate climbing steadily. From 58 beats to 69, then back to 61, then up to 72, then back to 68, then up to 76. Rising with every second.

"Nurse!" I cry. "Doctor Pasternak! Come! Look!"

They gather round as I stand next to my child, my hand covering his heart. Afraid to take it away, I am prepared to leave it there for as long as they'll let me. Bill places his hand next to mine, and we revert to being the kids we were, giddy with excitement.

"I prayed so hard."

"You see, Goldie," Dr. Pasternak says, smiling. "If only mothers would understand the power they have to heal their children. We see this kind of thing happen time and again. Your baby feels you. He smells you and hears you. I mean, after all, he was in your belly for nine months. He needs to feel your closeness and the comfort of his mother."

When Oliver is stable and showing sure signs of improvement, Dr. Pasternak places his hand on my shoulder and says, "He's going to be okay. It's time for you to get some rest, young lady."

It is so hard to leave. No one else could have persuaded me to leave my son. Nodding my reluctant assent, I lean over once more and whisper in Oliver's ear, "I'll be back soon, my darling. I just need to sleep. We both need our rest."

Down I go, sinking back into the chair, impossibly tired. As Bill wheels me back to my room, I feel as if the umbilical cord is being stretched all the way from Oliver's crib, along the corridor and into my room.

I had no idea then just how sick I was. I learned much later that for several days after the birth I had toxemia. I was being monitored as closely as my son.

Something remarkable happened the day that Oliver was born. I learned that day that miracles can happen. That prayer is powerful. That faith in something is extremely important.

It was one of the first times in my life that I realized that by focusing on something and willing it with all my might, I could actually change or re-arrange the course of events. This experience started me on a journey. It led me to a lifelong interest in these sorts of phenomena and in the theory of small things, which is called "the new physics" or "quantum physics"—investigating and exploring the new frontiers of consciousness.

We are all made up of waves of energy. The neurons that are con-stantly firing in our brains have small tentacles called "dendrites." Attached to the end of these little guys is a receptor like a radio. Scientists have now learned that these little radios can pick up informa-tion—even other people's thoughts. The brain is awesome. It has amaz-ing potential; it is far more advanced than any computer that man could make. We have resources that we are only now beginning to tap into.

We are all miracle workers, and we can all heal others. Sometimes it works, and sometimes it doesn't. Ultimately, I couldn't save others I loved from dying. They have had their time. In the end, we're all going through the same door in heaven. I continue to pray every day, not for miracles but for a peaceful and compassionate world. Maybe that will take a miracle. Who knows?

One truth we can be sure of: praying for someone's well-being while they are still on this earth, by reaching out and trying to help them in any way we can, by developing more compassion in our hearts and in our lives and in our spirits, will help make a better world.

Looking back on Oliver's birth now, I know that through prayer and love we both were healed. All these years later I can say that everything I promised Oliver that he would be he has become: a mirror of the heart of God.

I call him my "little man on the hill."

postcard

Rod Stewart rasps out "Maggie May" from the battered old jukebox that dominates a corner of Alice's Restaurant on Malibu Pier.

Sitting alone at a table, nursing a glass of wine, I stare out at the couples strolling hand in hand under the pier's swaying lights—happy people so close I can almost touch them.

It is 1977, and I am living out in my beautiful beach house perched on a cliff at Point Dume in Malibu. I designed it myself as our love nest. I had hearts embossed in the floors, stone hearts in the fireplace and heart-shaped balusters. But Daddy Bill is out on the road making his music, and little Oliver and I are together in our little house of hearts alone.

Seeing the sun setting orange and vibrant on the horizon, I am restless. Leaving Oliver in the care of his nanny, I take a drive down the Pacific Coast Highway for a closer look. The warm night's breeze tousling my hair, I head my car north as the pelicans rise majestically from the waves, dripping silver trails.

Something draws me to Alice's, an age-old Malibu landmark shaped like a lighthouse at the head of the pier. I feel the need to be among people for a while, strangers. I need to think.

Pushing open the door, I look around for a quiet table and hope that nobody bothers me. The one thing that celebrity has taken from me is my privacy in crowded spaces, which is especially hard for someone who has always enjoyed traveling in a party of one. I am in luck tonight; nobody seems to see me, perhaps because I am feeling so transparent.

Alice's Restaurant has always been a funky place to go. There is sawdust on the floor, a long bar, picture windows looking out over the ocean and dozens of little tables and chairs lit by candles. The bar is buzzing with people, some eating, some dancing and some—like me—seeking solitude. Wearing jeans and a T-shirt, I find a quiet seat at the back, order a drink and sit there staring out at the ocean, my diary open on the table in front of me.

I haven't worked for over two years. Not since *The Duchess and the Dirtwater Fox* in Colorado with Daddy. People warned me that once I hit thirty, I'd be history. Men and animals don't have that problem in this industry.

Being pregnant with Oliver, giving birth to him and then caring for him has kept me incredibly busy and fulfilled. Becoming a mother is one of the most amazing things that has ever happened to me. My son lights the fire of my deepest happiness and fills me with such joy, I feel my heart will burst.

It is the rest of my life that is making me sad.

Remembering the wise counsel of Dr. Grearson, knowing how important it is to face up to my fears, I have come to Alice's Restaurant to ponder my future.

Staring out at the ocean, I see that there are still a few fishermen hanging around, hoping for a late bite. The pier's pretty little lamps cast pools of light onto the contented people strolling beneath them, chatting, holding hands or kissing. I feel more of an outsider than ever.

So what next, Goldie Hawn? I ask myself silently, my pen poised over a blank page of my diary. What does the future hold? Because it seems you are pretty much done with the movie business. Or, at least, it seems to be pretty much done with you.

The frustration is the not knowing, the uncertainty. Am I done yet? I want to ask someone, anyone who might know. Is this it? An Oscar? Six more movies, and then it's over? Washed up at thirty-one? But I feel like I have so much more to offer. Please, someone, just let me know if that's it. Because then I can gain a sense of control in my life and move on.

And if it is over, I ask myself, then what next? I have gone beyond the stage of ever going back to Takoma Park to be a dance teacher. I am a Hollywood actress, like it or not, but now I'm married, with a small baby. If I can't star in any movies, I can only see a future for myself in producing them for other people.

I think of Daddy. "So what did you learn today, Go?" he always asks. What am I learning from this fallow time, this period of insecurity and uncertainty?

Staring up at the moon, just as I did when I was a little girl, I try to summon up my childhood determination to be happy, come what may. Who are you, Goldie? I ask myself. Who are you really? I order a second glass of wine. When I was small, all I ever wanted to be was a wife and a mother, living in a pretty house with a picket fence. But now that I have tasted the bittersweet pill of stardom, I am caught between its addictive lure and the world I used to belong to, unable to be fully in one or the other.

Is that who you are? I ask myself. Just your career? Then what will happen when you are left sitting by yourself at the end of your life, wondering where your friends and family went?

Picking up my pen again, I try to write but abandon the attempt. Sipping my wine and staring out at the ocean, I hear my father's words again in my head. "Go, whenever you feel too big for your britches just go out and stand in front of the ocean. Then you'll see just how small you are."

He taught me so much. He showed me how to stay real, keep grounded, not to rush through life too fast. Mostly, he taught me to keep that sense of wonder in my heart to sustain me through the hard times. Like now.

He's right. I throw some dollar bills on the table and happily slip out of Alice's Restaurant, completely unnoticed.

embracing strangers

*Sometimes we feel there is nothing new under the sun
and then suddenly springs a friendship like this,
a flower. Treasures are waiting just
beneath the earth, if only
we look for them.*

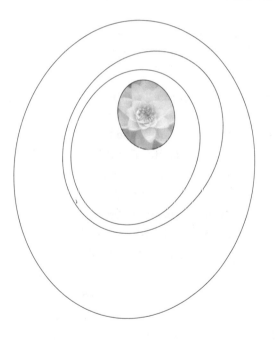

Oliver's not sleeping, Mom. He still has jet lag, and it's already been two weeks. Mom, this is so hard!" I sob across the telephone's long distances.

"I know, honey," Mom soothes, "but you're a working mother. You can't have it both ways."

"I know, Mom. I'm just so tired."

I am in Italy making a film called *Viaggio con Anita,* or *Trip with Anita,* with Giancarlo Giannini. It is back to back with my last film, *Foul Play,* with Chevy Chase, which came out of the blue just when I thought my career was over. I've brought Oliver with me since his daddy is in London making his music. I never sleep, and I feel like a walking zombie.

I have a nanny with me, but my Ollie wants only me. So I'm up all hours of the night, trying to find him pasta and bits of ham. Gosh, he is a picky eater. It is a scary time in Italy. The Red Brigade is terrorizing and bombing Europe, so I have been assigned twenty-four-hour bodyguards. It is great, I must admit. I like having someone sitting outside my door every night. They take Oliver, throw him on their shoulders and carry him around alongside me, all the while teaching him Italian. *"Ciao, Mamma!"* he says as I run off to the set. *"Ciao,* my bambino." Yes, my Italian is getting better too.

I look out the balcony of my room at the Hotel Palazzo in Livorno and down onto the busy Viale Italia and the Grand Quay. Ordinary

Italian life hustles and bustles below me, and yet here I am, trapped with a headache I could sell to science.

The Palazzo is a residential hotel with long corridors and high ceilings, like something out of *Sunset Boulevard*. It is furnished sparsely—a chair here, a vase there—and just a thought can create an echo. Rendered in pink plaster on the outside, it has big windows and small balconies with huge arches and colonnades, and PALAZZO in big letters across the front.

Every night after filming, I walk the long, empty hallway back to my room, to take over for the nanny and try to recover from another frustrating day on the set. To tell you the truth, I am getting a little tired of Italians patting me on the head and telling me everything is going to be okay.

"I find myself crying for no reason," I tell my mother unhappily. "I can't always be there for Oliver when he cries, and he hates it when I leave. Plus, the work is so hard. My director doesn't even speak English. To top it off, I was in the car today with Giancarlo Giannini, trying to discuss a scene, and, you know, he's just learning English. So I said to him, 'I think that this would be funnier if I reworked this line.' And do you know what he said, Mom?"

"No, what the hell did he say?" she growls.

"He said that this movie wasn't meant to be funny. I laughed and told him, 'No, honey, this is definitely meant to be a comedy.' And he said, 'No, this is a tragedy.' And you know, Mom, I'm beginning to think he's right."

My mom laughs. "Honey, you need some help right now. Why don't you send Oliver to Bill in London? He's there for a while, isn't he, making his TV show?"

"You know what, I'm going to do that, Mom. That's a great idea. He'd be better off there with his daddy. Although, it's gonna be so hard to be away from him."

With Oliver in Bill's care in London, I am left alone in Livorno to finish the movie, commuting to Bill's beautiful house in Regent's Park every weekend. This is working much better. However, there are still so many difficulties working in a foreign tongue, speaking a foreign language in a foreign land, and each day is filled with new frustrations. Not least that we are way over schedule.

So, here I am, facing new challenges daily, unable to express myself properly. Don't get me wrong, I love the Italians. They love your children; they love your dogs; they're always ready to feed you, house you and would give you the clothes off their back.

But the sexual politics are quite different there. For instance, in a scene where I fall into a fountain the director positions the camera so low that he is filming straight up my skirt. Then he attaches my sodden underpants and bra to the antenna of the hero's car. Or he takes my microphone away and gives it to Giancarlo Giannini.

"But who can hear me?" I complain. "You have to have sound."

"It's no problem," they say, *"mi amore,"* patting me on the head and hoping I'll just shut up. *"Domani.* Tomorrow. We fix it tomorrow. It is *non importante."*

Lunch goes on for hours. Wine, pasta, wine, meat, wine, dessert— and more wine. One day, I return to the set, but no one is there.

"Where is everybody?" I ask the only person I can find.

"Everyone have siesta," he tells me with a shrug.

Oh boy, I'm going to be stuck here for another year.

The siesta must have been good because the next day the director suddenly springs a sex scene on me, in which I am supposed to be naked.

"No!" I tell him vehemently. "I'm a new mother, and it was never in the original script."

"But you were naked before, in *Girl in My Soup!*" he exclaims, through an interpreter. "I saw you."

"That was different," I protest. "I was all alone, and it was shot very tastefully, through a gauze curtain. This is me and Giancarlo copulating openly in a hammock!"

With a frenetic waving of his hands and a look like thunder, the director cusses me in Italian. The only word I can understand is *"Madonna,"* which he now calls me for being too much of a prude. I am as stressed out as I have ever been, I miss Oliver terribly, and I am beginning to suffer the first major anxieties about my relationship, not helped by the long distances between us. Madonna wants to go home.

C oming back to my hotel every night, exhaustion drags at my feet as I cross that echoing marble lobby and climb the staircase to my room. Lifting my head against the weight of the day, I peep into the hotel bar to see if any of the crew are having a drink. I could use a good belt tonight.

Up at the counter, several young Italians are standing around a television set, screaming at a soccer match. I notice a man, sitting with his back to them, quite apart, in the corner of the bar. He is looking out onto the veranda. He seems to be staring at the flowers dancing in the breeze. The soft evening light illuminates his face.

Stopping in the doorway, I stare at him for a long time. There is something about him that I am drawn to, and it is not just the brilliant shaft of sunlight that seems to be pointing an ethereal finger at him from the window. He has an interesting face, deep with lines of experience and wisdom; his fingers are long like my father's and look as if they could play an instrument. I feel instinctively that this is someone I would like to know.

Impulsively, I, who has never been known to leave anyone a stranger, walk up and introduce myself. *"Buonasera."* I extend my hand. *"Il mio nome è Goldie."*

He places his hand on mine and says his name: "Aldo."

I look deeply into his face and realize that he must be at least ninety years old. For me, it is love at first sight.

I sit down and we begin our fumbling dance of words, a duet of Italian and French with a little German thrown in for the pas de deux. We mix and match the languages we know and listen in open wonder to the lyrical beauty of those we don't. In our faltering, fragmented sentences, we embark on a great love affair. Soon, he makes me completely forget the need for words.

Aldo is, without a doubt, the most romantic-looking man I have ever met. He is tall, lean, with a straight back and a shock of long white hair.

His face is craggy and crumpled, but he has high cheekbones, a Roman nose, a full mouth and a chiseled jaw. His blue eyes are droopy now and a little watery with age, but they still hold a sparkle that hints at the inner wonder of his great spirit.

Through our strange mix of languages, we gradually come to know each other. My Italian improves, and so does his German. Our French helps us when we're stuck. More and more, we are able to communicate. More and more, I am able to understand his incredible history. Having lived through two world wars and fought in the Resistance, he now lives in this hotel, waiting for the end.

"I met a girl in nineteen forty-two. She sold magazines at a stand in Paris," he tells me, his tongue curling deftly around his German. "Her name was Rosa. I bought a newspaper and I fell in love. After that, I see her almost every day. But Rosa was Jewish, and when the Nazis came she was very afraid."

"What happened?"

"The Nazis came for her, but I managed to get her away, into the network, where she could find safe passage out. I held her in my arms, just once, and kissed her. On my way back, I was nearly caught. A bullet nicked me."

"Did you ever see Rosa again?" I ask, hopefully.

"No," he says, sucking in a gulp of air that tells me the wound in his heart is still fresh. "I lost her forever."

Leaning forward in his chair, his eyes moist, he squeezes my hand. "We were like Romeo and Juliet." He pauses for a moment to compose himself. "I always hoped I would see my Rosa again, but I never did. A few years later, I met Fiorine, my beloved wife, who is now dying. But a little piece of my heart will never stop loving Rosa."

Aldo reminds me so much of my father. He is a dreamer and a born storyteller. Listening to him, I wonder if my father ever had a secret love, if Mom was his first and only sweetheart, or if, on his travels as a musician, he ever fell for anyone else, as Aldo did with Rosa.

Like Daddy, my new friend is also a great lover of music. He persuades the bartender, who stands drying glasses in front of a mirror pitted with time, just like Aldo's hands, to switch off the television when nobody is around and play his 78s. Side by side in this cavernous bar, with its elegant columns and ornate moldings, we listen to his favorite Italian opera—Puccini and Verdi, Rossini and Bellini—music that is both strange and wonderful to me, and very different from the Bruch and Bach and Tchaikovsky that Daddy always played at home.

Sipping a cappuccino, I sit in reverential silence while the amazing voice of the Italian diva Renata Tebaldi fills the room with an aria from *Tosca.* I stare and stare at Aldo's exquisite hands as they sway in time to the music, his eyes closed. Beautiful, gentle, expressive, they are so like my father's.

His physical fragility belies his inner strength. Hidden beneath a body that is crumbling and causing him pain beats a heart that has seen so much, has borne so much and knows so much.

K nowing Aldo is at my hotel in Livorno waiting for my return each night lifts my heart. I feel like a married woman scurrying away from her demanding husband to meet her grateful lover. He is my guru and my spirit guide on this earth. He is the one who, for the moment, seems to make sense of my life.

I can tell how much he also looks forward to our nightly chats. His whole being lights up when I come into the room after a hard day's filming. It fills me with such joy to see him so happy, it erases the frustrations of my day.

Aldo and I develop a fascinating relationship, incredibly deep despite the language barrier. I grow to love him more and more. He knows I am an actress who goes to work every day, and who flies to London each weekend, but he doesn't want to know any more than that. It's not *importante.*

What is *importante* is how much we have come to mean to each other. When filming in Livorno finally comes to an end after four months, I am stricken by the thought that I may never see Aldo again. Relieved as I am that the movie is over and that I can now spend a glorious summer in

London with Oliver and Bill (where our beautiful daughter will be conceived), it is still one of the hardest things I've ever had to do.

"Here, I bought you something," I tell him, unable to hide my tears as I hand him a large red geranium to remind him of us. "You have to water it regularly."

"Like our friendship, my darling," he whispers, "or it will die."

Knowing his time on this earth is running out, I write to Aldo soon afterward. He writes straight back. In his long, sloping handwriting he tells me of the sad deterioration of his wife, his own failing health and his sorrow to be old and dying. I keep every single letter he sends me, to remind me of his gentility.

My dear Goldie, I hope that you will remember me always. I will never forget Goldie, the little blond American, so very dear, who writes to me with her own hands. Her letters designed with the heart . . . I am older and tiresomely alone with my poor wife who is always more ill . . . I have perhaps made many sins, many errors and many mistakes in error. Now comes the time of reckoning, Judgment Day. I have lived a long course of life, now I close the book of lost debts. I have retired to a home for old men called "House of the Old." I want to try even this last experience. I am fascinated. To you, Goldie, a hug, a caress to your blond hair, an unforgettable look at your blue eyes, the fruit of the loom.

I write back:

Dearest Aldo, I have read your letter over and over again. It makes me so sad that I cannot be near you and comfort you. I picture you in my mind's eye and I see you walking the enormous hallways of the huge hotel and at times pretend that I am turning a corner and by surprise run into you. It always makes me so happy not to have missed you. I am planning a trip to Europe soon and I will try to come and visit. I must brush up on my French; my textbooks are collecting dust on my shelves.

You were so dear to bring me words of comfort. I care so much about you and feel as though I have found a kindred spirit. I feel you know so much about life. When you are having one of your bad and tired nights think of me because you are so valuable to me, as I am sure you have been to the many lucky people whose lives you have touched in your life. Please don't hesitate to write. Love and kisses. P.S. It is still quite warm here. I'm waiting for the cool breath of autumn.

In one of his final letters to me, Aldo writes:

My dear friend, I was happy to receive your unexpected letter. It gave me in my solitude a moment of joy. I am so very alone and I thank you. I would like to be listening to music and reading poetry with you, Goldie. I still have the little plant you left for me. Every day I look at it, and every day I think of you . . . The photographs (of your children) were very pretty. You say that with her smile Katie could stop a war. Well you, Goldie, with your words, could stop even death, perhaps mine.

Your letter is doubly propitious because I am tired, Goldie, so very tired. But I am still painfully alive. I live in this unhappy scene of the world; the same in sleep as awake and so often my thoughts take me to you like a distant dream . . . I think of you with affection. Aldo. P.S. I enclose a photograph of old Aldo, very old. It was taken by two German tourists who were kind enough to mail it to me. Look at my hands, so skeletal, as has become my life. In the words of an old Italian song, don't forget me.

I write to Aldo for more than four years, sending him gifts, flowers and photographs, and I visit whenever I am in Europe. One day, his letters stop coming, and I know in my heart that he is dead. I try to find him, to send flowers to his grave, but the world has swallowed this remarkable human being whole and closed over him like water, leaving no trace.

From the briefest of chance encounters, from a kind word to a stranger, Aldo and I ended up giving each other so much. To this day, I feel the light of his life illuminating mine. One should never be closed to new friendship, no matter how old or tired or busy. Every relationship has its unique gifts, and Aldo's gifts to me were priceless.

Blanche DuBois, Tennessee Williams's character in *A Streetcar Named Desire*, said, "I have always depended on the kindness of strangers." I feel that deeply. There is something about being vulnerable to a stranger. Not vulnerable in the sense of being endangered, but vulnerable in that you are in unfamiliar territory, a place where you need to avail yourself of the help and kindness of others. It not only helps you restore your faith continually in humanity, it is also so humbling.

I never want to get so comfortable that I forget the importance of those small connections people can make with other human beings. When you are comfortable, you can miss so much, and I for one don't want to miss a thing.

postcard

*Oh heart beat in my womb, pounding out
the rhythm to the music of my soul,
making me throb from head to toe,
giving each other life. I know in my
heart, as she will know in hers, that
we are separate people alone in this
world; but now we have each other as
close as two can be, sharing our warm
secret that we will always keep.*
—*A poem to my unborn daughter*

grief

Your joy can be measured only
by the depth of your sorrow.

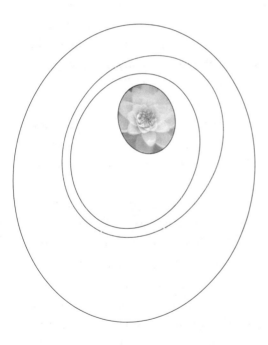

My eyelids flicker open and then close. I am in that delicious state of wakeful nothingness, floating weightlessly just before sleep. It is a warm afternoon in early 1982, and I am lying on my bed for a rare afternoon nap. Curled over into the fetal position, a blanket pulled right up around my neck, my mind drifts with the tide of my thoughts, back and forth, lapping gently against the inside of my skull.

Through the swirling water, something begins to emerge like an image on photographic paper. Only this isn't static; it's moving. It is as if I'm witnessing something but am detached at the same time. I can see my father. He is in his new apartment in Los Angeles, and he is busy in his kitchen with something.

I smile. What is Daddy doing? Is he cooking hush puppies? I wonder. Or is he creating something with his beautiful hands?

I continue to watch him as he walks from the kitchen into his dining area. Then I suddenly see him clutch his chest and fall to the floor.

In a blind panic, I awaken with a start, sit up and call his name.

What in the world was that? What have I just seen? I jump out of bed, hoping to dispel my bad dream and shake myself back to reality. I run to the bathroom to splash some water on my face. Looking into the mirror at my own reflection, I say, "I'm gonna call Dad."

Walking back into the bedroom, I pick up the phone.

"Hello?"

"Daddy?" I am so relieved just to hear his voice.

"Go? Hi, honey, how are you?"

"I'm fine." I exhale. "How are you, Daddy? Are you okay?"

"Oh, I'm fine." There is a weariness to his tone.

"So how was your day, Dad, on a scale of one to ten?"

"Hmm. Maybe a six."

"Why don't you come over for a cup of coffee?"

"Okay."

As I put down the phone, I think to myself, He sounds so uninspired. I hate that.

Out the kitchen window, I watch his Pacer idle into the driveway. That was fast, I think. I run to put the coffee on. I watch him saunter up to the kitchen door and hear it slam behind him. I am so glad he's here.

Sitting at my kitchen table, stirring his coffee, he sits opposite me with a wistful expression. "You know, Go," he says, "I'm not afraid of dying . . . but I'm so lonely sometimes."

I stare at him, my own spoon frozen in my cup. I feel like I could die. I can't bear to think of my dad feeling lonely; he has always been so self-sufficient, so self-generating and so creative. This admission knocks the wind clean out of me.

Maybe I should tell him I'd like to take that road trip we've always dreamed of. Just then, Oliver chases Kate through the kitchen screaming, reminding me how difficult it would be to get away these days. Instead, I change the subject and start to talk about my preparations for my next movie, *Best Friends*, with Burt Reynolds. That always cheers him up.

"Mom's going to meet me in D.C., Dad. You see, first we're filming in Buffalo, and then the company's moving to Washington. Isn't it neat? I'm going to be in our hometown, making a movie. Why don't you meet us there?"

"Nah." Daddy sighs. "I don't care to go back to Washington. Been there, done that."

"I'm gonna miss you, Daddy. I wish you'd think about that. But I'll call you, all the time, as usual. Give you the scoops. And when I get back, let's talk about that road trip we've been planning for so long." I've said it anyway.

He perks up. "Great, Go."

The call comes early one morning. I am in a hotel in Washington, rushing around trying to get ready for the day's shooting. My mom is in the next room, I'm late as usual, the kids are playing, and I haven't even washed my face yet.

The telephone rings and I pick it up while pulling on a shoe.

It is Patti. Her voice is shaking. "Goldie, Daddy's in the hospital. He collapsed in his kitchen last night. An aneurysm has burst his aorta. Please, you and Mom have to come home right now."

My world goes cold. I saw this.

Mom and I can barely hold each other up. We are both too scared to cry. We don't know where to go or what to do first. Norman Jewison, my director, somehow appears magically in front of us, hugs us both and says, "Just go. Don't worry about anything. This is only a movie. Go home and be with your father."

Mom and I hardly speak on that long journey back to Los Angeles and Cedars-Sinai Medical Center, the place where I gave birth to my children and where my father is now in critical condition.

Staring out the window of the plane, I pray to the God I prayed to to save my son. "Please, God, please let him live. He's only seventy-three."

When we arrive at the hospital we meet up with Patti and her two sons, my beloved nephews Michael and David. Shaken to the core, we are led into the Intensive Care Unit, a world of strange beeps and sounds, measuring the pulses of life. Daddy is hooked up to all sorts of machines. We have never known him to be sick; he hardly ever went to see a doctor.

Mom, my sister and the children and I visit Dad every day for eighty-two days. We are now shooting the movie in L.A., which allows me to be with my father as much as possible. I rush from the set every night after work, to sit with him and stroke his hair and whisper how much I love him. My mother, who never divorced my father and never met anyone else, rarely leaves his side. Patti and I do our best to shore her up. Those eighty-two days are some of the longest of our lives.

Sometimes when I arrive late at night, he is asleep and I scribble little notes for him. One night I write, "You know, Daddy, I want to tell you how important you are to me and how all your advice and your philosophy is part of all of us now. I know you thought it went in one ear and out the other but it didn't. See you tomorrow." I kiss him good night, and ask the nurse, "Please give him this when he wakes up."

Those final weeks of the film when I am trying to make people in front of the camera laugh, when I am secretly dying inside, are truly awful. One night, I am in the middle of the breakup scene with Burt Reynolds at the end of the movie when I get a call from the hospital.

"Come right away, Goldie." It is my father's favorite nurse who cares for him. She is a sweet girl who Daddy jokes he will marry one day. Tenderly, she adds, "He's not doing well. Could you come to the hospital?"

With the insistence of Burt and Norman, I flee the set, still wearing my costume. Luckily, this is one of many false alarms. But then, soon after the film wrapped, the inevitable phone call came. "You'd better come to the hospital, Goldie. Your father's blood pressure is dropping. This could be it."

After running every red light trying to get there for his final breath, I run into Intensive Care, but something is wrong.

The machines that had been whirring and ticking, bleeping and monitoring Daddy's life force, have fallen silent. All I see is his beautiful body lying there—lifeless. I throw myself over him. I can't believe he's gone. I'm hurting inside. I've lost my best friend. This isn't possible. I wanted to say, "Come back, Daddy." It was too late. All that can be heard is the sound of the nurses, who loved him, weeping softly. My mom, my sister and my nephews all run into the room. We hold each other hard, and we cry. We cry for an unusual man who did unusual things.

This loss feels unbearable for a while, as if no one in the world has ever felt this much pain.

He wasn't the best husband, and I guess he wasn't your all-time perfect father either, but he was an unusual man who did eccentric things. In truth, perfection is only something we can strive for. I am so lucky to have my memories, to be able to feel his love from this distance, to share in the wonder of his spirit. That will never leave me.

I have since come to learn that loss is part of being alive; it's part of loving. Sadness is just as important as joy. Letting go of someone we love is the hardest thing we will ever do. Pain provides us with the vital ingredient in the genetic makeup of our character; it is part of the DNA of our philosophy. Some people never surrender to love for the fear of being hurt. But to not have loved, to not have felt the immense joy it brings, would have been a far worse kind of death.

To the tune of a lone fiddler, we buried Daddy.

"My father was a king among men," I told the assembled throng. "His crown was studded not with precious stones but with love, kindness, humor, music, dignity, honesty and integrity . . . From the day he hocked his violin for a sax and took it into the woods and worked at that instrument until he learned to play it, he was committed to a philosophy that carried him through the rest of his life. It kept him learning and discovering new things up until the day he left us.

"When he met our beautiful mother, they gave us life. He learned to change our diapers at the same time he taught himself to repair watches. He opened a watch shop and became an institution in our small city. He played the fiddle at night for all the great world dignitaries and repaired watches by day. We were so proud of him . . . He taught us the simple pleasures and curiosities of life . . . Daddy kept us laughing. His sense of humor was a gift from God as well as his gift to us.

"He was a man of few words, but when he spoke we listened. His words of wisdom to me when he sent me to New York will ring in my ears forever: 'Always look like you know where you are going . . . Keep your feet on the ground. If you need me, the umbilical cord is stretched to wherever you are . . . Don't pick your nose in public. And remember to put the butter back in the icebox.'

"He has passed these philosophies to each of us in his own way. We have grown straight and tall because of him . . . This was our father, the tenderest, most gentle person I've ever known, and I was so proud that not only did I understand what he felt but that I agreed and I rejoiced and thank God for him and his influence in my life and the life of my family.

"Not only did he see his loved ones clearly but also himself without illusions. He loved without pomp or pretense, and he never stopped loving all of us even when we let him down. He told Patti and I time and time again to stop rushing and don't forget to smell the flowers along the way. Well, Daddy, you'll see, we will take your advice and continue your dreams. I wish everyone on earth would follow your dreams and objectives, then for sure we would have more peace on this earth and goodwill toward men. Daddy, your light will always shine inside your children, and we will never stop loving you."

grief

fate

*You often meet your fate on
the road you take to avoid it . . .*

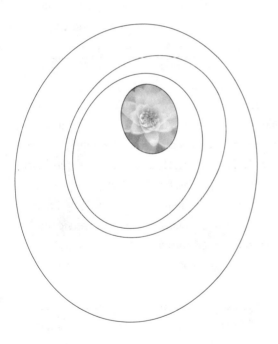

I watch the brown leather riding crop as it slithers down my chest, carving a path around my breast, trailing lower and lower. I don't dare look up at the person who's holding the crop. I'm holding on for dear life. I bite my lip until tears come from my eyes. I am helplessly losing control.

Inadvertently, I catch the eye of the perpetrator, "Captain Lewis"—otherwise known as my friend Eileen Brennan—and that's it. I collapse into howls of uncontrollable laughter. Eileen, who can't hold it together either, joins me, as do the entire cast and crew of *Private Benjamin*.

"Cut!" the director, Howard Zieff, yells out through the laughter, his own face creased with mirth. "Okay, now, let's try this again."

We do the scene ten times before we can do it without cracking up.

Eileen and I are on the same wavelength, hearing the same music that connects our timing without words or need for translation. It's like having a dance partner you're at one with: no matter where he takes you, he never throws you off balance.

Comedy has its own special language, and in sharing the same rare and unspoken understanding of what's funny you feel that in some way you have met a soul mate. That's what Eileen is to me, my comedic soul mate.

Our joyful time working together ends all too soon, and we promise never to lose touch as we do so many times when we fall in love on movie sets only to get caught up again in our lives. Before we know it, years go by without even a phone call.

It is now almost a year later, and Eileen and I have made a plan to meet for a long-awaited dinner and keep our promise to never lose each other.

My children and I are living alone now, in my new beach house in Malibu, while my house in Pacific Palisades is being remodeled. Broad Beach is far from town, and even farther—around forty-five minutes— from my planned rendezvous with Eileen in Venice Beach.

I feel strange tonight, and have a weird feeling that I should cancel. I'm really tired and just don't feel like going. An indefinable heaviness presses down on me. I'm unable to settle on anything, listless and restless. I so want to see Eileen and share our times together; I haven't seen her for far too long, but, for some reason, I just don't feel like it tonight.

Maybe I'm just dreading that long trip down the Pacific Coast Highway late at night. It's a horrible road, one of the most dangerous in Southern California. Looking out my window into the dark, I shiver. I pick up the phone and try to call her to cancel, but she's changed her number, as I have many times. Frustrated, I walk around my bedroom, trying on this outfit or that, discarding them all on the bed as I decide what to wear. I try to reach her again, this time through other people, to tell her I don't really want to leave my children in this house we've only just moved to. She'll get it, being a hands-on mother herself; she'll understand, and we'll just rearrange our dinner for another night. But no one has her number.

Finally deciding on what to wear and realizing that I am already late, I kiss the kids good night reluctantly and jump in my car. I secretly hope that she will have given up on me and gone home. Then I could turn around, head back home and shake this ominous feeling.

It is totally dark. I have never known it to be so completely black. Looking up at the night sky, I see that there isn't a moon. My fingers gripping the steering wheel, I have such an uneasy feeling nagging away

fate

at me. I say to myself, You'd better be careful driving tonight, Goldie. Something bad could happen. Even though I am already an hour late, I drive well below the speed limit.

I turn down Washington Boulevard in Venice Beach and search for the restaurant down a dark street. There it is. I've passed it. I look both ways and make an illegal U-turn in the middle of the street. Porsches are good for something. I find a parking spot right in front of the restaurant. Lucky me.

Dashing out of my car, I run straight through the door and see her shining face. She's here; she's waited for me. It is so good to see her. Her great big smile makes my heart sing.

"Get in here, girl, and sit down," she says. "Where the hell have you been?"

"Eileen, I am so sorry. I tried to call you, honey, and cancel. I don't know what's with me today. But you changed your number, I couldn't reach you."

She throws her head back and lets loose that cackling laugh of hers. "Well, I'm glad you didn't. Now, have a glass of wine and tell me everything."

"My God, where do I start?"

We talk about our children; we laugh about our time together on *Private Benjamin*; we order food and play catch-up. We talk about our recent trip down the red carpet when we were both nominated for the Academy Awards. We recall how we both came away empty-handed. I tell her of the sadness of my separation, and we speak of her love life. She makes me laugh, as she always did.

Dinner is great, but it is getting late. I look at my watch and then up at her smiling face. "My darling Eileen, I'm pooped, and I've got a long ride home."

"Okay, let's go."

We argue over who pays the bill and I win. We kiss all the waitstaff as we wend our way through the tables and out the door. They close the little restaurant behind us. Wandering out into the pitch-black night, lingering on the sidewalk, neither of us wants to say good night. Hugging me warmly, she says, "Kiss the kids for me," and peels off to cross the street.

"Kiss the boys!" I call after her.

Watching her cross the street, backing up to wave good-bye, I feel like there's a long cord of energy connecting the two of us. Unlocking my car door, I hear her call.

"Goldie!" I turn. "Let's not leave it so long . . ."

But she cannot finish her sentence because a car flies out of the night, seemingly from nowhere, slamming into her sideways and tossing her into the air like a rag doll.

I am paralyzed. I can't speak. I can't even scream.

Time stops as I watch the car lift my dear beloved light, my joy, my friend into the air. I want to run and catch her, to break her fall. I want this not to be happening, but I am frozen stiff in a waking nightmare.

Her body slams to the ground and lies there, completely still. I begin to shake, my body vibrating from head to toe. People come running out of their homes and the restaurants. But I cannot move. I'm afraid of what I will see. I am afraid that dear Eileen is no longer alive.

I start walking around in circles upon circles upon circles, always the same circle. The owner of the restaurant, the one we were just joking with, comes and puts his arm around me. He tells me he's called an ambulance. He tries to break my repetitive circling, but I can't seem to stop. "It's okay," he says. "The paramedics are on their way. Everything is going to be okay."

"No, no, it's not going to be okay," I tell him. "No. No. This isn't happening."

Looking across the street, I see people crouched beside Eileen. Strangers. Breaking the momentum of my little circles, I find my feet running toward her at last, not wanting anyone else to touch her. I lower my eyes, finally finding the courage to see her face. She looks like she's sleeping. Her beautiful face seems to sink into the asphalt, as if it were a pillow. The only indication that anything is wrong is the blood trickling from under her head.

"Eileen," I call softly. "Eileen?"

But she doesn't respond.

"Oh my angel. My sweet angel."

Just a few moments before, we were so alive, so happy, so joyful, and then, the next second, everything changed. In the blink of an eye, in less time than it took for her to say good-bye, a darkness descended on our light, extinguishing it.

I see her chest rise and fall, and relief floods me.

"Thank God!" I sigh. "She's still breathing. Thank you, God."

I am shaking so violently that my teeth are chattering. I can barely speak. The restaurant owner takes his coat off and puts it around my shoulders. "Come away now," he says, pulling me away. "The paramedics are here."

I watch them as they insert intravenous tubes into Eileen with breakneck speed, clamp an oxygen mask over her face and attach her to a lifeline. They lift her onto a gurney. They slam the doors behind her and take off, flashing lights and sirens clearing their path. I start to run after them as she disappears from sight. Standing in the middle of the street, I pray with all my heart. "Please don't let her die."

A policeman comes up and takes me by the arm.

"I have to go with her," I tell him, running to my car.

"You're in no condition to drive," he says, pushing my car door shut. "I'll take you."

We follow the ambulance, and he asks me lots of questions, but I can't answer one of them. When we get there, they wheel Eileen through one door and me through another. Looking down, I see that I am clutching her purse. Trying to steady my hands, I go through her phone book for numbers of her family. I call her sister, and I call her ex-husband.

I don't know how long I sit in the corridor. Nurses keep bringing me cups of coffee, but I let them go cold. Every time the door swings open from the ER, where they are working on her, I stand up, hoping for good news. Finally, a doctor comes to me, his hands limp.

"She's asking for you."

The news lifts my heart out of the dark hole it sunk into in that deserted street in Venice. I want to burst in that door and kiss her and hug her and thank God that she made it.

The doctor warns me, "Prepare yourself. Her face is pretty smashed up, Goldie."

At that moment, all I can hear is that she is alive. I run to her room, lean over her bed and kiss her badly swollen face. Her eyes flicker open, and she looks up at me. She is still so beautiful.

"What happened?"

"Oh, honey, you were in an accident. But don't worry. You're going to be okay. You're going to be okay."

W hy didn't I follow my instincts that night? Why didn't I listen to what my heart was telling me? If only I had, this might never have happened. Eileen would have waited, eaten and gone home. I would have apologized profusely the next day. I couldn't stop thinking about that. Why didn't I listen to my mind?

During her long convalescence, sitting with her and talking to her meant so much to me. It helped relieve the guilt that I carry to this day. While she struggled with the consequences of her terrible injuries, I asked myself over and over what I could learn from this.

"What is it about us?" I asked her one day. "What is the magic of our friendship? And why is it that we felt so deeply connected, even before this happened?"

Then Eileen told me what happened in the back of the ambulance that night. How she left her body and was drawn to the light. How she sensed the warmth and felt her ego falling away, and how she was surrounded by nothing but pure, unconditional love. It wasn't dissimilar to my experience when I left my body many years before—hovering, witnessing events with a strange emotional detachment.

Now I understand our connection. Our spiritual paths have grown in tandem. It seems that neither of us was supposed to die. We both still have things left to do. Eileen has raised two incredible boys, and she has continued to shine her remarkable light along her deeply spiritual journey.

Our love has left an indelible imprint on my soul. I shall carry it forever.

fate

left-hand turns

Joy is something we each have inside us.
If only we take the action to awaken it.

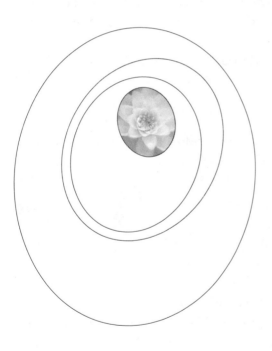

The day is orange, and the smoke from cow-dung fires hangs like a pall across the scorched African earth. I arrive in a cloud of red dust in my Jeep to find a remote mud hut settlement full of statuesque nomads from the Turkana tribe.

The hot wind, laden with dust under an equatorial sun, stings my eyes. Rubbing them, I see a group of half-naked men sitting on their haunches around a smoldering fire. Beyond them, their scrawny goats stand motionless in the glare of the sun. The scene is almost biblical.

I have agonized about leaving my children behind in search of this serene tranquillity that my soul is deeply in need of. It is something that seems to get lost in the Western world I live in.

On my way to this Dark Continent, I sat staring out the airplane window at the vast ocean below and wondered if this was too selfish, leaving my family for a short time, just to escape the shackles of my emotional life. But something drove me on; the gypsy in my heart told me I needed to place myself outside my own environment for a while, to make a left-hand turn.

As soon as the cabin door opened and the warm African air blasted me in the face, I knew I was right. Suddenly, I was in another world, on a continent I had never seen before. It felt instantly exotic, instantly different. I could feel my pores opening and releasing some of the stresses of my life.

I hired a small single-engine plane, piloted by a beautiful woman. For a moment, I thought I had been transported to the pages of a novel.

"Have you ever been to Africa before?" she asked. I shook my head. As the engines spluttered to life and we took off down the runway, she added, "Then you're in for a treat."

We lifted off through the clouds. This was really higher up near heaven.

The first touchdown was on a thin, very bumpy dirt landing strip, setting off a stampede of what seemed like thousands of zebra, sending up billowing clouds of dust. It was the first time I had ever seen so many wild animals roaming free. I screamed, "Look at that! I can't believe what I am seeing!"

The door opened. When the dust cleared, I came face-to-face with dozens of men from the Masai Mara tribe. They greeted me with megawatt smiles that just knocked me off my feet.

"*Sopa.*" They grinned. "*Sopa, madam.*"

"Hello," I replied. "*Sopa.*" I didn't know people could smile that big.

Each night, I slept out under the stars, listening to the sounds of the jungle, reveling in the peace I felt inside. Each day, I did things I have never done in my life before. I ate food I'd never normally eat. I went on safari in a Jeep. I took a balloon ride across the Serengeti, watching the animals from a hundred feet up, the silence all around us as we heard their galloping hooves and inhaled their red dust.

After each new adventure, I sat on the edge of a dirt strip in the middle of nowhere waiting for my plane to appear. Sometimes the weather would be bad, and I would wonder, Where is she? Is she in those ominous clouds? Then my fear would kick in. Maybe I shouldn't be flying in this. I'm a mother, after all. Am I being irresponsible? As always, I was torn between the agony and the ecstasy.

I could hear the droning of the plane's engine long before I could see it. As if by magic, it found its way through the clouds, circled overhead and floated like a bird to earth. My pilot, looking very romantic in tight pants, a man's shirt buttoned low and her dark hair pulled back in a ponytail, stepped out of the cockpit. She looked like a *Vogue* model as she stretched her legs.

"Ready to go?" she would say with a smile, throwing me a bottle of water.

I would climb aboard and take the right-hand seat next to her. Then we took off effortlessly down the bumpy strip. Soaring above the clouds, I looked down through their beauty and felt such freedom. I had never seen a land like this before.

"Oh, I live for this!" I told my pilot. "To experience these moments."

"Yes." She laughed. "Africa is a land full of moments."

We touched down next in a place called Turkana in eastern Kenya. The plane kicked up the dust over the high-desert floor, full of boulders, rocks and escarpments. A single hotel sat on a hill above the landing strip, overlooking an encampment of tribesmen on the shores of Turkana Lake. A strange place for a hotel, I thought, but when I got there I discovered why. The few guests who were there were doing the same thing I was. They were people who lived in a busy world and wanted a break.

I was shown to my room—a cot on a cement floor, with a toilet, and a shower that was connected to the hot springs beneath the earth. My father would have loved this. No frills.

That night, the hotel staff invited some dancers from the Rendille tribe to perform for all of us. We sat around a campfire while a series of handsome young men formed a circle and started to jump and writhe and move to the sound of a drumbeat. They were wearing orange loincloths and had orange fabric draped over their shoulders. Some carried ornamental sticks.

The drumming was hypnotic, and the men danced in time to it, jumping up and down, moving their hips backward and forward. Every once in a while, a dancer would go into the center and perform a solo, or others would join him and they would do a movement in unison. I wondered if they were improvising. I know what that feels like, just moving to the sound of a beat. It was so enlivening and stimulating. Watching them dance by the flickering fire, listening to the rhythmic beat, it was all I could do to stop myself from jumping up and joining in.

A moment later, two of the dancers seemed to go into a trance. Their eyes rolled back in their heads, and, I must admit, it was a bit frightening. I couldn't tell if they were in a state of ecstasy or if I was witnessing an epileptic fit.

I watched a young boy begin to convulse. I later found out that he was filled with the spirit. Then others followed, losing themselves and becoming possessed, and gyrating. For a moment, the cynic in me wondered if it was all theater. But it wasn't. It was the real thing. I truly was in another world. I couldn't help but think how extraordinary this experience was. I hoped that one day my children would be able to witness this, and that Africa still would be as unchanged by then.

Early the next morning, we set out from our hotel in a Jeep into the barren desert full of rocks, with no particular path to follow. We were journeying to remote villages, or *manyatas*, as I learned they were called. We had a Rendille and a Turkana tribesman with us. It seems that they don't speak each other's language. We first stopped at a settlement with only women and babies, all of them more beautiful than the last. Bony camels stood incongruously on the periphery of the encampment, and I was told they provided the staple food: milk mixed with blood, called *banjo*. I got out of my Jeep and walked toward these women, secretly hoping they wouldn't offer me any.

"*Sopa!*" I cried to one woman, holding my camera up to take her photograph. But she screamed at me unintelligibly and began to throw rocks at me.

My Turkana tribesman told me, "They believe that if you take their picture you steal their soul."

I understood. On the occasions when I have been cornered by the paparazzi taking one picture after another, I know what that feels like. It strips me of something deep inside. It is as if all the color has been drained away, leaving me feeling like a negative.

We scurry on over the rocks and hills to the next village. Here, there are nothing but nomadic men, of all ages. Young and old. Some are sitting on their haunches in front of their reed huts, and I feel as if I have walked backward through the pages of the Old Testament. Goat hides are draped over the roofs of the huts to dry. There are flies everywhere. I swat them off angrily, but everyone else seems completely unaware as they cluster around their nostrils, eyes and mouths.

I walk up to the men crouched on the ground, and they look at me as if I have just landed from Mars. I say hello, and they all say hello back, I think. In order to become part of the group, I decide to crouch alongside them, hoping to speak with them through my interpreter. But, unbeknownst to me, I am on a slight slope. No sooner do I squat down than I lose my balance and find myself doing a backward somersault in the dust, my bare legs helplessly in the air. Ass over teakettle.

Before I can restore both my balance and my dignity, the men around me begin to chuckle, the deep creases of their laughter lines forming fascinating three-dimensional maps across their faces. Looking up at them from the earth, I start to laugh too, and I can't stop.

My strange companions can't stop laughing either. I clutch my stomach. One of them imitates me. Tears stream down my cheeks and theirs too. Several of them flop back onto the earth like me. We are all equals. All dignity forgotten. For several blissful, powerful moments, we are all helpless with mirth. How about that? No one speaks the same language, but we all share this common language: the language of laughter.

I realize in this poignant moment that laughter is a sound. It is not a word. It transcends every language on the face of the planet. It needs no translation. It comes from an unknown sameness—a primordial innate sound that all human beings share regardless of language: It is a sound. *Ha-ha*. It is the sound of joy.

My journey continues as I ride in the back of our Jeep, intensely moved by the strange beauty of this sunbaked, barren land; this vast wilderness stretching endlessly beyond sight.

Suddenly, out of nowhere, I see a flash of orange in the far distance lifting off the earth. I screw up my eyes. "What is that?" I ask my driver. "Look, over there. Let's go toward that color." I point, and he heads the Jeep in the direction of this mirage shimmering on the horizon.

The closer we get, the more the band of color separates, until we can see that it is comprised of six Rendille warriors strolling along in the middle of the desert. Draped in orange cloth, and seven feet tall, they walk toward us with bare feet, flatly.

As we get closer, I see that they are adorned with handmade jewelry and beautiful hand-carved sticks. They look so vibrant in this bleak landscape. What an exquisite contrast they make. Stopping the Jeep, we step out and say hello as they approach. These six young gods smile at us with those bright grins and flashing eyes. I can't take my eyes off their jewelry. It is beautiful—red, blue, yellow, white and green beads hanging from leather strips around their necks. There are large bones threaded through their earlobes, stretching the skin. Ouch! I think. This definitely gives new meaning to body piercing.

I stare at their jewelry. They stare at my Rolex. For a second or two, I actually wonder if it is a fair trade. At which point one of the men bends his statuesque frame at the waist, takes off his necklace and hands it to me as a gift. I am in a state of bliss.

They speak to my Rendille guide, who nods. They pile in—all six of them—hunched over in the back of our Jeep. Knees and elbows, legs and hip bones dig into one another as we each squash up and try to find our spot. They bring with them the pungent scent of the earth. We drive off, and the rhythmic bounce of the bumpy road settles us into our seats like spring bulbs planted in soft earth.

Suddenly, I hear a sound. One of the men begins to sing. It is rich, a tone that emerges from deep within his throat. Another man quickly takes up the joyful tune and begins to harmonize, filling the space around us. Then the others join in. All six of them are singing now, the sound all around. It is clear to me that they must have spent a great part of their lives sharing notes, learning to harmonize. It is a very different harmonic arrangement than any I have ever heard before. I think it is the music of the gods.

As we bump along the ancient escarpment, the tribesmen sing and sing, the baritones and the tenors, their voices rising and falling like the swarms of flies that dance in tall columns by the water holes.

I can't help it. I sing along with them, trying to pick up the tune as

left-hand turns

best I can. Somehow, they make room for my voice in the tight company of theirs, blending it into a rich tapestry of what is now a Western and African sound. We laugh and sing together for all we are worth, our voices trailing out of the Jeep behind us like a gaily colored kite.

When it seems like we are truly in the middle of nowhere, with not a significant feature to be seen in any direction, my companions suddenly stop singing and ask the driver to let them out. But where are they going? I think. This piece of dirt looks no different from any other piece. It is a great puzzle to me.

Disappointment creeping into my heart, I watch as one by one they unfurl their long limbs from the back of the Jeep and pull themselves up to their full, impressive height. One by one, they smile and say their shy good-byes.

The tangerine sun is dipping below the horizon as I watch these beautiful orange-clad warriors walk off into the distance. Majestic in the sunset, they merge back into the sand and the dust and the sun like the mirage that they always appeared to be. I have rarely felt such happiness.

This was an important journey for me because it reconnected me with the simplicity of life. I cleared my mind. I laughed and sang with strangers. I spent quiet moments of reflection counting my blessings. These experiences filled me with a light that shines inside me to this day.

Sometimes, when life gets too hard and crowds in on you and you become desensitized, you need to remember to just take time. Go away. Change your surroundings. Put yourself in a situation where the outcome is uncertain. Give way to the kindness of strangers. Humble yourself on your road untraveled.

I have found that when we go on a journey, we buy time, because we give our full attention. We are present and conscious because all the newness of our surroundings keeps us sparked and alert. Travel prolongs our time, I think. I like to call it "rubber time." How often do we say to ourselves, Where did that year go? Hey, where did that week go? But if we go away to some place that holds a little interest for us, every moment will be filled with wonder, and our brains will peak.

Like Daddy always said, "Slow down, Goldie, just slow down."

Now there was someone who knew about rubber time.

297

left-hand turns

postcard

*It is the simplest things in life that hold
the most wonder; the color of the sea,
the sand between your toes,
the laughter of a child.*

The glass beads on my sarong catch the light and sparkle like jewels as I hang it out to dry in the sun. Drawing water from the well, I stop to watch the children playing under the olive and almond groves that sweep down to the turquoise Mediterranean Sea.

We are on the island of Ibiza, Spain, in a two-bedroom, whitewashed finca my children call "the Rock House." It is 1982, and I am having the most perfect summer of my life. We have no electricity, no hot water and only the most primitive accommodations in the house I have bought up in the mountains above San Miguel. The windows are tiny, the stairs are bare cement, and the courtyard is cracked and shabby.

My kitchen is a former goat pen with a battered two-burner stove to cook or heat water on. My closet is a series of old hooks on the wall of my tiny bedroom, on which I hang sarongs, scarves and bathing suits. We pick white figs from the trees that surround the house, and sit by candlelight at night eating bread and cheese, fruit, chicken or fish from the local *mercado.* Amid such simplicity, we have found incredible peace.

Each morning, I fill a big blue plastic tub with water from the faucet that connects to the well and leave it out in the sun to warm. One by one, I bathe my children and towel them dry. They are naked as jaybirds and brown as berries, and their hair is bleached white from the sun.

I pile them into my little Spanish car, and we wend our way down the mountain to Benirras Beach. Our beach. The beach we go to every day. Twisting down the little road, we reach the glittering azure cove. A huge rock like a clenched fist rises out of the water.

Some of our new friends wave from the rocky beach as we pick our way to our spot, carrying what we need for the entire day. They are mostly hippies who have come to Ibiza to play music, smoke pot and make love under the stars.

We have frittatas for breakfast and fish for lunch, and the children eat an occasional hamburger. I drink cappuccinos all day. The fish is pulled fresh from the sea. Smoky and salty, it is some of the best I have ever eaten. All the food is cooked in our own special kitchen, a funky little lean-to bar right there on the rocks.

Every full moon there is a celebration in honor of female energy. Huge driftwood fires are lit as musicians gather around to play bongos and drums. As the moon floats full and high among the stars, we sit around the fires and drink yerbas. Oh, how I love yerbas. It is a drink made from all the herbs on the island—and very potent, I might add. We watch bodies gyrating to the drumbeat, backlit by the moonlight on the waves. I am filled with such joy and contentment, without a care in the world.

We love Wednesdays, the hippie market day, when I cram the kids in the back of the car and drag them to a busy corner of the island. Battered campers and painted psychedelic vans line up, from which people sell exotic wares from their travels to India, Asia and the Middle East. Clothes and fabrics and beads, saris and sarongs, which I buy and tie around my waist, or my hips, or my head. One size fits all.

Coming home each night, we bump along little twisting

roads lined with rock walls. We wend our way back up the mountain past dazzling white houses and shady glades of fragrant pines to our secret little hideaway. Pushing open the heavy wood door, I light the candles and prepare some food, and the children and I sit together, miles from anywhere. We play games and I sip wine, our skin tight and tingling, until the night weighs heavy on our eyelids and we fall into bed.

Rising late, the sun floods in through my little window. I lie across the sheets listening to the bells tinkling on the sheep that are herded through our olive groves by a woman in a long black dress and an old sun hat. The same woman who sits alone beneath the almond trees on the fringes of the village. Looking out, the day already offers a sultry promise of heat, and the rich soil glows like red ocher in the morning sun.

Washing the salt from my clothes each morning, I drape them over a line of rope slung loosely between two fig trees. Stepping back, I marvel at the way they sparkle as the breeze lifts the fabric and the sun catches their beads. Nothing will erase the beauty and color of that vision.

When that idyllic summer is over, we return reluctantly to our beach house in Malibu, and my life as a solitary parent. But I can't bear to break the spell. It feels so strange, this bustling world of cars and people rushing to get places. Trying to hold on to the magic of Ibiza, I follow my old routine for a while. I play with the children on the beach; I wash my own clothes and hang them out to dry on the line. I light the candles each night for dinner and sip some wine.

For just a little longer, I don't want to be anything other than the nameless mom of two small kids living in our beautiful little rock house by the blue-green sea. For a few weeks more, I desperately want to stay in this place of simplicity. Part of me never wants to return to the real world.

power

Power is sometimes misinterpreted as strength.

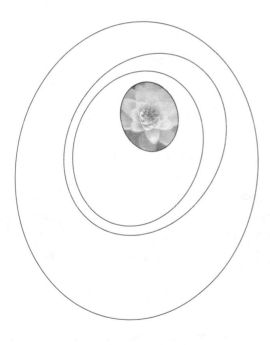

Striding across the lot of Columbia Pictures, I have a script tucked under my arm that I am very excited about. Making my way up the stairs to the first floor, I am ushered into the opulent office of the studio's head of production and handed a ritual cup of coffee.

"Thank you for finding the time to see me," I tell him, taking a seat opposite his enormous desk, "but, as I told you on the phone, I think this is a movie you might really be interested in making."

"You certainly sounded passionate about it on the phone," he says, smiling. "I am interested to hear why."

"Well," I begin, placing a copy of the script on his desk and taking a deep breath, "I fell in love with this movie for many reasons. This is a heroic woman's story. But it's not just about one woman, but all the women who stayed home during the Second World War. For the first time in their lives, they had to learn how to do man's work—build airplanes, fix toasters, mend cars. They took care of themselves while their men were off fighting the good war.

"When it was over, these women were expected to lay down their tools and put their aprons back on. They were lured back into the kitchen by new washing machines and appliances, but it was very hard for them to give up the liberation they had experienced, both sexually and personally. That is what this movie is about."

The head of production sighs. "The problem we have here, Goldie, is that this is a period picture. As I'm sure you're aware, period pictures are sometimes difficult and expensive to make, so I'm curious about why you think this one would work."

"Oh, but I see the movie in a way that is much more modern," I counter. "The clothes should be fabulous, the swing music should be great, and I think we need a director who is young and fresh and edgy, who can really give this an up-to-date feel. This shouldn't be your usual forties movie."

The studio executive sits and listens to me patiently, drumming his fingers contemplatively on his desk. When my time is up, he thanks me warmly and escorts me from his office.

"That was a terrific pitch." He grins. "Very impressive. I'll be in touch."

By the time I return to my office on Westwood Boulevard, at Hawn-Sylbert Productions, the message is waiting for me that he has turned me down.

"Why don't you try Warner Brothers?" my business partner, Anthea Sylbert, suggests, seeing my crestfallen face. An Academy Award–winning costume designer turned producer whom I first met when she designed my costumes for the movie *Shampoo*, Anthea always makes such sense. "After all, we do have a deal with them."

"Oh, I don't know," I tell her doubtfully. "They want me to do fish-out-of-water comedies. See, this film isn't funny. It's an ensemble picture and not at all what they seem to have in mind for me."

To my surprise, Anthea is right. Warner Brothers agrees to make this movie, which is called *Swing Shift*. Having cut a nonexclusive deal with me to produce movies for them on the back of my success in *Private Benjamin*, they give me the green light.

Within a few weeks, I am sitting in my cozy office, excitedly waiting for a young new director to walk through my door. I have just seen his latest movie, *Melvin and Howard*, which I loved, and I just know he's the right guy to direct *Swing Shift*. My assistant shows him in, and the first thing I see is his big colorful tie. Above it is the beaming face of Jonathan Demme. Straight in from New York, this guy has tremendous style. He looks as if he has stepped out of a movie. I love him instantly—the way he looks, the way he talks, the way he thinks.

"I've read the script and I think it needs work," he tells me candidly. "I have some ideas, and we'll have to do some rewrites. I like what it has to say."

"I have found the guy who should direct our movie," I tell the head of production at the studio excitedly the minute he leaves my office. "He's awesome and he's available and I love, love, love him!"

They know Jonathan and hire him immediately. Before I know it, he has an office on the lot, and our movie is on the fast track.

"This is going to be so much fun," I tell Anthea. "I've just got a great feeling about this guy. He's young and enthusiastic, and, best of all, I'm back in the chorus again. This is one picture I know I won't be carrying by myself."

Warner Brothers organizes a series of meetings and brings in a producer who is attached to a group of financiers. "We want to bring these guys on board to help pay for this movie," the studio heads tell me, "and it would really help if you would chip in here. Would you relinquish your producer's fee and take your name off the production, Goldie? It will leave room for the others."

I don't even have to think about it. "Sure," I tell them. "No problem. I'll do that." Honestly, it is a relief. No strings, no producing, no walking on eggshells. Just to work on a film I believe in with other actors is a joy beyond belief. I can just be an actress again.

Jonathan and I read with a number of actors and actresses. A young man named Kevin Costner is among them, and he's great but, sadly, not available when we need him. Dozens more men and women pass through our door. Sitting eating sandwiches in Jonathan's office, I am having the best time, back in the trenches.

"Who's next?" I ask, my mouth full. It is the end of a long day, and I am snacking before going home to bathe the kids.

"A guy called Kurt Russell," Jonathan replies, running his finger down the list.

The moment Kurt walks in and sits down, I am suddenly on full alert. We have an instant, easy connection.

"You know, we've met before," he tells me, his eyes twinkling mischievously.

Uh-oh, I think. "Where? When?"

"We did a movie together called *The One and Only, Genuine, Original Family Band*."

"You're kidding! But that was, like, my first part in a movie, even before *Cactus Flower*."

"I know. You played the giggly girl. I was sixteen years old and the drummer boy in the band. I had the biggest crush on Lesley Ann Warren."

I laugh. "Oh my God!"

"No, but it gets better than that," he says, rocking back on his chair and grinning. I don't think I've ever seen a man more comfortable in his own skin.

"It does?"

"Do you remember you were lost? On the Disney set, when you arrived for the audition?"

"Well, kind of."

"And you stopped and asked a woman sitting on a bench for directions?"

"I did?"

"Well, that was my mom. She was a dancer, and when she came home to dinner that night she told us, 'I met a girl today, and she's going to get the part.'"

"Oh my God! Your mother's a dancer? I met her? This is un-believable."

He smiles. "Yes, you remind me a lot of her, actually."

I can feel light beaming out of my body. The muscles that control my smile ache. When he gets up to leave, I don't want him to go. As he reaches the door, he turns around and looks at me and says, "You know, if I don't get this part I'd still like to take you out for coffee sometime."

"Oh, great . . . I mean, yeah . . . okay."

He closes the door, leaving a big empty void.

Remembering that Jonathan is in the room, I turn to him in a daze. "Oh boy," I say, my heart still pounding in my chest. "He's pretty great, isn't he?"

Jonathan smiles. "I think we just found our Lucky."

I'm married!" I yell at Kurt, pushing him away, my face flushed.
"Don't you understand? Don't you get it?" Spinning on my heels, I
run away from him, turning my back on temptation.

"And cut!" Jonathan shouts. "Thanks, Goldie, Kurt. That's a wrap."

Looking across at our director behind the camera, I wave and smile.
"Okay, then, Jonathan. Great. Thanks, honey. See you tomorrow."

Pulling off the forties-style scarf that holds my wig in place, I brush
down my factory dungarees, eager to get out of my costume. Turning, I
give Kurt a broad grin. Oh boy, am I falling in love.

When we reach the makeup room, Kathy Blondell, my hairdresser,
sits me down and starts to unpin my wig. Peering at myself in the mirror,
I grimace. "I hate this wig. It always seems to go on the wrong way. I
wonder what it really looks like in this film. I haven't seen it yet."

"Well, why don't you ask Jonathan?" she suggests, glancing out the
window of the trailer. "Looks like he's on his way to the dailies."

"Great idea," I say, jumping up, my wig half off. "Hey, Jonathan, are
you on your way to the dailies?" I call out to him.

"Yes, yes I am," he says. He pauses. "But I would really prefer it if
you didn't see the dailies, Goldie."

I feel a little sting. Looking into his eyes, I realize for the first time
that despite our great working relationship, I still pose some kind of
threat to him. I have tried so hard not to step on any land mines; I have
been so aware not to say anything that might make him feel defensive
or unsure of my true intentions. "Oh, okay," I say. "I just wanted to
check my wig out on film because sometimes I think it looks a bit funny
on my head."

"Okay," he says. "I'll check it out."

"Hey, thanks."

I watch him walk away and feel yucky inside. I wander back to the
makeup trailer. Flopping back into my chair, I rip off my wig and stare
at myself in the mirror. A skullcap flattens my hair to my head, and my
big ears are sticking out, and I think to myself, How could he be threatened by this?

308

Pregnant with Oliver, but happy to be on the cover of *McCall's*.

With Patti as my bridesmaid, and heavily pregnant, I finally get married in the backyard of my parents' house in Takoma Park, Maryland.

(AUTHOR'S COLLECTION)

Patti and I having fun in Italy, and on a boat near Capri, after I received the David di Donatello Award for *Cactus Flower*.

(AUTHOR'S COLLECTION)

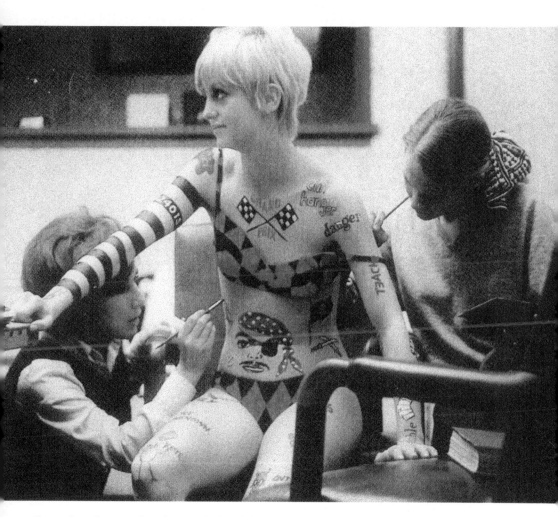

Learning the art of patience while working on *Laugh-In,* as artists painted my body for a sketch, a process that sometimes took up to three hours.

(GEORGE SCHLATTER PRODUCTIONS)

I enjoyed every minute of being Private Judy Benjamin on the set of *Private Benjamin*. (© 1980 WARNER BROS. INC.)

Director Howard Zieff and me on the set of *Private Benjamin*. (© 1980 WARNER BROS. INC.)

During a break in filming *There's a Girl in My Soup*, the mad but adorable Peter Sellers took me to visit "some friends" of his—at the zoo!

(© 1970, RENEWED 1998 COLUMBIA PICTURES INDUSTRIES, INC.)

Happiness, for me, is a place called India. (PAUL MASSEY/K2/KATZ)

I loved every minute of being back among India's children.

(PAUL MASSEY/K2/KATZ)

OPPOSITE: A contemplative moment in India during the shooting of the documentary about Asian elephants, *In the Wild.*

(PAUL MASSEY/K2/KATZ)

Traveling rickshaw-style in New Delhi. (PAUL MASSEY/K2/KATZ)

On location during work on *In the Wild*.

(PAUL MASSEY/K2/KATZ)

Getting to know Tara, the love of Mark Shand's life, an elephant he bought from traveling beggars when he found her emaciated.

(PAUL MASSEY/K2/KATZ)

Feeding time for Tara.

(PAUL MASSEY/K2/KATZ)

Sharing my directorial vision with Kurt on the set of *Hope* in Texas.

Learning the ropes as a director filming *Hope*.

Nobody said this was going to be easy. Directing *Hope*.

With Juan at an Operation Smile gala. (HAL AMBROSE WASHINGTON FOR OPERATION SMILE)

Putting on the Ritz with Kurt for the 1997 Academy Awards.

(COURTESY OF DOLORIS HORN)

With my spiritual guru, my stepson, Boston, in India.

(AUTHOR'S COLLECTION)

Kurt and Juan messing around in the lake at our cottage in Canada.

(AUTHOR'S COLLECTION)

On a family vacation to the Eiffel Tower in Paris. *From left to right:* Oliver, Kate, Kurt, Wyatt, Boston and me. (AUTHOR'S COLLECTION)

Oliver, Wyatt, me, Kurt and Kate at the American Museum of the Moving Image tribute to my career. (COURTESY OF MUSEUM OF THE MOVING IMAGE)

"What's the matter?" Kathy asks as she unleashes my own hair.

"Well, that was strange. Jonathan doesn't want me to see the dailies."

"Ah, well, you don't like to see the dailies anyway," she reminds me.

"No, I know," I tell her sadly. "But he doesn't know that." Looking up at her concerned expression, I muster a smile. While brushing out my hair, Kathy says, "Jonathan doesn't know you well enough yet."

The next day on the set is one of the most perfect of my working life. Jonathan agreed at the beginning of the movie that my mother could have a small part, playing Ethel, the landlady who owns the garden houses where the principal characters live.

Today is her big day. She has to speak a few lines and make a few moves all by herself. She is surprisingly nervous as she is manhandled into her forties costume and has her hair and makeup done.

Jonathan is incredibly sweet with Mom. He really gets to her, and they make each other howl with laughter. He approves her clothes and escorts her to and from her dressing room as if she were the Queen of England. But, bless her, no matter how many takes he allows her in a scene where we are all listening to the radio for news of the war, Mom can't remember her lines.

Sitting at the kitchen table filing her fingernails, all she has to do is look up at me as I walk past and say, in that incredible voice of hers, "This American's going to die with perfect nails."

She tries it over and over, but she gets it wrong every time. She looks at the camera, she looks at Jonathan, she looks everywhere but where she's meant to be looking. When she finally looks at me, she flubs her lines. Jonathan laughs and laughs each time she gets it wrong, and so does the rest of the crew.

I am mortified.

"Oh my God, Mom, this is taking so much time!" I finally tell her in a whisper. "Just try and concentrate on what you have to say and where you are meant to be looking and let your lines come out naturally."

My mother scowls at me. "This job! My God! Oh, for Christ's sake, Goldie, you say them!"

"But I can't, Mom!" I laugh, as everyone breaks up around me. "I have my own lines to say."

Finally, after I don't know how many takes, she gets it word-perfect, sitting in exactly the right spot and looking up at me like she's supposed to. The entire crew breaks into spontaneous applause. We are one big happy family. My mother smiles and nods, gets up and walks off that set like Tallulah Bankhead.

Walking down the path toward my trailer after my scene, I spot Kurt getting ready for his. He is sitting astride a 1940s motorcycle with a funny little sidecar, looking like a gazillion-trillion dollars in a leather jacket and a smile that could melt an army. I am so in love from my head to my toes, I am tingling.

"Come on, hop in," he says. "I love this machine."

"But I can't! I have to change my costume."

"That's okay, get in," he insists. "I'll take you for a ride."

Climbing into the sidecar, I let him take me for a ride all the way around the lot. I feel so stupid sitting down below him, like a character out of the Keystone Kops. But looking up at him, the wind ruffling his curly hair, I know I am looking at the man I hope to have in my life for a very long time. I love him for being so smart, so real, so loving and so unaffected by this business. I look up to heaven and wonder if my dad has not sent him to us.

The film is over, our happy troupe of players has disbanded after a sad last day and a bittersweet wrap party. Jonathan had his photograph taken kissing every member of the cast and made them into a collage for his wall. I still have the photos of us puckering up.

It's six months later and the night of the studio screening of the first cut of our movie, *Swing Shift*. As usual, we are all a little anxious as we file into the Warner Brothers screening room. As actors and crew, we have all given our best, but—as with every movie—they are ultimately assembled and made in the editing room, leaving us completely helpless.

I arrive with Kurt, and wave at a beaming Christine Lahti and Ed

Harris. I return Holly Hunter's wink. I raise a hand in greeting to a nervous-looking Jonathan. Kurt takes my hand, and we sit side by side as the lights dim and the film begins to flicker at us from the projector.

The movie that I was so passionate about, that I first sold to Warner Brothers, unfolds before our eyes. I take Kurt's hands. We watch our faces up on the screen, our mouths opening and closing over our lines. There is the airplane factory, the pretty little garden houses and the buzzing, jumping jitterbug bars where I first felt the pangs of love for Kurt. Our costumes look great. My wig doesn't look too bad after all. But something is wrong. Very wrong.

When the final scene rolls and the screen flickers blank, you could hear a pin drop in that screening room. I sit staring up at the screen in silence.

"What happened?" I finally say to Kurt, a lump in my throat. "What happened to the honor of the women in this movie? My character has no conscience. I look like I'm almost enjoying it when I swan off with my husband and leave Lucky just standing there. There is no struggle there at all! And that masturbation scene should never have made the first cut. It didn't feel right when I did it. Oh my God, I had no idea! I should have said something sooner."

I had such high expectations for this movie, for how it was going to look and feel, but now all I feel is a mass of butterflies in the pit of my stomach. I say to Kurt, "Even if I hadn't been playing the role of Kay, I still would have hated her. She had a very complex character, and the editing of her scenes needed to be handled with great compassion, wisdom and experience. It was all a matter of someone else's perspective, I guess—it always is—but I just wish I had known the vision of our director. Maybe I never asked in the first place."

Everyone else looked good; their characters were rounded and believable and true. Christine Lahti, as my best friend, was outstanding (and later won the New York Film Critics Award for Best Supporting Actress—and deserved it, I might add), but my character doesn't look like the character I thought I was playing.

Holding myself together, I stand as the lights come up, and cling to Kurt's arm.

power

The audience seems to be unusually quiet. Half smiles are being thrown at one another as we all head toward the exit.

Heads of studios file past, faces somber, their eyes cast down. One of them, catching my eye, throws over his shoulder, "We've got some work to do."

We! I thought I wasn't producing this movie!

T he following morning the studio calls me.

"We'd like you to come in for a meeting this afternoon, Goldie. We're all going to sit down and talk about what needs to be done to fix this movie."

Despite my sadness at how things turned out, I feel intense relief. It's the studio heads who will now help us do whatever we can to get this movie back on track.

Jonathan arrives silently and takes his place at the conference table. He can barely look me in the eye. He hates me already, I can tell. My heart sinks to the pit of my stomach, and I wish I could somehow get us back to the place we were when we first met and fell a little bit in love. But there is no getting around this feeling of sadness.

One of the studio heads opens the meeting. "I guess you both know why we're here. We'd like to talk about some changes we want to make, because, to be honest, this isn't really working for us, guys. We have some notes; we'd like to hear your thoughts; and then, between us, we can decide what needs to be done. We know this is the first cut, but we think that some of the characters need more defining, and the timeline is a bit confusing."

I feel horrible. I keep hearing my pitch to them almost a year ago. It will be fresh, new. We can merge the forties into the eighties. It should feel like a musical. It's going to be great. I cringed at how much I sounded like a producer with all the shuck and jive and all the radda radda. I know in my heart that I have dramatically let them down.

"Goldie, we know that you've got some things that you want to say, so why don't you go ahead."

"Okay," I begin, clearing my throat. "Well, clearly, I'm not happy with the way this movie turned out. It isn't just that I'm unhappy with my character—that's a small part of that—it's that this is not the movie I sold to this company."

Turning to Jonathan, I tell him, "I never wanted to stand in your way or be the squeaky wheel, Jonathan, and I deliberately tried not to do that. But I guess that I'm just going to have to say at this point that because I promised a certain movie to Warner Brothers, and even though I relinquished my producer's role, I am now going to have to take off my blond wig and put on my producer's hat."

Jonathan hardly says a word as the discussions continue and I vent my frustrations about the film. I become a lot more vocal and much more heated than I ever intended to be. My emotions undoubtedly get the better of me. Jonathan sits there expressionless, but I can see in his eyes how offended he is. In fighting for the integrity of my promise to the studio, I know in my heart that I have lost a dear friend. Worse than that, I have become his worst nightmare. The idea of being that person in his mind upsets me greatly.

A small part of me, however, can't help but wonder how he would have reacted or if things would have been different if I had been a man. Would he have sat and listened if I had spoken my mind frankly and expressed my opinions forcefully? This isn't about Jonathan; this is a Hollywood problem.

But it is too late. I cannot change my gender, and I cannot take back what I have said. I have been tiptoeing around for so long, afraid of standing tall and giving credence to the things that I know. In fearing that the suggestions I might make would be offensive, I didn't make them, even though they were based on my own experiences and point of view of character development, my understanding of the story lines and the film's overall social commentary.

The next few months become *my* worst nightmare. The studio expects me to help fix this movie, so I become the go-between. They ask me to approach a new writer and work with him on script changes. Despite still not having the producer title or credit, I spend the next few weeks running back and forth in the middle of the night with new pages. When we finally come up with rewrites that the studio is happy with, they commission one full week of reshoots, a very expensive proposition that involves bringing back all the actors and starting from scratch. Nobody is happy at the prospect, least of all me.

Jonathan is invited to come back and direct these new scenes, but when he arrives on set I can feel nothing but loathing from him. All I can think of when I look at his face is the joy we once shared, the laughter and the kisses and the hugs. I remember the hilarious casting sessions, the late-night sandwiches, choosing Kurt as Lucky, the fun we had during the jitterbug scenes, the way he was so darling with my mother. I so admired his energy and his passion and his vision. There is now so much misunderstanding between us, and I don't know what I can do to repair it.

Equally distressing for me, I can feel huge resentment from some of my fellow actors too. I am sure many of them think this is just a huge ego trip for me, to make my character look better, but they are really missing the point. To try to defend myself and what I'm trying to do for the movie would only fuel the flames, so I say nothing and just try to get the work done.

I have never felt quite so disenfranchised. Jonathan, whose help I would have loved, sits in a corner watching us work our way through this whole ghastly experience, completely rudderless. At one point, when Kurt and I finish a scene, I turn to Jonathan and say, "How was that, Jonathan?"

He looks at me with a passive expression and says, "Well, I don't know, Goldie, how was that?"

It is all I can do to stop myself from running off the set. I feel so completely isolated. I started out with such good intentions for this movie, and I can't believe that this is how it has ended. I'm not doing this to spite you! I want to scream. I'm not doing this for myself. I'm doing this because Warner Brothers might ditch our movie.

The revised script trickles in. The final pages are delivered on the last day. We shoot them mechanically, trying to make them work. In the end, some of them do and some of them don't, but there is no more time and no more money. I drive off the lot that night, wondering how I allowed all this to happen. After all, we create our own realities. And my fear created this one.

When the movie finally comes out later that year, 1984, Jonathan stays away. His publicity people issue a disclaimer saying that he had nothing to do with the final cut.

I'm hurt. I go away for a while, to get away from Hollywood and all the hype. I fly to Santa Fe, New Mexico, to visit the eight Indian children I sponsor on a reservation, to get back to what really matters to me.

Sitting in a street café in the most beautiful surroundings one morning, sipping coffee and reading the newspaper, I feel much better. The scenery is breathtaking, the air is so clear, and the waitress comes to my table and pours me another cup. Just as I am about to take a sip, I spot a headline on the Entertainment pages: GOLDIE FIGHTS FOR CONTROL.

It takes me so off guard, I stop breathing. I read through the text about how I snatched control of *Swing Shift* because I didn't like the way I looked. Over the next few days and weeks, the stories start to repeat themselves, appearing all over. Some claim that I thought Christine Lahti outshone me in the first cut, so I insisted that her performance be reduced. In each case, when approached for a quote Warner Brothers replies, "No comment." This is what really pierces my heart.

No comment? Is no one going to defend me? I realize then that the studio's relationship with the director is sacrosanct. It is the one relationship that they protect above all. My blood freezing in its veins, I also fear that this could be the end of any chance I ever had of working with another great director.

Needing to run, to escape to somewhere pure and clean and clear, I jump in my car and drive out into the arid desert. I need to remind myself of the world outside my industry, of the ancient rituals and customs that ground me to this life. Collecting one of my adopted children from the reservation, I take him to a Hopi Indian village to watch the ritual corn dance. Snuggled next to this beautiful seven-year-old boy, sitting with our legs dangling over the roof of an adobe building as the sun sets warm and golden over the purple mountains, I watch the men dancing beneath us to a hypnotic drumbeat, celebrating the fruits of their harvest, which this year have been pitifully meager.

They work hard for a living, I think.

It was a great leveler. That no matter who we are, sometimes things don't always work out the way we want.

R ight or wrong, I acquired a reputation after *Swing Shift* that to this day I'm not sure I don't still have. One director who was approached to do a movie with me a short time later actually called the studio and said, "I've heard she is difficult to work with. Is this something I want to get into?"

When I heard what he'd said, I thought I was going to die.

It is not just a question of mudslinging, but a little bit of who I am too, I suppose. I guess in my wish for things to be the best they can be, I don't play that game so well.

The question is how do we as women become realized, how do we deal with our own power? Whether it is in our relationships or in the workplace, it seems we are always negotiating for our own voice and always afraid of speaking what we feel. As a little girl, I was shy. I wasn't comfortable with my own ideas, never believing they were worthy of being heard. As I grew older, I was afraid of my own strength and worried that if I showed too much power it would make me less attractive to men, or a threat to women.

But now, after all this time, I throw down the gauntlet. The only path to happiness is to really be all that you can be. To be secure and unafraid of speaking your own mind. If your intentions are not just to win the game, then you can feel good that you have spoken your mind without malice or anger but just from the depths of your truth.

The more we can feel emotionally liberated, the more whole we can feel as people. We might say to ourselves afterward, Gee, I shouldn't have said that, or maybe I should have said it differently. Well, okay, maybe you need to work on your presentation—it is important to be conscious and compassionate and act with great civility—but don't forsake your own wisdom because you fear you will lose something.

What is more important? Losing your face, or losing your integrity?

I've seen Jonathan Demme many times in the years since *Swing*

Shift. I think we have come to understand that we were both placed in an impossible situation and that neither of us handled it quite as well as we might have. We were both young; we were both growing. We were both fighting for our positions. We both had strong beliefs as well as our own insecurities. To be less seasoned is to be less tolerant and more afraid. The more seasoned you are, the more willing you are to let others shine.

If I knew then what I know today, I might never have burst out at him like that in front of the studio heads. I would have tried to be more sensitive and more mindful of his role in the process. I now understand all of his reasons for feeling so threatened by me. Although I became the scapegoat, I can see why he felt undermined both creatively and as a man.

When Jonathan went on to direct *The Silence of the Lambs* and won an Oscar, I rushed to see the film and loved every minute of it. I mean, what a brilliant piece of filmmaking that truly was! I sat down and wrote him a heartfelt letter, telling him what an amazing job he did and what a fantastic filmmaker I believed he was. He wrote me a beautiful letter back.

By reaching out to each other in this simple way, by showing tolerance and kindness to each other and putting all the pain and misunderstanding behind us, we achieved closure on what was, for us both, a very bittersweet experience.

And, best of all, I learned one of the most important lessons of my life: that the power to forgive is the greatest power there is.

keeping the flame

*The keys to maintaining a healthy
relationship are respect, desire,
forgiveness and love.*

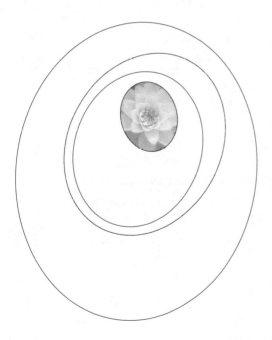

postcard

Oh, give me a warm and flattering light to shine on my face as I confront myself in the mirror to take a deep howling look into the troubles that have lined and distorted me. This reflection is slowly looking more and more clouded and grotesque as the ending draws near of yet another lover who passionately ejects out of my life to become another memory unforgotten. The streaks and shrieks of anger are sometimes like firecrackers exploding from small ignitions so minuscule that they are barely visible and, after the blast, there is no trace of their existence. A series of random booms that make my head ache in its total circumference. The heaviness in my chest and back is reminiscent of times where similar feelings of sadness and aloneness were brought upon by the hard realities of the utter futility and uselessness of a relationship and how the ending is so close and yet so damn difficult to realize.

Why must we always get to a point in an incompatible relationship that we become demolition experts and blow up the other person's self-esteem and paint them to be valueless and worthless human beings? The act of destroying self-image is such a devastating part of the denouement of a passionate love story that it almost makes it not worth the experience. How many times must one live this story before one can reroute the landing and make it smooth and without too many bumps on the runway? My mind is sound and sensible, but to realize that I am still human is most painful. To recognize my state of constant instability is maddening.

What creates these weaknesses, and what prevents us from improving our choices? When will the roads I choose be paved with concrete instead of quicksand? When will I stop feeling guilty for who I am and for being intelligent? Or when will I cease to cringe when I am more quick-witted than a man, and when will I stop protecting the ever-so-fragile egos of my men and start to stand up to the truth? The painful thing about enlightenment is that you cannot go back to the warm safe place that ignorance keeps so impenetrable for us. Oh cursed are the enlightened, for the only protection from knowledge and experience is more knowledge and experience.

—*Diary entry, 1982, when my life seemed to be falling apart*

My first marriage lasted six years. My second, four. I was never to marry again. Relationships, even ones once as happy as these, often hit insurmountable problems. It is easy to point the finger, to blame the other person. Sometimes we're right to do so. I suppose I could easily blame my career, my money or my power and leave it at that. But that's too simple. I remember what someone once said to me: whenever you point a finger, there are three fingers pointing back at you.

It is important to remember the good things about my marriages, the happy memories that still fill my heart. Gus was such a sweetheart. He was with me when I was first discovered, and he helped me deal with so much. I loved being his wife and taking care of him.

Bill helped me through one of the most fearful times of my life, the prospect of losing Oliver. He comforted me with his humor, and was tender with me as a vulnerable new mother. He also gave me the gift of his grandmother, Tessie, whose rose never seemed to fade. She was full of life and vitality and joy—a window into the spirit of his soul. Being with his big Italian family in Portland, Oregon, was like going home for me. It gave me a sense of normalcy when there was so little that was normal in my life. Sleeping in the attic with baby Oliver, a statue of Mother Mary at my side, allowed me the privilege of witnessing a whole new family culture that reminded me so much of my own.

But it is also important to remember what went wrong in those relationships. I asked myself over and over what I could have done better to make them work. I'm not perfect. I want to know how I can grow as a human being because of what I faced as my truth, what responsibility I take. If you don't take responsibility, then you'll never grow. You will never learn. And you will only repeat your mistakes.

By the time of my divorce from Bill, I had two small children who were both losing a daddy. I couldn't believe that everything I had planned had come so unraveled. I always thought that when I got married and had children, I would stay with their father no matter what. Divorce wasn't something anyone did in my family. Even at the end, my parents never divorced; they just took leave of each other. It was such a bittersweet time, for I truly believed I was doomed to live a life as a single parent. I tucked my kids in each night, wishing they had a father to do it too, and then I cried myself to sleep, wondering where it had all gone wrong.

I was trying to do it all—work, make movies, be a good mother, be a soccer mom to Oliver, take Katie to dance classes and keep a happy home. Juggling all this in my life, I was devastated. Was I now living my worst image of how Hollywood stars end up?

I couldn't imagine how, approaching my mid-thirties with a demanding job and, by now, celebrity status, I could ever meet someone who would be prepared to take me on, with all my baggage. More important, I feared I would never find someone who would love my children as much as I do, and give them a normal family life.

But I was wrong. A miracle happened. Kurt Russell was sent to us by God.

Here was a grown man who was capable of loving fully, with all of his heart. The most vital, playful, joyful human being, with an energetic life force born of a strong family upbringing. He makes every day a new day.

His young son, Boston, created from the union of his first marriage, brought even more joy to our family, adding a petal to our flower.

Kurt's love for my children thrilled me to no end. They flourished under his nurturing. His honesty, devotion and unconditional love bound us together in an inseparable state of familial bliss that has been unshaken to this day. He drew a circle around us in the sand, and its powerful alchemy has protected us ever since.

I have been asked time and time again, "Why, Goldie, haven't you and Kurt ever married?" I laugh it off and say, "Been there, done that. It didn't work for either of us." But, in truth, that's just a glib response.

I believe that the only true vows that we must make are vows to our own truth, and to our own initiation of our own kindness to someone else. Not to a promise to be there forever, but a promise to be there fully as long as we are there. We are not married to our children, and yet that is the greatest love there is. What is it about a piece of paper, a marriage certificate, that holds so much importance?

It is vital to remain cognizant of the fact that we are born alone and we die alone. Whoever we choose to share our life with is just someone we choose to share our life with. Not someone who has turned the key in the lock and said, Okay, now we are married. We are mere mortals. We're not perfect. We all make mistakes. In order to move forward, we need to forgive ourselves.

I understand that some people desperately want to get married. There is an innate part in all of us that needs ritual and ceremony. I am happy that I did, and I don't think anyone should miss out on what is essentially a beautiful day. But, through my experience, I have come to understand that the day after the wedding is just the next day. It's a new day, and then the next day is just the next day after that.

And if that sounds like an excuse not to work at the relationship, it isn't. If anything, it makes us work harder. I wake up every day with the intention to be loving and happy and the best I can be. I try to make each day a new day without carrying over the baggage from the previous day. I try to remind myself each morning why I am in love. And when there are differences, I try to put myself in the other person's shoes, so I can feel what they're feeling, not just what I'm feeling. I try to look with four eyes instead of just my two.

I know it isn't always easy to keep the flame burning. People grow comfortable with each other, or they become creatures of habit. And they are not always in tune with their partners. Sometimes when you have been in a relationship for a while, you get bogged down with a lot of negativity and dullness, and you get tired of dealing with all that stuff.

One trick when you're feeling down about your relationship is to imagine life without the other. It is a very scary thing to ask yourself to do, because when you do it you really get a sense of what your world looks like. Maybe you'll like it better, in which case the relationship is probably over. But, more often than not, you will see a huge void.

If you feel that void, if you feel a sadness, then take out some pictures and remind yourself what you were once like. Laugh together at how young and stupid and how crazy you both were, or even how you looked. Photos are great triggers of memory and emotion. Ask yourself if you too have changed.

Have you tried to make your mate what you want him or her to be, rather than rejoicing in your differences? What is it that you have sabotaged by trying to rewire the substance of the relationship to suit your needs?

The philosopher Kahlil Gibran once wrote about marriage: "Stand together, yet not too near together. For the pillars of the temple stand apart." That's a tough one for a lot of people to buy because, for some, there always has to be a chief.

There is nothing more unpleasant for me than to see a man stripped of his power. Even though we sometimes feel like the weaker sex, wake up (as my mother would say), nations have fallen because of us. Women have the power to diminish. I have watched it happen in my own home. It is far better to respect a man who has his own life, his own excitement, his own passion. Celebrate that in him; honor his variety and his power. The next time you ask, "Why didn't you call? Why were you late for dinner? Why didn't you pick up the milk? Why don't you ever take out the trash?" or continue to jab at what you view as his weaknesses, ask yourself: is this what you want to end up with? Is this your intention, to tame the beast? Is that the prize? The man who just says, "Yes, dear," and falls asleep in the armchair every night? Be careful what you wish for, because you might end up stripping away the vitality, the sexual energy of the man who you once thought of as your knight in shining armor.

The key to all of this is that one person may do all they can to keep their relationship as healthy as it can be, but it's not enough. No matter how healthy you become, your partner has to be working alongside you. If he doesn't, then it's like one hand clapping. It has to meet the other hand to make the sound of applause.

faith

What you believe isn't important.
What's important is that you believe.

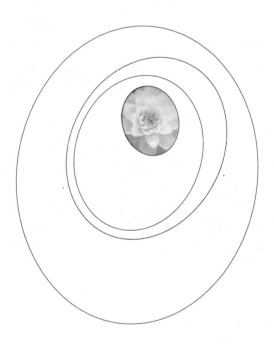

The swishing back and forth of the windshield wipers lulls me into a jet-lagged sleep. I half close my eyes and rest my head on the backseat of my chauffeur-driven car as it wends its way toward the holy city of Jerusalem. I am hypnotized by the ticking of the flapping metronome as it takes me deeper into the recesses of my mind. I see in the back of my mind a perfect picture of my beloved agent of fifteen years, Stan Kamen—the reason I am here.

Once so dashing, with a shock of dark hair, he's almost bald from chemotherapy. He's laughing as he tells me how funny he looks in the football helmet filled with ice that the doctor recommended to stop his hair from falling out. He is alive, happy and positive. He is the agent to the stars, adored by everyone, and he is now dying in the hospital.

My brain flickers back to the last time I spoke to him, more than a year ago. I'm standing at the stove, cooking breakfast for Kurt and the kids. My belly is swollen again, this time with Baby Wyatt.

The telephone rings.

"Hello, Goldie, it's Stan."

"Stan! It's so good to hear you! How are you, honey?"

"I just called to say I love you, Goldie."

His voice is soft and full of emotion. He sounds so weak.

"I love you too, Stan," I reply, turning away from the stove and staring out the window. "I love you so much."

I'm scared. I have never heard him like this before. He's giving up.

"Stan, where are you?"

"In the hospital."

His voice is barely audible. "Goldie, I want you to tell the children that I love them . . ." He can't finish his sentence. He's crying.

Oh my God, he is saying good-bye! Choking back tears, I blurt, "I'm coming to you, Stan. I'm coming right now."

"No! Don't . . ." His voice trails off. "I don't want anyone to see me like this."

"Oh, Stan . . . what can I do for you? I'll do anything."

"Just be happy, Goldie. Be happy." After a long pause, I hear surrender in his quiet tone. "I'm going to take a nap now."

My chest tightens. I want to wail; I want to scream, Don't go! Stay positive, and feel the love that will heal you. But nothing comes out. I am silenced by the truth. Almost gagging on my tears, I find just enough voice to say what I feared would be my last good-bye.

He died the next day.

W e're almost there, Miss Hawn."

My eyes pop open and my neck snaps to attention. How long have I been out?

"Is this your first trip to Jerusalem?" my driver asks.

"Yes, it is," I say, trying to get my bearings. My baby is now six months old, and this is the first time I have been away from him. Hopelessly in love, I packed his dirty T-shirt in my suitcase to remind me of his scent. The only thing that could drag me away from Wyatt is my promise to Stan to help him realize his dream of opening a cinematheque in Tel Aviv. At the gala opening of the Stan Kamen Theater—an institute he set up to teach young people about cinema and give them a place to exchange creative ideas—I'll have the privilege of cutting the ribbon. I'm also here to see something of Stan's beloved Israel for myself.

In the front seat of my car sits my bodyguard, Shalom, a huge, barrel-chested man with a soft heart. He's assigned to me for protection.

Protection from what? I wonder. Someone else has organized my schedule, a bit more demanding than I'd have liked, but, hey, I'm just drifting
with the tide.

"Get ready," Shalom tells me. "There will be a crowd of photographers waiting to shoot your first visit to the Wailing Wall."

My heart sinks. I forgot about the photo ops. It would have been nice
to experience my first visit to the holy city without such scrutiny, but I
remind myself of the reason I'm here: to bring light and awareness to
Stan's dream. I wipe the spittle from the corners of my mouth and take
out my makeup bag, with my face nicely tucked inside. I apply my base,
eyes and blush. Suddenly, our car makes a hairpin turn up the hill, and I
nearly poke my eye out with my mascara wand.

Looking out the window for the first time, I feel my heart starting to
race as we make our last turn before reaching the sacred city I have only
read about in the Bible. The closer I get to Jerusalem, sitting atop its hill,
bathed in its own unique light, the more I wonder at the visceral palpita-
tions I can feel.

Arriving at the wall, and seeing the paparazzi waiting, ready to shoot,
I take a deep breath and put on my smiling face. I let Shalom open the
door. The rain is now a light drizzle. I pull my scarf up to cover my
head in respect, as the cameras fire off like toy pistols, clicking and
flashing at breakneck speed. I can't see a thing. Slowly, Shalom guides
us through them.

The wall is enormous. Higher than I imagined, it was built from
giant slabs of pale yellow stone, carved centuries before. I stop and
take in its height and breadth.

Touching my shoulder, Shalom hands me a pen and a tiny piece of
paper. "Here, Goldala," he says, using the affectionate nickname he has
given me. "The tradition is to write a prayer to someone you love, fold it
and stick it between the bricks."

I take his pen and paper, sit down on the steps and write my prayer:
"Dear Stan, may you rest in the love and light of the Almighty."

From deep within me, I can feel a great swell of emotion.

"Shalom, may I have another piece of paper? Can I write two prayers?"

He tears off another piece.

"Dear Daddy," I write, "I miss you in every moment of my life. I pray that you will talk to God, and ask for more peace for the world. If anyone can do it . . . you can. I love you. Kink."

At that moment, something strange happens. I can no longer hear the cacophony of cameras. I lose all sense of my original purpose. As if in a trance, I walk to the wall, folding my little pieces of paper until they are two small squares of love. I wedge them deep between the cracks of the giant limestone slabs at the base of the wall and hang my head in prayer.

All around me, I can hear the murmured words of those who have journeyed to this place of pilgrimage. They come to mourn the loss of Jerusalem. They come to pray for the restoration of their holiest of temples, bowing repeatedly, white prayer shawls draped around their shoulders, moving their lips quickly as they repeat passages from the Torah.

Droplets of rain trickle down my neck as I listen to the reverent murmurs.

Staring down at my feet, I realize I'm standing on the smooth stones of King Solomon's Temple, a site where temple was built upon temple upon temple. I'm as close as I can be to the Holy of Holies, the temple's most sacred chamber. Not far from here, a priest would have stood on the mount and blown his shofar, the ram's-horn trumpet, to call the people to prayer.

White-hot roots seem to be growing from my toes, branching out, snaking through the cracks in the stones and deep into the soft earth beneath me, connecting me to some part of my past.

Overtaken with emotion, I rest my head on the wall and let go. The palms of my hands flat against the stones, my fingers hooked into the crevice where my notes are wedged, I cling to the wall, my shoulders shaking. The cold, wet wall absorbs my tears, as it has for so many others who have cried for their losses and their joy, connecting with God in such a holy place.

Shalom approaches cautiously, places his head beside mine and gently says, "Goldie, would you like to sit down?"

I peel my head from the wall and meet his tender eyes. Mascara streaming down my cheeks, I nod.

He takes my arm and leads me to the steps. We sit quietly.

"Why am I crying, Shalom? I didn't expect this."

Still staring at the wall, he says, "Many people cry here. I was once sitting right here next to a man who was also crying. I gave him my handkerchief. He blew his nose and said, 'I'm not even Jewish. I'm a cabdriver in New York City. Why am I crying?'"

Shalom turns and looks at me. "We cry, Goldie," he says, his own eyes filling. "We cry for many things."

Suddenly, in the distance, from somewhere far across the Old City, I hear the chant of a muezzin calling the Islamic faithful to prayer. His lilting voice—guttural, deep in resonant beauty—floats out from the top of a tall minaret.

Simultaneously, the bells of a Christian church burst to life, clanging and chiming across the rooftops, and a group of Hasidic Jews descend the stairs behind me singing songs of devotion. All I can hear in my head is this perfect harmony of sounds: the muezzin's glorious descant, the sonorous church bells at the core, and the prayers of the devout Jews providing the humming bass notes. It is the music of God. Of all our gods.

"This is the most beautiful symphony I have ever heard, Shalom."

He listens and nods.

Somewhere inside me, I feel a heave from the pit of my stomach that connects right to the center of my heart. I think of the blood that has been shed in the name of God, of the centuries of conflict and hatred and misunderstanding. How it has seeped into this barren earth and tinted it red. No wonder I am crying.

Turning to Shalom, sitting quietly beside me, I ask, "Why must man insist that his faith is the best faith? Aren't we all praying to the same hole in heaven?"

Shalom slips his handkerchief into the palm of my hand. He has no answer for me. He pauses, then looks at his watch. "It is time to go to Yad Vashem. They are waiting for you there. Are you ready?"

"Yes." I turn to him and ask, "Will you do something for me?"

"Of course."

"Well, whenever I visit a holy city I like to find a spiritual teacher and sit with him. Is it possible to find someone I could meet with at the end of this day?"

Shalom smiles. "Yes, I know someone, a wonderful woman. I will call her and see if she can see you."

He gives me his hand to pull me to my feet. I look up at this giant of a man and tell him, "You're not just a guardian of the body, you know, Shalom."

"I'm not?"

"No. You are also a guardian of the spirit."

He throws his head back and laughs.

"Yes, Goldala, we need that too."

"You can say that again."

We share a moment of levity as we walk through the entrance of Yad Vashem. At this Museum of Tolerance on the Mount of Remembrance, the excruciating images of the sufferings of the Holocaust are beyond my worst imaginings. The lists and lists and lists of the dead. The cattle car that stands alone in the grounds, once used to herd unfortunates to the concentration camps.

Already spent, I walk through this living nightmare, taking in the unbearable images of torture and pain. I see photos of mothers singing to their children, distracting them, while they stand in line for the gas chamber. I pass a glass case filled with the tiny shoes of babies and children who died in those chambers of hell. I see too many photos of emaciated men and women, lying on their filthy cots, at the moment when the Allied forces told them that the war was over. Their faces are blank, devoid of any emotion—a haunting reminder of how the human spirit can die inside the living. Men who have nothing left to live for, who have lost everything, including their god.

Limp as a rag, I walk out of this world of sorrow. I feel helpless and filled with a sense of futility, knowing this kind of torture is still going on in other parts of the world. By now, my face is distorted and swollen from crying. No longer paying attention to the clatter of the photographers' cameras, I let them click away. Who cares what I look like? How can I complain about anything in my life, ever again?

Shalom hands me a new hankie, and I blow my nose. Feeling weak, I say, "I think I need to eat something." He takes me to the King David Hotel for a lunch of eggs, until I feel restored enough for my next port of call: a visit to the Israeli prime minister.

Taken to his office, I walk down a long hallway followed by my growing entourage. Secretaries peek out from their doorways to catch a glimpse of me. I wave and smile as I walk toward the big double doors at the end of the hall. Behind that door is a man who, I have been told, was a ruthless fighter in his youth, leading many battles against the Palestinians. He is considered by many a hero, and yet, by others, a terrorist.

The door opens magically, and Yitzhak Shamir is sitting at his desk, nose buried in a document. He raises his head and jumps up to greet me. His hand reaching for mine, I am surprised to see that he is only five feet four inches tall. I take his proffered hand in both of mine. He leads me over to his sofa, and we both sit down.

Why am I here? I think. What am I supposed to talk to this man about? As the photographers motor their cameras, I realize that this is really only a photo opportunity. Nothing else. A setup. I am growing increasingly uncomfortable.

He turns to make polite chat, expecting perhaps some general questions about Israeli politics, or perhaps about more global issues relating to the relationship between Israel and America. But I am far more curious about his psychology.

"How do you sleep at night, Mr. Shamir?" I ask.

Caught completely off guard, he looks up at me with surprise in his eyes.

"I sleep pretty good," he says, studying me with renewed interest. "It's a tough job, you know."

"Yes, I can imagine," I say. "It's important that one can sleep and feel some peace while leading a country through such difficult times."

Little more of value is said. We exchange idle chatter until the obligatory photographs have been taken. We rise from our seats and prepare to say good-bye. On impulse, I bend down and hug him close. I'm not sure what makes me do this. Perhaps I feel for his life and for his struggle. Surprisingly, he hugs me back. I pull away, smiling, to discover that he is smiling back at me. This is good.

The next day, our picture will appear on the front page of every newspaper in Israel. It will show Shamir's side of our embrace, his eyes closed, his mouth sporting a blissful smile. Soft and sweet, like a koala bear, his is not the face of an old war dog but that of a loving grandfather.

T he day has turned to dusk, and my celebrity tour of the Holy City has come to an end. Abandoned by the gaggle of clicking photographers, I am emotionally drained, and, thankfully, finally alone.

Our car comes to a full stop in front of a small gray cement house, wedged between other humble homes, on the outskirts of the city. It begins to pour rain as I step onto the curb. Pulling my shawl up over my head, I pick my way around the puddles to the door. I knock. I turn back and wave to Shalom, who sits patiently in the car. He gives me a thumbs-up.

An elderly woman opens the door. She's somewhere between seventy and eighty years of age; it is difficult to tell. Her manner is soft and free of stress. A large, welcoming smile spreads across her face, and her eyes dance with joy.

Yes! I think. This is just what I need after this long, long day.

She ushers me inside her dark living room and introduces me to her elderly husband, who sits reading a newspaper beside a fire.

"Come, my dear."

I follow obediently into an even darker room. A flickering candle is the only source of light. It sits tall on a round table on which also sits a beautiful quartz crystal ball. She pulls out a chair for me to sit on. I don't know what to expect. I wonder if she will read my cards, or speak some words of truth—her truth, of course. Whatever, I am ready to bear witness to what is in store. I love not knowing.

I sit in silence with my hands in my lap, watching the flame dance in the air. I figure she will speak to me when it is time. I feel a familiar sense of peace and comfort in her house, just like I did in my mother's house. I hope that one day my children will remember the peace and safety of my house too.

Finally, she speaks. "Dear one, you have had a very difficult day, haven't you?"

"Yes," I reply with a sigh, relieved that the session has begun. "It's been so emotional. I have cried so much today, for so many reasons."

She nods knowingly. "You carry a lot of stress. Many people take more from you than you have to give sometimes."

She pauses.

I don't say anything for fear of interrupting her train of thought.

"I want to give you a meditation to help you cleanse yourself of the feelings that are left unsaid, that are locked in your heart. There are so many things that we hold here."

She puts her hand to her breast and goes on. "These unexpressed emotions crowd the spaces in our chest and make it sometimes difficult to breathe. You feel like you want to cry and don't know why?"

She's hit a nerve.

"Yes," I admit. "I do hold back my true emotions sometimes."

"Of course. We all hold back, because it may not be the best course of action to go forward. You are mindful of hurting other people."

She stops and stares at me as if she were looking deep into my soul.

"Okay, now let's begin. I would like you to close your eyes and follow the images I describe to you and see them in your mind's eye. This will help give you a way to focus your attention inward. That is important. This process will feed your soul and wash away your fear, your anger and any emotional pain you may have tucked deep inside of you."

Closing my lids over my eyes, I try to think of what I fear, what makes me angry, what pains me. For the moment, my mind is a complete blank.

"You are standing in the middle of a warm, golden desert . . ."

And so my spiritual guide begins. Gladly, I listen to her words and focus on them.

"Take off your shoes and feel the warm sand on the bottom of your bare feet. You stand there, alone. Not a person in sight. Your breathing becomes quiet. You are safe. As you stand on the desert floor, you see in the distance an oasis with rich foliage and one large tree. Walk to it. Wrap your arms around its trunk. Hold it close to your chest. Feel its power and strength. Envision its roots reaching into the center of the earth."

I see the oasis, force myself to touch the tree.

"Now, imagine the soles of your feet have roots just like the tree. See them reaching down, creating a hook that holds you firmly to the earth. Stand there feeling the power of stillness while being fully connected to solid ground. Unshakable and strong. Let the warm desert wind brush across your face and hair. Be still."

I can feel my heart rate slowing; I can sense the familiar physiological changes within me—the calming of my body and my soul.

"Behind you is a rock formation. From the top of the rocks falls a steady stream of pure, aquamarine water. Walk over and stand beneath the waterfall. Let the cool, soothing water wash away your stress and ease your tired muscles. It feels like silk as it rolls over your skin. Now, lift your head and let it run over your face, smoothing out the tension. You look like a baby. Smile and feel good."

I can feel the muscles of my mouth expand into a smile.

"Look down. You see a fire burning near an ancient cave that's carved out of sandstone. You see a strip of red paper lying beside the fire. Pick it up. Write on it. Write down all of your hopes, your fears, your sorrows, anything you wish to change or rid yourself of, and then throw it in the fire and watch it burn to ashes."

Okay, this is where I am stuck. Squeezing my eyes tight, I try to do as she says. I was into this big-time until she mentioned the paper. I could see the desert, the tree and the water. It felt so good. But now I have lost the flow. This is the second time today I have been asked to write on paper, the second time I have had to confront the sadness in my heart.

I want to tell her, But my life is good, and I am so grateful for the gifts I have been given. After a day like today, I have never been more aware of how lucky I am.

I'm not sure I want to do this. But she is waiting.

Okay, Goldie, think harder, I tell myself. With an imaginary pen, I write on my fantasy red strip how I want to rid myself of my most self-centered actions. I want to banish my self-doubt and my fear of failure. I wish to eliminate my terror of death and dying, and of losing my mother. I toss the piece of paper into the fire and watch as it turns to ash.

I open my eyes and see that our candle has burned to a stump. The flame still seems to be dancing, however, with the shadows on the walls. For the first time in a long time, I feel totally relaxed and at peace.

I look into the kind shining face of my storyteller. "That was wonderful. Thank you so much."

She places her hand on mine. "You must always remember this guided meditation and use it when you feel drained. It will be a source of regeneration."

At last, I am heading back to Tel Aviv after this day of days. I am now running on fumes. The torrential rain still pelts our car as we make the hairpin turns back out of Jerusalem. Feeling safe and warm and sleepy, I lean my head against the headrest and reflect.

I think of the Arab families I met at the Druze village I was taken to, of the beautiful children, with their dark eyes and olive skin and big smiles, who offered me thick creamy yogurt made from the milk of their goat. I think how their bright eyes will be dulled with hatred by the time they are grown, and how some will dream of martyrdom before they can even read.

I think of the showcase Jewish schools I visited, of how music and art and culture are instilled in every child. I think of my encounters with those whose brave attempts to create tolerance between Arab and Jewish children have provoked controversy.

I think of the Jewish mothers I saw feeding their children the food they had prepared; I understood my own need to mother, to nurture and to feed. How I sit at the table, as Mom did with me, staring at my children's mouths chewing as they eat the food I have lovingly made for them. This is me. This is my mother. This is my tribe.

I think of the sorrow and the sadness and the pain of this troubled city and how it has so overwhelmed me. I think of the pity of a world where these three faiths, these people who each profess a fervent love of their god, can't live together, pray together, in the same sort of exquisite harmony their calls to prayer beckon each day.

I think of the reason I am in this holy land: the death of dear Stan.

The more I think of all I have witnessed in this mystical corner of the desert, this land of milk and honey, of fractured hopes and dreams, the more I hurt. No wonder I cried. I was crying for those yet to die needlessly in the name of God, or Allah, or whatever people choose to call Him.

The ground beneath me felt as if it were vibrating, pulsing, with the years and years and years of desecration. I could see and feel the truth: that man wants to annihilate his fellow man. Nobody has learned how to get along. Nobody has learned how to truly forgive. And nobody has learned enough to know that we have the power to either destroy this earth or be the caretakers of it.

That is the pain of mankind.

I crawl into my bed at my Tel Aviv hotel at last and pull the covers up over my shoulders. The rain is still drumming on the window, but I no longer care. I take my baby's T-shirt and press it to my face, inhaling his smell. This is my elixir for sleep, bringing me back to maternal bliss.

One day, I'll tell him about Mommy's first trip to the holy land, I think as I begin to drift off into a deep, deep sleep. One day, I'll tell him about Stan Kamen and his wonderful dream, of the powerful effects of the Wailing Wall and Yad Vashem.

One day, I'll tell him everything.

There is nowhere quite like the Middle East to exemplify the global conflict between human beings, the misunderstanding and intolerance growing out of our differences.

Jesus Christ said it. Walk in the shoes of your enemies, because only then will you understand who they are. Similarly, Buddhists practice compassion for the benefit of all sentient beings. The Koran states that every Muslim must revere and bow down to the Christians and the Jews, because they believe without them they would not have Abraham and Moses. And on and on.

We live in a world of tremendous polarization. Life is either black or white, right or wrong, good or bad. You're either Jewish or Muslim or Catholic or Protestant or some other religion. But these faiths are merely vessels. They hold no prejudice or anger. Their philosophies are pure. It is we who project our own fears onto them, our own intolerance and hatred, born of our need to identify and belong to a tribe.

In defending who we are and what we believe in, we have to assume that members of a different tribe are opposed to us. When will we learn that it doesn't matter which tribe we belong to? When will we understand that we all belong to the greatest tribe there is: the human race?

removing obstacles

The only way to remove obstacles
is to face them head-on, just like
the buffalo stands facing the wind.

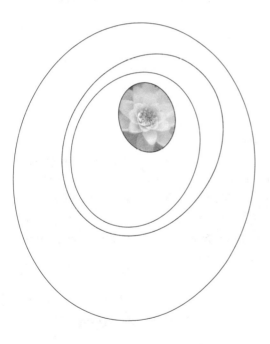

W elcome to India. What is the purpose of your trip here?" the immigration official asks me at Delhi International Airport.

"Work."

"And what would you be working on?"

"A documentary."

"Oh, are you going to Bollywood?"

"No. Actually, it's an English documentary."

"And how long will you be staying?"

"Oh, I don't know. Two weeks."

He nods and stamps my passport. As I gather up my papers, he asks, "What is the subject of your documentary?"

"It's about the Asian elephant. I'm highlighting its plight and doing what I can to save it."

"Very good." Touching a small statue of Ganesh, the Hindu elephant god, which sits on his desk, he says, "This will bring good karma."

I walk out of the airport into the middle of a sultry Indian afternoon. I'm immediately hit by a wall of heat, the pungent smells of cooking and burning, the crush of humanity, welcoming me back to a place my soul calls home.

A driver is waiting for me, my name misspelled on a card he is holding up.

"Miss Horn?" he says, and I laugh. That's my secretary Deloris's surname.

"Yes." I smile.

Taking my seat in the back of his old black Ambassador, I laugh to myself. Bumping and rolling through the crowded streets of Delhi to my hotel, I have no idea why these ancient cars have managed to survive the rigors of the Indian infrastructure.

At my hotel, I meet up with the rest of the team from Tigress Productions, my new troupe of traveling documentarians. Dizzy with jet lag, I have a quick dinner with the crew, who are all fabulous and fun and full of life. As we all retire to our rooms for sleep, the director, a lovely English gentleman named Andrew Jackson, advises us to eat a hearty breakfast before we leave tomorrow. It sounds a bit ominous to me. I wonder what we have in store for us.

In bed, I lie awake for a while, too jet-lagged to sleep. This is my first documentary. I'm happy to be documenting my personal story to find "my" elephant, Belly Button, a blind mother I first set eyes on seven years before on a game reserve deep in the south of this amazing country. Wonder if I'll find her. I close my eyes and count elephants.

The next day, we fly to Nagpur, in the heart of India, for the start of our journey to our first port of call, Kipling Camp. I am greeted by my new driver, and, much to my chagrin, am led to yet another old Ambassador. How long is this drive? I ask.

"Five and a half hours," he answers.

I now understand why we needed to eat a big breakfast. I'm glad I did. "I've been in these cars before, you know, and they nearly always break down."

He nods and smiles but nonetheless carries on organizing our convoy of six Ambassadors, dividing us all up with our luggage into separate cars, as is the custom, and for comfort's sake. Game for anything, I climb in my car and off we set on our caravan, honking horns and waving cheerful good-byes. After my hearty breakfast, all I have with me is some bottled water, a packet of crackers and a tiny jar of peanut butter.

Setting off, I'm quickly reminded of the exhilarating chaos of driving in India, swerving left and right to avoid rickshaws, children, street beggars and sacred cows. There are elephants, and giant Tata trucks, their cabs adorned with effigies of gods, tinkling bells and vibrant garlands of marigolds—all the while belching vile black exhaust.

Out my window, I see stalls selling great pots of spices: saffron and cumin and turmeric. I peer into shops cascading with the most exquisite silks. I watch women in gaily colored saris walking down the street with children on their hips and baskets on their heads.

Trying to keep up with the convoy, we *chug, chug, chug* past trucks and slow-moving oxen, lucky to reach a speed of thirty miles per hour, cars heading straight toward us all the while. I close my eyes. With no shock absorbers, we bounce in and out of every pothole, which are more numerous than people. After just a short time, I feel like my gallbladder and liver have swapped places. Jumping and jolting around on the back-seat of the car, here I am, embarking on yet another harrowing road trip across this country that I love, taking my life in my hands.

"What in the world am I doing?" I laugh out loud.

But after a few hours, I'm not so happy. "How much farther is it?" I say over my growling stomach.

He smiles at me in the rearview mirror, his head bobbing on his shoulders like a chicken. "Not far."

Alarmingly, our car has started to make a terrible coughing sound and I'm getting steadily more concerned.

"I think there's something wrong," I say, tapping him on the shoulder. "Maybe you should pull over before the engine explodes."

He bobs his head and smiles. "Yes please, madam."

Our convoy pulls off the main road into a small village. My driver gets out and opens the hood of the car. Unscrewing the radiator cap with a rag, he is greeted with hot steam jetting up into his face. "Oh," I scream, running to my bag to get something to help him.

Just then, everyone suddenly crowds around my car. They are twenty men deep, and at least ten more are underneath the vehicle, banging and crashing. Someone produces ice from a dilapidated building, and I tend to my driver's scorched face. The remaining men of the village circle us, just staring at me, smoking fiercely, making me feel increasingly uncomfortable. I think our arrival must be the biggest thing to happen in this village since Gandhi walked through.

"What's going on here?" I finally ask the rest of the crew. "What exactly are we waiting for?"

"A part."

"Really? I thought the engine just overheated."

"No, not for your car. For another car."

"Oh, another car has a problem? Okay. Do you have any food, by the way? I'm starving."

"No, but some of the guys are sampling the samosas being sold at the side of the road. Would you like some?"

"No. No thanks." I think to myself, Not on your life! I've known people to get really sick eating from roadside stands.

After an hour of waiting, they decide to swap my ailing car for another lovely Ambassador. Lucky me.

When we continue, the bumps seem to be worse than ever. I speak to my driver: "Excuse me? Excuse me?"

He turns around and smiles.

The road becomes increasingly more rural, dirty and bumpy, with ever more potholes. If I thought I had no shocks on my first car, this second car is unbelievable. My gallbladder and my liver have now changed places again.

By now, we're *really* out in the boonies.

"Excuse me? Excuse me? How far is it now? I'm really getting hungry."

The driver turns and smiles again. "Yes," he replies.

Oh my God, he doesn't speak English! Not a good feeling when you're in the middle of nowhere. I'm horrified. It's pitch-black, and I feel like I'm traveling down a narrow, bumpy road to nowhere.

We just keep on going, on and on into the darkness. I watch the other cars whiz past us. We're going much slower than the rest of them.

"Excuse me?" I ask my driver, hopelessly trying to talk with my hands. "Can you go faster, please? Faster?"

Soon afterward, and to my enormous relief, he pulls the car over to the side of the road.

"Are we here?" I ask hopefully, looking around. But he simply gets out, pulls a mat from the trunk, kneels on it by a roadside mosque and begins to pray to Mecca. I feel like joining him at this point. Maybe it will help.

Back on the road, we carry on driving for at least another two hours. I'm still starving, even after I polish off what is left of my peanut butter and crackers. There isn't a drop of water left. There is no sign of our convoy, and I have no idea where I am or where I'm going. I look at my watch; this journey has taken seven hours so far, with no end in sight.

I keep thinking that just around the next corner we'll see a sign pointing to Kipling Camp, or at least find the rest of the group waiting for us by the side of the road. I secretly wish another one of their cars had broken down.

Tapping the driver's shoulder, I tell him I have to use the bathroom. With much sign language, I eventually make him understand.

Unfurling my stiff limbs awkwardly, I squat down in the moonless night. All I can hear around me are the sounds of the jungle. A few paces behind me, I hear a twig crack. Oh my God, a tiger could creep up and bite me on the ass! Please let me live to tell this story! I pull up my pants quickly and race back to my car posthaste.

Back on the road, traveling at what seems a snail's pace, my driver is looking around furiously.

My blood sugar is low, my body is exhausted from traveling and I'm losing my sense of fun and adventure. "My God, what if he is lost and doesn't know where we are?" I ask myself aloud. At that very moment, my driver stops the car, looks right and left in panic and does a U-turn. I knew it, he *is* lost.

"Are we lost?" I ask, trying to stay in control. Is that what we are? He is not answering me. We are lost in the middle of frigging India? The cat in me is rising.

Finally spotting lights in the distance, I throw myself over the front seat to attract his attention. Pointing, I say, "Lights! Lights! There! Go down there!" This looks right to me, and, even if it isn't, at least there are people there.

We turn down a long road and drive noisily and dustily into a clearing in which a huge open fire burns wildly, illuminating the faces of our distinguished English crew. Ah, there they are. I see them all gathered around the flames, happily eating platefuls of curry and rice, drinking beer, talking and having fun. Unfortunately, my blood is now boiling.

Mark Shand, my elephant guru, who is a part of our team, opens my door to greet me. A tall man with a shock of blond hair, he stands there with a broad grin and dancing eyes.

"Welcome to Kipling Camp," he says in his impeccable English accent. "Where have you been?" He is way too happy for me at that moment. I jump out of that car disheveled, dirty and steaming mad.

"Where have I been? Where have I been? I have been with a driver who doesn't speak English, and who stops to pray every fifteen minutes. I've been in a car that has shaken my bones to powder. I've been lost in the middle of the jungle with no food or water. Where's the director?"

"Oh. He's by the fire."

I stomp over as everyone stares up at me in silence. "Could I speak with you a second, Andrew?"

This lovely, gentle man, who is so sweet and kind, dabs his mouth with a napkin and stands.

"Andrew, it's only by luck that I'm here. Next time, I'll need a map, some food and water, and an English-speaking driver."

Andrew says, "I'm sorry. This is terrible. You must be hungry."

I'm now spitting fire.

"I'm not hungry. I'm past the point of being hungry. I want my room, I want my bed, I want to go to sleep, and I want to forget about this day."

I don't usually act this way, but to my shame, I become like Joanna, my character in *Overboard,* before she loses her memory.

I'm in a snit and I march past the campfire, the crew and the delicious-smelling food. They all sit staring intently into the flames.

The director leads me with a flashlight down a dark path to a small wooden cabin in a clearing. He pushes open the door to my little cottage and takes leave. I look around at my room suspiciously. I see two cots, one draped with a mosquito net. A door leads to a small bathroom off to the left. Sitting pretty in its own web, on the leg of my bed, is a large, poisonous-looking spider. My eyes narrow.

"That's it!"

A spider! A spider in my room!

I slam the door shut and run back out toward the campfire.

I can hardly believe what comes out of my mouth, but, as I stand there, frightened and upset, I announce: "I need someone to go and clean my room. There are little poisonous animals around my bed and other little furry, four-legged crawly things in there, and I need them taken out of my room . . . because . . . *this is not my habitat!*"

This is not my habitat? Am I serious? If anyone had started to laugh right then, I swear I think I might have broken down and laughed too, which would have been the best thing for all of us. I had become completely possessed. And I guess my mother would have said, "Goldie, you're overtired and you need a nap."

Unfortunately, nobody laughs. Instead, the director and his crew take me very seriously. They hurry to my room and clean it all up, spray it with bug spray and tell me when it is safe to return.

I walk back with as much dignity as I can muster. I check under the bed and in every crack until I'm satisfied that there are no potential roamers who will emerge when the lights go out. I get undressed and climb between the cotton sheets. Sleep. Please, just let me sleep.

Just then there is a gentle knock on my door.

"Come in," I call.

The door opens, and the director stands there, looking decidedly nervous, poor thing.

"I'm so sorry, Goldie. I hope everything is all right now? Is there anything else I can do you for?"

"Yes," I reply, my sheet up around my neck. "Would you mind tucking me in with the mosquito net? I'm a little scared. I don't want any insects sleeping with me tonight."

What a love. He does exactly as I ask, tucking the net tightly around me so that there isn't even a chance for anything to crawl up inside my bed.

"Okay, then," he says, looking at me through the gauze curtain, "is there anything else you would like?"

"Yes. I want you to sleep in the bed next to me."

"Wh-what?"

"I don't feel safe sleeping alone tonight. Would that be a problem?"

Oh my God, the look on that man's face! I can only imagine what he's thinking.

"I am sorry," I continue, "that I am so nervous about the spiders and snakes and bugs."

Just then a loud thump on the roof makes me jump out of my skin.

"What was that?" I sit up with a start, my eyes popping out of my head.

His brow furrows, forcing his eyebrows to meet. "The monkeys, I should think. They live here too, you know."

Bless his heart, he goes to his room, gathers his belongings together, comes back and fixes his mosquito net, and then turns to me bug-eyed.

"There are a few things I have to do. I have to sit with the crew for a bit and plan our shots for tomorrow, but then I'll be in. Okay?"

"Okay," I reply, "and thanks. Thanks a lot."

Worn out by my exhausting day, I sink back into my tented haven and I'm gone. Lights out.

When I wake the next morning, the bed next to mine is crumpled but empty. Did he ever come in and sleep next to me after all? Or did he just crumple the sheets to make me think he had? I'll never know, but it is the beginning of a lovely friendship.

Emerging from my cabin, blinking into the dappled sunlight, I find that I am in paradise. All the fear and anger and distress of the previous day melts away. Hundreds of birds crowd the treetops, squawking and twittering as a mist lifts itself through the branches. Monkeys chatter beneath them, dangling their young and eating fruit. The canopy of the jungle forms a lush green umbrella high above me, through which golden light streams in brilliant shafts.

There is nobody around, but there is a fresh pot of coffee bubbling on the fire, and some folded chapatis warming on a plate. Pouring myself a cup and eating hungrily, I wander away from the fire, down a slope toward the sound of voices and splashing water.

Kipling Camp in Kanha National Park is the home of Mark Shand's famous elephant, Tara. Having bought her, emaciated, from some traveling sadhus, or beggars, he crossed India on her back, writing a book about their experiences. I read it on the plane over, having first met Mark at a dinner in London for the Asian Elephant Appeal. He had always planned to sell Tara when his journey came to an end, but, by then, he was in love and couldn't bear to.

Down at the waterhole, I find Mark shirtless and in shorts, sitting astride a recumbent Tara, scrubbing her wet skin with a pumice.

"Good morning, Goldie!" Mark yells exuberantly. "Come and join us."

Embarrassed by my behavior the previous night, I step forward shyly and watch from the bank. I've never seen an elephant lying down before. Tara is six thousand pounds of flesh and bone, all of it just a few feet from where I'm standing. She is a wild beast, however domesticated, and I'm secretly terrified. She looks like a mass of gray boulders lying in the water, and just as heavy.

"Come on," Mark encourages, holding out the pumice. "Climb on up and help me bathe her."

"Yikes!" I say, backing away. "No, I don't think so."

"Come on, Goldie, it's okay." He laughs. "Come closer."

Tara's trunk reaches out toward me, its sensitive tip probing and smelling my outstretched hand.

"She's just checking you out," Mark says, "Don't worry. I'm right here with you."

"Oh God, I don't know. I mean, what if she gets up?"

"She won't. Now come on, get closer and you'll see."

Removing my shoes and socks and wading into the water up to my knees, I find Tara's eye and look deeply into it. She has beautiful long eyelashes, and she is almost in a trance as her eye slowly opens and closes as she enjoys her massage. I know she won't hurt me.

Swallowing my fear, I wade in deeper, and Mark lifts me up on top of her belly. Perched up on top of an elephant for the second time in my life, I once again feel the prickly skin that tore my tights during a *Vanity Fair* photo shoot. Taking the pumice from Mark, I begin to slowly rub it over her rough folds of skin, increasingly at one with this beast. Washing behind her enormous pink-speckled ears, I watch as she closes her eye in contented delight.

The crew are on the bank filming us bathing Tara. We're soaked to the skin, but we're laughing and having the best time. Once she is washed, Tara pulls herself upright and steps majestically from the lake, dripping water. I back away, still in awe of her huge bulk.

Mark and I climb up onto a rock and watch her as she eats her dinner.

"Aren't elephants dangerous?" I ask him.

"Naturally, no. Naturally, they're peace-loving herbivores. Indian mothers often leave their children in the care of their elephants, guarded between their huge legs."

"Like prehistoric babysitters?" I laugh.

"Exactly. But, sadly, there is a new phenomenon happening, as elephants are pushed farther and farther from their habitat, and that is when they turn nasty. Four hundred people were killed by elephants in India last year. In northwest Bengal, a young elephant calf was hit and killed by a train. His mother waited by the tracks, and when the train came by the following day she deliberately derailed it."

Mark's story doesn't ease my mind the following morning when he breaks some news to me: "We're going to get Tara ready for you to ride her today," he yells from his position astride her ears as she strolls into camp.

"Oh no!" I say, shaking my head vehemently. "I'm drawing the line at that. I'm not going to ride a wild elephant in the middle of the jungle. What if she suddenly takes off? I have a family. I have a career. I don't want to die in India."

Mark laughs. "But, Goldie, this is going to be wonderful. You'll be great, and I'll be right up here with you. Tara's a pussycat. She took me all the way across India, remember?"

I go cold. This isn't possible, I think. No one warned me of this. I can feel my hackles rising again. Don't go there, Goldie, I tell myself. Be nice.

To relax my nerves while they fit Tara with a howdah, a kind of saddle, I play a quick game of cricket with the English crew. Sitting in the peanut gallery, a family of monkeys watches us play. Hitting the ball right out of the park, I meet my fellow players' indignant cries of "But, wait a minute, we invented the game!" with a shrug of my shoulders.

"It's just like baseball," I tell them as the monkeys chatter their encouragement.

Mark is one of the most charming and persuasive men I've ever met. With the cameras following my every move, he woos me into agreement.

"Hey, guys, I don't really think that I actually need to be up on the elephant," I protest as I'm led reluctantly toward Tara for the shot. "I'll do a lot of stuff. I mean, I washed the elephant, and that was good. I can feed the elephant. I can be by the elephant, but I'm not sure I really have to be up on top. I'm sorry, you know. I don't think I can do this."

"You'll be perfectly all right," Mark calls down to me from her back, his eyes twinkling. "She's my baby. She wouldn't hurt a fly."

At that point, a tin of Altoids mints drops from my pocket, and Tara grabs it with her trunk. Before I can stop her, she stuffs the Altoids in her mouth. Her mahout, or trainer, opens her mouth, reaches right inside her gullet with his arm and pulls out the completely flattened tin. I still have it as a memento.

The mahout taps Tara's legs and makes her go down on all haunches. Before I know it, I am climbing up her backside and into the howdah with Mark. My heart is pounding right through my T-shirt.

"*Mahl! Mahl!*" Mark shouts, and Tara gets up as I cling on for dear life.

"Oh my God!" I exclaim.

It's like going up in a Ferris wheel, up and up, tilting back and forth, side to side, precariously. Suddenly, I'm touching the bottoms of the treetops. So much for drawing the line.

"See, now, that was fine, wasn't it?"

"I-I guess."

Mark positions me behind him, and makes me watch carefully to see exactly how he drives his elephant. Sliding down just behind her head, he gives commands with his bare feet tucked in behind her flapping ears. Then he makes her stop, and he turns to me.

"Now kick off your socks and slide forward to where I am so that you're sitting right behind her ears," he instructs. "I'll move back to where you are."

"You want me to drive her?"

"Of course."

"But my dogs don't mind me," I say, shaking my head. "Why would an elephant?"

"Let's give it a go."

"Oh my God, you tricked me!"

Sliding forward gingerly, I now have my toes behind Tara's lovely pink ears and am pressing them into her flesh.

"Ooo-h, I don't know. I don't know, Mark, this doesn't feel very safe."

"Just lean back and hold on tight. Right. Now use your feet to touch her ears, and tell her which way you want to go. That's right. Now yell *'Agit! Agit! Chi!'* and kick her left ear with your foot."

To my complete astonishment, Tara not only begins to move, she moves in the direction I want.

"Oh my God, Mark! Oh my God! This is awesome! I am driving a frigging elephant! I am a mahout!"

I'm in a state of bliss. I can hardly believe the swaying movement of the elephant, her enormous bones shifting left and right beneath me with such grace. I can see everything from my elevated position, the beauty of the jungle and the streams and the wildlife. Dear Tara is so gentle with me, so patient.

We prepare to leave Kipling Camp early the following morning. All the people who cooked for us and took such good care of us gather around to say good-bye. As our convoy pulls out of the camp, dear Tara literally runs after us with her trunk in the air, trumpeting. She is saying farewell to Mark, clearly distressed to see him leave. It is so beautiful, like something out of a Disney movie.

The owner of the reserve kindly lends us his brand-new Land Rover, which is just as well because we have to retrace our journey down that bumpiest of bumpy roads. But this time we float along in style, the most comfortable ride I've ever had in India.

During the worst storm, at the beginning of the monsoon season, we fly to Bangalore, on our way to the next and most important stage of our documentary. We're headed for the Kabini River Lodge, eighty kilometers outside Mysore, once the hunting grounds of the maharajahs. My new guide is Aditya, whom I love instantly, the handsome friend and former traveling companion of Mark's. A photographer and adventurer, he takes very good care of me.

"Ah, Goldie, I am so happy to meet you," he says, in an accent that sounds more English than Mark's. "Get ready for the second part of your magical mystery tour."

"Thank you, I will."

"So tell me why you came to India to make a documentary on elephants?"

"Well, first of all, I love India," I tell him. "I first came here in nineteen eighty. And then when I came back in nineteen eighty-two with my nephew Michael, for some crazy reason I ended up at Kabini River Lodge, to see the wildlife. One morning, on a safari, we came across a clearing, and standing in the most beautiful light was a female elephant grazing, her little girl ellie at her side. They were all alone. I noticed that she had a big white circle around one eye. Our guide told us that she was blind, and that her baby daughter stood watch while she grazed, acting as her eyes, ready to warn of any dangers.

"He called the mother Belly Button, because she had such a prominent one. It was an incredible sight, this mother being protected by her daughter. I was so moved by the connection between these two beasts. I'm coming to try to find her again."

Aditya smiles. "Well, my dear, you're in India. Anything is possible. You must trust in destiny."

At that point, our old car—yes, another Ambassador—coughs and splutters to a halt once again. A huge explosion out of the rusty exhaust pipe makes its own singular contribution to India's pollution crisis.

"Trust in destiny? Are you kidding? How about trusting in a mechanic every now and again!"

We both burst into peals of laughter. I never thought I'd find someone who laughed as much as me, but I've met my match in Aditya.

A few hours later, we pull up to a government warehouse, where our crew has set up the camera ahead of us. They start rolling as Aditya helps me out of the car.

"This is something you must see," he tells me. "*This* is why you're here."

The camera follows me into room after room, stacked floor to ceiling with tusks and ivory and elephant skulls, big and small. Wandering through this vast skeleton graveyard, which smells of the sandalwood they've also confiscated, I've never seen anything like it. How can they slaughter these beautiful animals just for their tusks? What a terrible waste. I didn't expect this part of the journey to be so sobering.

We move on and eventually reach the beautiful reserve I remember so well, where I first saw Belly Button seven years before. Arriving at night, we find a guard jumping around like a madman in the middle of the road. His ashen face glares pale in the headlights of our car.

"What is it?" asks Aditya, frowning.

"A lone tusker, sahib," he replies panic-stricken, pointing down the darkened road. "He's been standing there for over an hour. It is most unusual, sahib. Most unusual."

The driver turns our car so that the headlights pick out the big bull elephant standing regally across the road, ears flapping, his tusks glowing white. In India, only the males have tusks, and the lone tuskers are considered the most dangerous.

"He's come to welcome you, Goldie," Aditya whispers. "He has come to thank you for what you are doing. This is his salute."

As I turn to look at the tusker again, openmouthed, he lifts his great trunk into the air, blasts a trumpeting call into the warm still night and lumbers off into the jungle from which he came.

Kabini River Lodge is a little more run-down than I remember it,

357

with its peeling Raj villas and rickety ceiling fans set in a forest of rosewood and teak. Thankfully, dear Papa is still in charge. Having chosen to stay on after independence, he is now older and a little frailer, but he is still full of such passion for the creatures he loves. It's wonderful to see him again.

Later that night, I sit around the campfire having dinner with Papa and the crew, learning more and more about elephants. Papa is full of wonderful stories, many of them from firsthand experience. He tells me that when an elephant goes into labor, she is tended to by three or four other female elephants, who act as midwives.

"And when an elephant is dying, the rest of the herd try to hold it up. Using their trunks, they lift and caress and encourage, until they can do no more. Then they hold a funeral. They cover the body with leaves and twigs; they gather around in circles and they weep. Later, they return to draw the tusks, burying them deep in the jungle or smashing them against trees, almost as if to defy the ivory traders."

Listening to his stories, I can't help but wonder. "What if my Belly Button is dead?" I ask him. I can hardly bear to think about it.

"Well, if that is so, then it would be the natural cycle of things, but she would not be forgotten," Papa tells me. "Not by you, and not by her herd. Elephants cannot pass the bones of a dead elephant without stopping to examine the remains. They seem to be remembering how their loved ones looked. I once found an orphaned baby elephant, dehydrated and weak after days of standing over its dead mother, rhythmically caressing the bones of her face."

I can't believe what I'm hearing. "I had no idea they had such a strong emotional life," I say.

"If they feel so deeply, then why do they kill?" the director asks.

Papa nods sadly. "Elephants rarely kill unless they are threatened. I knew of one who accidentally killed his favorite mahout, thinking he was the one who abused him. When he realized what he'd done, he circled the body and wouldn't let anyone near it. Bereaved, he wept real tears. He even tried to revive him. Only when he realized there was nothing he could do did he let the family take the body away."

We listen in stony silence.

. . .

Early the next morning, the crew are up and out before dawn. "Stay here," they tell me. "We're going to look for Belly Button." They have been speaking to the wardens on the three vast nature reserves, and several reports have come back of a blind ellie living in the same area where I saw her before.

When they return, several hours later, I cannot tell from their faces if their search has been successful or not. No one tells me anything. They just ask me to go with them, and they lead me to the riverbank and a boat. We speed down the beautiful Kabini River, past crocodiles and cormorants and fishing eagles, all the while looking, searching for my elephant.

We see many elephants, but, sadly, not Belly Button. As the day goes on, the sun beating down on my neck, I grow steadily pessimistic. Is it possible that I'll come all this way and miss her? When the water becomes too shallow, Aditya and I shift into a tiny coracle boat made of bamboo and buffalo hide, which spins and twirls out of our control, a metaphor for life.

Farther down the river, which has been dammed, we come across the ruins of an old Ganesh temple, a shrine to the elephant god. Aditya and I swirl and spin around it, getting close enough for me to reach out and touch the sacred stone, asking for its blessing.

I float precariously down the River Kabini. It's so peaceful here, but, instead of relaxing, I feel my eyes darting right and left to each muddy bank, desperately looking for this elephant. My heart is in my mouth. What if we don't find her? We already have plenty of material for the documentary, but everyone agrees that it would be dramatic to wrap it up with the rediscovery of my Belly Button.

Spotting another wild herd covering themselves with mud against the sun and bugs, we clamber out of the coracle and straight into quicksand, where I sink up to my ankles. Trudging through it with Aditya holding on, I feel like I have moon boots on, the wet mud is so encased around my feet. Reaching drier land, we creep quietly on through the brush and trees to the edge of a clearing.

"Shhh!" Aditya whispers, pressing a finger to his mouth as we crouch closer and closer.

I must admit I'm a little frightened. I don't know what to expect. I've never been this close to a herd of wild elephants before. My breathing becomes more and more shallow.

Aditya leads me forward through the grass, our crew filming a few paces off to one side. Through my binoculars, I spot three tuskers at the top of the hill, looking down on their family of female elephants.

"Do you think she's in there somewhere?" I ask as I watch them grazing and bathing at the water's edge.

"I don't know, Goldie."

I press my binoculars really hard against my face. "Look at that, Aditya! Look at that circle of family. There are aunts and cousins and sisters all together. There's a lesson there, isn't there?"

Quietly in my ear, Aditya replies, "Yes, yes, there is."

"Oh my God!" I cry suddenly, pointing wildly. "Oh my God, Aditya! I think that's her! I think that's my elephant! Yes, there she is! Oh, Aditya, there's my elephant!" My heart is racing. I want to jump up and down and scream. "I see her! There's that ring around her eye. It's Belly Button! She's alive!"

"Shhh! They'll hear you!"

"But it's her, Aditya!" I squeal, tears streaming down my face. "Oh my God! It's Belly Button! I can't believe it."

"And do you see anything else?" he asks in his deep voice.

"What? What?"

"Do you see anything under her legs?"

Straining through the binoculars, I see it. A tiny calf, hiding between her legs. "It's a baby!"

"Yes, a son. Less than a week old."

"Oh my God! How do you know that?"

"Well, actually, we've had a crew out here for weeks. They found her and her child. We wanted to surprise you."

"You did? Oh my God, I don't believe it. But I wonder where her other baby is?"

"You see that young elephant by her side?"

"Yes."

"Well, that's her!"

"No! Really? You mean, you knew this all along?"

"Yes, I'm a trickster." Aditya grins wickedly. "But I didn't know about the baby until yesterday. That baby was born just as you arrived in Kabini."

I stare and stare at my elephant's new calf, her tiny boy. He's so small that I can sometimes hardly see him as he takes baby steps between the massive tree trunk legs of his family. Just like his sister before him, this new infant will grow up to help act as his mother's seeing eye, shepherding her through life. My elephant will have another elephant, and that elephant will have another, and so the cycle will continue. The herd will perpetuate.

I feel such deep joy, watching this family taking such good care of each other in times of birth, life and death. Just like my family.

As one, the herd moves to the river to bathe. I watch as the little baby frolics in the water, happily playing, his tiny trunk up like a periscope. His older relatives flank him to protect him from crocodiles. They also take care of the disabled Belly Button, nudging her gently to the riverbank, making sure she doesn't slip. She has not been cast away because she is useless; instead, she is being helped, assisted and loved.

My knees weakening under me, I slump against a tree stump and watch breathlessly.

"Now do you believe in destiny?" Aditya asks me.

"Yes," I say emphatically. "Yes, I believe in destiny. I have to. Because in India, anything can happen."

Not knowing the outcome of an experience can be incredibly humbling and refreshingly liberating. Especially when we have to trust in strangers or lean on them for help and guidance when our course shifts unexpectedly.

We like to think we have things completely under control. We hold on so dearly to the things that define us—our houses, our cars, our clothes, our belongings, and even sometimes our opinions. But when we become lost or are suddenly out of our element, we not only have to face up to the unknown, we have to do it without any of the things around us that we think are important.

If someone had told me how things would start out on that trip to India—that I'd be lost and frightened, or that I'd have to sit on top of a wild elephant—I probably wouldn't have gone. But I did. That journey provided some of the greatest memories of my life. I learned so much. Mostly, I reminded myself how to surrender to the moment.

Letting go like that reminds us of the simple beauty of play. Children don't plan. They don't control. They laugh, they have fun, they go with the flow. There is a lesson for us all there.

Kurt and I go on bicycle trips where we are completely free. We don't do what many of our fellow cyclists do: get up at dawn, pedal directly from A to B, have dinner and go to bed. We meander. We get lost. We stop at remote farmhouses to ask where we are. We have to try to find our way back, or hope, as darkness descends, that the support truck will eventually find us. It always does. It's fun to be lost for a while; it's humbling.

If we can just let go and trust that things will work out the way they're supposed to, without trying to control the outcome, then we can begin to enjoy the moment more fully. The joy of the freedom it brings becomes more pleasurable than the experience itself.

postcard

Oliver, Kate and Wyatt burst out of our kitchen door in a dead race toward our car.

"I made it first! I'm in the front seat!" calls Ollie.

"No! It's mine!" Kate hollers back.

Wyatt, six years old, and ten years younger than Oliver, trails along, picking up the rear.

I am still in the kitchen, waiting for the star of the night: my mother, Laura Hawn. It is almost sundown, and we should have left for the synagogue fifteen minutes ago to make the High Holy service.

I smell her heady perfume before she even rounds the turn of the stairs. Celia, our dear housekeeper, holds Mom steady from behind so she doesn't fall. Her red lipstick is perfectly applied to her once-full lips. Her cheeks are finely dusted with pink blush, and her soupy brown eyes are adorned with a smattering of mascara.

"You look beautiful, Ma."

"Thanks, honey. Celia did my makeup for me. I can't see a damn thing anymore."

Celia beams. There is so much love between them you can almost touch it.

"I could smell you before I could see you." I laugh. "You smell real good."

"It's Shocking." She smiles, enjoying the pun. I think fondly of the neatly wrapped bottles of perfume my father used to place under the Christmas tree for her each year.

Struggling to put on her coat, Mom looks around the room. "Where are the kids, already? We'll be late."

"They're already in the car, Ma. Let's go."

Celia appears from the garage with a wheelchair. Mom's face drops.

"I hate that damn thing! I don't need it!"

She was always so independent, always so active. It pains me too that she needs to be pushed around, dependent on the kindness of others. But I have to be practical.

"Well, Mom, let's bring it along, just in case. It's a long walk, and maybe you'll get tired."

Laura Hawn gives me one of her black looks. Like the ones she used to give to Daddy, or Patti or me when we were bad. Boy, they burn right through you like a hot iron.

Oliver may have won the race to the car, but he is soon dethroned from the front seat when I open the door. Standing with Grandma, I tell him, "In the back, Ol."

"Oh, let him sit up here," Mom protests. "I can get in the back."

"No, Grandma, you sit in the front," Oliver insists, holding her arm, steadying her for a soft landing.

Katie leans over and touches her grandmother's hair. "You look so pretty, Gram!"

Mom puts her hand on top of Katie's. "Thanks, honey. I love you."

"Love you too, Gram."

Oliver jumps in the backseat with Katie and Wyatt. The car shakes as Celia slams the trunk shut, securing Mom's chariot. She waves us off—one grandma, one mom, three children and one wheelchair—as we pull away from our house on a warm September evening. We are on our way to pray to God for forgiveness for our sins. This is Rosh Hashanah, the holiest day of the Jewish year.

We wend our way down Sunset Boulevard. The kids are unusually quiet in the back. I glance furtively over at my mother as she looks out the window. She has a beatific expression on her face as she watches the hustle and bustle of life beyond her cloistered world. It makes her happy to reconnect to the life outside her four walls.

She had her first heart attack six years ago during the

Christmas holiday. They had to perform emergency bypass surgery days later. Patti and I rushed to the hospital. Panicking, we clung to each other and didn't let go. Dazed, we were both bewildered that this could happen to our strong and willful mother.

We walked into her coldly lit room in the same hospital where Daddy had died. Once again, we heard those horrible beeping machines that he was hooked up to ten years before. This couldn't be happening, we thought. Not again. Not to Mom. Looking down at her, we tried to act as normally as we could. Hoping to cheer her up, we fixed fake smiles. But, of course, she saw right through us. She could see the fear in our eyes. Nothing gets by Mom.

"Why don't you both go away now, so you can have a good cry?" she told us. "It's all right. I know. Go."

Our bodies stiffened in unison. We both bent down and kissed her. Our tycoon, our sage, our get-it-done mother.

"Okay, Mama."

Glued together, still holding hands, we went outside to the hallway, grabbed each other and sobbed our pain and fear. Our sorrow flowed between us. We were one.

All these years later and Mom is still with us. But her health is on a downward spiral.

W here the hell is this place, Goldie? It's almost dark already."

Katie spots the sign to the synagogue. "There it is, Mommy."

I pull up to the entrance and the kids pile out. Wyatt and Kate open Gram's door and help her out, as Oliver and I manhandle the wheelchair out of the trunk. We struggle together to open it, while Wyatt and Kate hold on to their grandmother from either side, acting as her stanchions.

Oliver takes the wheelchair from me finally and pushes

it toward Mom, Indy 500–style, stopping on a dime at her feet.

"Come on, Gram," he says. "Get in and start your engines."

She smiles her crooked smile, all protests forgotten, sits down and raises her funny fist up at him as he pushes her along. I feel so blessed, so lucky to have my children and my mother all together on this night of forgiveness and prayer.

Oliver does a few wheelie-type moves. Katie laughs her contagious belly laugh, and Wyatt is running after Ollie, trying to push too. Under my breath, I try to make them all behave, but I can't help laughing at the sight of my mother weaving around in the chair she hates so much. She is smiling that proud grandmother smile.

Entering the temple, we move down the aisle as one looking for our designated row of seats. Wyatt suddenly spots a box full of little white hats. He watches people take them out of the box and put them on their heads.

"What are those, Mommy?"

"They're called 'yarmulkas,' honey. Take two. One for you and one for Ollie."

Wyatt looks happily down at the box of hats. He loves hats. "Okay, Mommy."

We park Mom in the aisle when we find our designated row. Katie takes her customary place next to Mom, and Oliver and I shuffle farther down the row.

"Where's Wyatt?" I ask.

I look back and see him headfirst in the yarmulka box. He emerges, grinning, with three, one on his head and two in his hand. He runs down to Oliver and puts one on his head, and then he runs to Mom and plops one on her head too.

"Grandma," he cries at the top of his lungs, "you need a Yamaha!"

We all fall down laughing, trying to stifle our giggles as the rabbi clears his throat to speak. Oliver tries to snatch it back from Grandma to save her embarrassment.

Poor Wyatt looks confused.

Seeing his crestfallen face, my mother says, in her gravelly voice, "To hell with it, give me the Yamaha!" and plonks it on her head.

Kate and Oliver can no longer control themselves.

"Looking goooood, Grandma," Oliver laughs, giving her the thumbs-up.

My mother replies by turning around and looking down the row, shaking her fist at him with a look that says, Don't think for one minute that I'm too feeble to get out of this damn chair and put you over my knee.

The rabbi begins to recite the prayers, but we are so far back it is difficult for us to hear. My mother's face a picture of frustration, she says, "I can't hear. I can't hear!" To Katie, she repeats, louder, "I can't hear!"

"What is it, Mom?" I ask along the row.

In a voice nobody has trouble hearing, she says, "I can't hear! I can't hear a damn thing!"

"Mom! Shhh!" I say, looking around at all the faces turned toward me. I smile apologetically, and they smile back.

"Well?" Mom barks.

I whisper in Oliver's ear: "Go back and get some of those special earphones they have for the hard of hearing." He jumps up and runs over to where the temple fathers keep the special apparatuses. Rushing back, he puts a set in his grand-mother's lap.

Mom fumbles with these earphones noisily and finally at-taches them to her head upside down: the earpiece is on top, pressed against her yarmulka, and the clip part is under her chin. The rest is blocking her sight. She looks at Katie and says crossly, "Now I can't see a damn thing either!"

By this time, we are just losing it. Katie reaches over and tries to put them on properly.

"No, Grandma, like this," she says, patiently trying to figure out how they go. Parts of the contraption poke into my mother's ear, up her nose and in her eye.

"I hate this!" Mom spits. When the earphones start to make a strange high-pitched whistling noise, like feedback, deafening her, my mother rips them off her head angrily and throws them into her lap. "I hate this thing!"

None of us are even listening to the rabbi by now. We are just watching Mother. Oliver is beside himself.

Up comes the fist and that familiar scowl. "Shut up!" she tells him. "Just shut up!"

I am almost under the seat by now, holding on so tight that I can barely see through my tears of mirth.

Dear Kate comes to Mom's aid yet again and snuggles up real close to her. Not wanting her to miss the service, my darling daughter leans over in her gentle way and puts her little mouth close to her ear, her head pressed against Mom's, and painstakingly repeats the rabbi's every word.

My heart fills with such love at the sight. My mother's only granddaughter, the only girl in our family of this generation, sits there helping her grandma so tenderly. I see in her such nurturing, such loving, such strength, that my mother passed to me, and that I now realize I have passed to my daughter. Their two little heads together is all that I can see for the rest of the service.

After it is over, we file behind Grandma's wheelchair, Oliver pushing. Outside, we all stand around in communion with the rest of the congregation. I go to fetch the car, and when I look back I see my children surrounding Mom—an elephant grandmother with her children and grandchildren all around her. We are all, in our own way, holding her up until she dies.

A woman I don't know passes me and says, "You have a beautiful family."

Looking past her at this perfect tableau of family unity, I reply, "Yes. Yes, I do."

As I climb into the driver's seat, I silently pray that we can have one more year like this together with Mom.

Taking her home, we help her up to her room. We cross our hands and make a chair and carry her upstairs with an encouraging, "Come on, Laura, here we go."

Wyatt runs ahead up the stairs to turn down Mom's bed for her, to make her landing there more comfortable.

I tuck my mother into bed and kiss her good night. Walking to the door, I turn just before I switch off the light and look back at her.

Propped up on her feather pillows, still looking like the movie star that she could have been, she locks her eyes with mine with a look that penetrates my heart.

"I love you, Goldie."

"I love you too, Mom . . . With all my heart."

Later, I tucked little seven-year-old Wyatt in bed and began singing my usual song, "Raindrops on Roses." Interrupting my aria, he asked, "Mommy, what are stars made of?"

"Mostly gases, I think," I said.

"No, I don't think so. I believe that stars are people who died long, long ago who did great things for the planet."

I covered him up, kissed him and told him that he just might be right. I turned out the light, softly shut the door behind me and left him alone with his kind thoughts. Children's minds are a fertile ground for beauty. Flowers grow there, I think. It's up to us not to trample on them.

going back

If we only take time to go back to the wonder
of our early years, we can rediscover
the child inside us all.

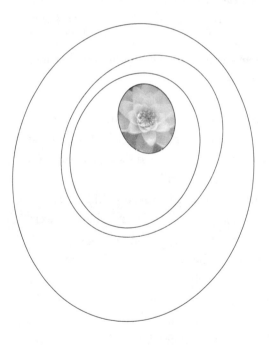

I squeeze Jean Lynn's hand as we watch her little sister's casket being lowered slowly into the frozen earth. In step, we both walk over and throw our single white roses into the grave before she is covered with dirt to be marked by just another headstone like all the rest.

It's a cold November day. Family and friends huddle together in a steam of mist to say good-bye to our Lyla, taken in her forties. When we were children, it never occurred to us that she might be the first to die. We teased her mercilessly, calling her "Illa" and making fun of her transparent skin and brown teeth. A chronic diabetic, she was fragile even then. But we didn't think of that. She was just the kid sister who suffered the teasings of her older siblings and their friends.

She had a great big laugh, and she followed us around like a devoted puppy. "Stop trying to copy us," Jean Lynn would say when we were stirring rocks into our mud to make pies. "Leave us alone."

She had the worst kind of diabetes. She gave herself a shot every day. Now and then, we were witness to her diabetic reactions, which were scary to see. But we were just children, and like all children we thought she'd live forever, no matter what. We were wrong.

Standing around the casket are the cast from my childhood. Jean Lynn is married now, with kids of her own, and she works in a bank not far from here. I look over at David Fisher, my first boyfriend, from the age of two. My, how he has changed! That first set of teeth has long since gone, and the boy I used to interpret for has grown into a handsome, middle-aged businessman.

I see his brother Jimmy, now a university instructor, standing to his right. I remember those languid summer afternoons when we'd camp out on their wraparound porch playing game after game of red canasta while his mother baked in the kitchen. He was the trickster of our clan, breaking up our lemonade stands, eating all of our homemade cookies and blowing bubble gum in my hair. But I loved him so much, it didn't matter.

Then there was Joey, Jean Lynn and Lyla's older brother, now a nuclear physicist living in California. The one who knocked over our Christmas tree. He made fun of me too. He'd joke about the way Mom would call me in for dinner. "Go-All-Day!" he made me repeat over and over, faster and faster. "Go-All-Day! Go-al-day. Go-al-die!" breaking it up phonetically until I eventually sounded just like her. He made me so mad.

So here we all are, the core group, the tribe that helped define who I was and who I've become. Our eyes to the ground, we silently drift away from Lyla's grave and into our separate sadnesses. This is clearly a passage we're not ready for, this sharp reminder of our own mortality. Truly the end of childhood.

Jean and I catch up with David and Jimmy, and we embrace each other in a group hug.

"Hey, guys, let's go to Gifford's," David says suddenly.

"Gifford's?" That was our favorite ice-cream parlor in Silver Spring. "Is it still there?"

"My mom thinks it's moved, but I think I know where it is."

I look at Jean to see how she feels about this. "Come on, honey," I say. "Let's have a hot fudge sundae for Lyla."

We share a conspiratorial look, and, jumping into my rental car, the four of us are on a journey to retrace our past, starting with a childhood treat: a visit to the ice-cream parlor.

We get lost, of course. The old signposts are all gone. We drive around and around in circles looking for familiar landmarks, the laughter beginning to bubble up inside us. It feels so good to be together again, as if no time has gone by.

"This is weird, isn't it?" Jean says, echoing all our thoughts.

Just then, Jimmy yells, "There it is, over there!"

I spin into a little strip mall and spot Gifford's sitting between a 7-Eleven and a computer store. How life changes. Only, right now, it feels as it always did. My car feels like a time capsule where everything is just as it was all those years ago.

We order ice cream—the same way—Swiss chocolate hot fudge sundaes with marshmallows. The four of us sit at a table and stare at each other, all grown up, and yet we can still see the kids we once were. My best girlfriend Jean Lynn is still my best girlfriend Jean Lynn, David and Jimmy too. It's as if no time has passed at all. One by one, we start to laugh. One by one, the laughter turns to tears. Giggling, crying and remembering, we are alternately rolling with laughter and hanging on to each other. When we are spent and have dried our eyes, we sit and eat our ice cream in silence, each one lost to the memory of past times.

"Hey!" I say, breaking the silence. "Let's go back to our old stomping ground. I want to see my old house."

Everyone agrees, and we scramble eagerly back into my car and drive to our old Victorian neighborhood nestled on the other side of the tracks. I can't wait to see the dead-end street I grew up on.

We cross the tracks into Takoma Park, and I can feel our excitement growing. It's been far too long since we traveled in this pack, down the sidewalks of our tiny lives.

Seeing the sign for Cleveland Avenue, I make the turn. I can hear my mother growling at the cabdrivers, "It's that sharp left on the corner." We drive down my quiet street, still filled with potholes, past mountains of leaves piled high on the roadside.

"Oh my God, guys, remember how we used to jump in the leaves after we raked them up from the lawn?"

"Stop!" Jean Lynn yells. "Stop the car. I want to get out."

I have hardly brought the car to a halt before she throws open the passenger door and jumps feetfirst into the pile of leaves outside Mr. Morningstar's house. "I just had to do it!" she shrieks, her face almost obscured by the leaves she is throwing up all around her. We all join in, laughing like children, tears in our eyes. If it wasn't for this day of death, this gathering of loved ones for dear Lyla, we would never be experiencing this bliss. Go figure.

Brushing ourselves off, we look around. There's my house, number 9. Over the back fence, we can see the Fisher and the Sror houses, side by side. Nothing much has changed. As one, we walk over to the redbrick duplex that was once my castle. It looks so tiny. I don't think I ever really noticed before that it was attached to another house. They both look much smaller than I remembered.

We walk up the steps to my porch, our minds replaying childhood memories.

"Jean, do you remember when we cracked rocks open and dried them here, just to watch them sparkle in the sunshine?" I ask.

Before she can answer me, David chimes in, "Yeah, I remember when we played out in the backyard tent 'I'll Show You Mine If You Show Me Yours'!"

I howl with laughter. "Oh, David, you were my first!"

We knock, but there is no one home. Our hearts sink. One by one, my friends begin to turn away.

"No!" I cry. "No! We have to go in, guys. We just have to!"

"Let's try the door," Jean says, her eyes brighter than they've been all day.

"You're kidding! You think?"

"Yeah," encourages Jimmy. "Why not? It was your house first."

I turn the handle. The door is open, just as it always was. "Hello?" I call. "Hello? Is anyone home?"

I half expect to hear a reply from the nice lady I know who bought the house from Mom, but all I am met with is silence.

"Come on, guys," I say, leading the way.

The whole gang obediently follows me inside. The house still smells the same: slightly musty. In our funeral garb, we walk through the rooms, touching everything, remembering happier times. I can almost hear the voices coming out of the walls—Dad's, Mom's, Patti's—and Nixi barking his greeting.

In the kitchen, my eyes fall on the old butler sink where Mom bathed me when I was little. "Oh, great, she didn't get rid of it!" I cry, running my fingers over its smooth ceramic surface.

"It's probably a valuable antique now," David laughs.

Looking at the wall by the telephone, I'm sad but not surprised to see that the new owner has wallpapered over the phone numbers we scribbled straight on the plaster—the collage of names and numbers from my past. Aunt Tootsie, Uncle Charlie and Aunt Sarah, the school, the store, Hawn's Watch Shop. Now all hidden beneath the pretty floral paper.

Walking upstairs, everyone following, I look down through the balusters, remembering the Christmas parties and all the pretty lights. "Hey, Jean, let's go look in our closet!" I cry as we rush to my old room and open the door to the closet we used to hide in, tucked in side by side, lighting candles and burning the sashes to my dresses. Trying to sit inside again, we can't even close the door.

Down in the basement, where I found my dear Nixi dead one day after school, I look longingly at where my father's old workbench stood and wish it was still there.

"Come on," Jean says, pulling me away. "Let's go over to my house."

We scurry out after leaving a note for the owner, telling her we were there and apologizing. I hope she isn't mad.

Walking down Cleveland Avenue in our little troupe, just as we did every year for trick or treat, we peer at the houses of all the neighbors we used to know and the doors we used to knock on dressed as ghosts and ghouls. The scent of wet leaves takes us straight back to the damp fall nights and going back to school.

Jimmy starts to laugh. "Oh my God, Goldie, remember that naked lady you and Jean used to carry around the neighborhood?"

"That wasn't a naked lady, Jimmy, it was my mother's sewing form she kept in the basement."

"Her name was Mrs. Tookey!" Jean Lynn screams with laughter at the memory. "Oh my God, do you remember we left her in Mrs. Tyrrell's yard and waited around the corner to see what she would do? We were insane!"

"All I remember about Mrs. Tookey is that she had huge breasts," Jimmy says.

"Oh my God, Jimmy. You're still sick."

Pushed to the front, I tap gently on the front door of Jean Lynn's old house. A young mom with a toddler at her side opens it. Recognizing me instantly, she opens her mouth in surprise.

"Hi," I say, smiling. "Listen, I'm really sorry to trouble you, but this used to be my girlfriend's house, and we all used to live in this neighborhood and . . ."

"I lived here," Jean adds wistfully, peering in beyond the new owner. "With my brother and my sister, Lyla. We buried her today."

Jimmy chips in, "And we were wondering, well, could we possibly take a look around?"

"It would mean so much," David adds.

The woman looks from one to the other and doesn't know quite what to say. "Well, sure," she says, finally. "Come on in. I'm afraid it's all a bit of a mess."

We troop in, our little crew, and stand awkwardly in her hallway. She stares at us for a moment and then retreats to the kitchen to let us look around. Tiptoeing through our past, we move as one from room to room, inspecting every nook and cranny, remembering the wild parties Jean Lynn's parents used to have, the music and the fun. Piling down to the basement, which has been completely remodeled, she and I look laughingly at where we hid under the oilcloth, afraid of the bomb.

"Oh my God, remember the shows we used to put on for the whole neighborhood in your garage?" I say, looking out the back window.

"We used to make poor Lyla run around after us like a little slave," Jean recalls.

"She was always so willing to help, so happy to be with us."

"We could never have done it without her."

"Do you remember when we found the squirrel that was dying in the garage?"

"Oh my God! We put him into a wheelbarrow under your doll blanket and wheeled him all the way into Silver Spring over the railroad tracks to the animal hospital. But then they said he could have rabies. Rabies! We couldn't get out of there fast enough!"

There is so much history in this house, in all of our houses. The sleep-overs. The Oreo cookies and milk in bed. Watching scary black-and-white movies. And staying up late. Walking into David's house next door, I can literally smell the chocolate chip cookies David's mother seemed to make all day long. She was the Betty Crocker of the neighbor-hood, the stay-at-home mom.

"Are you remembering our games of miniature golf?" David asks, standing at my side as I stare out longingly at his old backyard.

"Yes, but mostly I'm remembering the fence," I say. He follows my gaze and smiles. There it is, the chain-link fence, just where it always was, dividing his world and mine. It is all I can do to stop myself from running out and climbing it, just as I always did, hooking my toes back into each link.

Our journey into our past now over, that night I go back to Jean Lynn's house in Silver Spring, not far from where we grew up. Tired, wistful, I take a long, hot shower and slide between the cold, crisp sheets.

There is a gentle tap on the door. It's Jean Lynn.

"Hi, Poo-poo-face," she says, using our childhood language. "Can I come in?"

Sitting on the edge of my bed in her nightgown, she pulls the scrunched-up face we practiced for hours as children, "Our Face."

"Are you giving me 'Our Face'?" I say, pursing my lips around my teeth similarly, just like Bucky Beaver.

"Don't go tomorrow," she says, her lips still puckered up. "Stay, Poo-poo."

We both laugh.

"Seriously, honey," she adds, "I can't thank you enough for coming. I really needed you here today."

"You know what, Jean? I really needed to be here."

We hug, each one unwilling to let the other go.

Joey peeks his head round the doorway into the room, his eyes mis-chievous. "Good night, then, Go-All-Day!"

Pulling apart, we dissolve into laughter, and then Jean Lynn gets up to go to her own room. "I love you so much, Goldie," she tells me, turning to look back at me from the doorway.

"I know. And I love you too, Jean Lynn."

She switches off the light and closes the door behind her. So happy to be home, I drift into the blessed sleep of a child.

A s we grow up, our lives become so cluttered. We become shackled with responsibility, and bogged down with work and kids and the daily rituals and problems of our everyday lives. We forget how to play.

When we were children, we lived entirely in the moment. We knew no greater pleasure than to jump in a pile of leaves, ride bikes through muddy puddles or make crazy faces at each other with mouths full of ice cream. And tomorrow was only tomorrow.

Somewhere along the way, we grow up and suddenly feel self-conscious doing these things, perhaps because the adults around us start to tell us, "Act your age!" But what does age have to do with play? How can we relate a number to a full-on expression of abandonment and joy?

I remember one day, not so long ago, when I pulled my car up to a stop-light in Los Angeles, on Wilshire and Twenty-sixth Street, right near where I lived. I was by myself and an Elton John song I love, "I'm Still Standing," came on the radio. I began to move my body to the music, bouncing up and down on my seat, singing at the top of my voice. But this wasn't enough.

"The hell with it!" I cried, and, opening my car door, I jumped out, stood in the street and really let myself go. I started to really dance with abandon. I didn't care what I looked like. I was feeling the rhythm, feel-ing the joy, and I went with it. The man in the car behind me started to laugh. Before I knew it, he jumped out of his car and he started dancing too. The two of us strutted our stuff and shook and wriggled and danced until the stoplight suddenly changed. Then we dashed back into our cars, laughing, and went our separate ways.

All you have to do is unleash the child in you, and watch how it un-leashes the child in those around you. As Einstein said, a person starts to live only when he can live outside himself.

So dance that dance. Sing that song. Go to the park and ride the merry-go-round. Remember back and try to rediscover that place deep within you that is pure play. It is still there. And when you find it and open up to it, you'll discover that others around you will do the same. It will give them the permission they seek to be a child again too. Life is too short. Go for it!

postcard

The whistle blasts from the kettle just as the doorbell chimes. Celia and I are in my kitchen, all atwitter. We are expecting a very important guest. Master Lu, a renowned Chinese healer, is coming to help my ailing mother.

"Oh, they're early!" I say, putting down my red teapot on the kitchen table.

"Go! Go!" Celia says. "I'll bring the tea." Laughing, she raises an eyebrow. "Are you sure your mother's up for this?"

"Yes. She's up for it. Anyway, she knows I'm crazy," I add over my shoulder as I run for the door.

Standing in the doorway is Master Lu and his beautiful Chinese wife, Alice. I have used him many times before and have always benefited from his energy healing. We hug before I lead them into the living room, tiptoeing past the library, where my mother is napping.

"How is your mother feeling today?" Alice asks.

"Not very well. Her heart's getting weaker and weaker."

Celia arrives with the tray. Master Lu, a sturdy man with a large face as round as the moon, smiles broadly at me all the time. He speaks to me in Chinese, and I listen as if I understand every word. Alice interprets. "Master Lu is going to bring your mother energy."

"Good, thank you. Follow me."

I lead them into the library, where my mother is lying fast asleep on her side, her mouth wide open. She must have heard them come in. Something tells me she's faking it.

As Master Lu and his wife stand like Eastern monoliths in the doorway, I bend down close to her face. "Mom, Mom? Master Lu is here to see you. Mom?"

My mother stirs a little under her bedclothes, but she

doesn't open her eyes. Instead, she slides even deeper. Oh, this is great, I think.

Master Lu stands patiently in the doorway, while I sit on the edge of my mother's bed and shake her gently. "Mom? It's Master Lu. Remember? I told you he was coming?"

My mother's eyes pop open. The bedclothes flip down, and she stares up at me. The look is undeniable. It says, Oh no, Goldie, not now. Spare me from all your crazy stuff!

"Come on, Mom, let me help you up."

Reaching around behind my mother, I lift her into a sitting position. Her hair is disheveled, her face screwed tight. Alice comes and sits down next to her, and, smilingly, takes her hand.

"Master Lu is going to make you feel better," she tells Mom. "Now please to stick out your tongue."

"Stick out my what?" Mom growls.

"Your tongue, Mom, stick out your tongue."

My mother sticks out her tongue in such a way that I hope Master Lu doesn't consider rude. Taking no notice, he bends down and examines it carefully, checking its color and coating. He mutters some words to Alice in Chinese, which, of course, is all Chinese to us.

"Now, Mrs. Hawn," Alice says, "lift your arms, please."

"What the hell for?"

"Mom, shhh, please. Just do it!"

I can see this isn't going to be easy. Mom eventually does what she's told, glaring at me all the while. Master Lu runs his hands along the sides of her arms, over and over, never once touching her.

"What's he doing to me?" She scowls.

"I don't know. I guess he's getting rid of negative energy."

Master Lu takes my mother gently by the hand as Alice says, "Now please, Mrs. Hawn, let's get up."

Kicking out her legs with energy I didn't think she still had, Mom stands up, her big toe pointing straight to heaven.

As Master Lu begins to lead my mother across the room, Alice instructs, "Please come over to this chair and sit down." Turning to me, she says, "Would you please fetch a bowl of water?"

"Oh yes!" I cry happily. "Right away." Running out of the library, I call, "Celia! Celia! We need a bowl of warm water."

Celia comes running. This is a big event. She pulls out a plastic bowl from under the sink, and I fill it with water, checking the temperature. I hurry back as quickly as I can without spilling a drop.

The scene that greets me is like something from a pantomime. Mom is sitting in the chair in her nightgown staring at me, an eyebrow arched, as Master Lu conducts an elaborate ritual before her, working the energy fields. Waving his arms around dramatically, he is pulling the energy one way and then the other and drawing the energy from the top of her head. He looks as if he is conducting the *1812 Overture*.

Mom is now enjoying the attention, I can tell. Her spirit seems lighter, and there is a playful expression in her eyes.

Alice places my mother's feet in the bowl of water. "Mrs. Hawn, Master Lu will bring you energy now."

My mother sparks up and looks at me with those big brown eyes.

"Mom, are you feeling good yet?" I ask.

She forms a perfect circle with her mouth and says, "Oooooh!"

I eye her suspiciously. I can't tell if she's serious, or if she's just having fun with us.

Alice, all excited, rushes out. "I get washcloth!"

She runs to the guest bathroom and fetches one. Master Lu takes it from her and plunges it into the bowl of water with my mother's pointy little feet. Lifting it out, wringing it almost dry, he places it, with great ceremony, right on top of my mother's head.

She looks up again and chortles another "Oooooh!"

I stare at her agog. She looks like Ishkabibble.

"Mom?" I ask, trying to hold it together. "Are you feeling the energy?"

"Oooooh," she repeats. "Hmm." She lifts the edge of the washcloth and peers up at me. I half expect her to give me the fist.

Master Lu and Alice exchange some more words in Chinese, and Alice takes Mom's elbow. "Please now, Mrs. Hawn, get up. Get up! You have energy!"

My mother stands, her feet still planted firmly in the bowl of water. I hover close by, afraid she might topple over, but she stays steady.

"Wow, Mom! Look at you!"

"Now step out of the water," Alice instructs.

Still nervous, I watch as Mom does as she's told, stepping out of the bowl without so much as a wobble. "I swear to God, this is a miracle!" I cry.

My mother stands ramrod straight, her wet feet flat on the rug, that crazy washrag still on her head. A single eye peers out at me, and I can tell she's in her own world now. She is having a ball.

"Master Lu says to please walk around the room," Alice says, taking Mom's hand. "In a circle."

Mom stares at me from under the wet facecloth, her hair flattened to her head, and smiles sweetly. Uh-oh. Now what does she have up her sleeve? But she walks the most perfect circle around the room in her nightgown, arms out, hands turned to the ceiling, looking like Loretta Young. I feel sure that some miraculous healing has happened.

"Mom, Mom, how do you feel now?"

She rolls her eyes, makes one more perfect circle and gives us another "Oooooh!" Her skinny little ankles peeking out beneath her nightgown, she stops, puts her hands together and stares at us. I'm laughing, Master Lu is laughing and

Alice is laughing. I feel like I've gotten a little piece of my mother back.

"Mrs. Hawn!" Alice cries. "You got the energy!"

"Hmm." Mom nods and smiles. "Very nice."

"Mom, this is great, this is so great." I run over to Master Lu and give him a big hug. "Thank you so much."

Master Lu gives me a ceremonial bow, to tell me that his work here is done.

"Mom, stay right there!" I tell her. "I'm just going to see Master Lu and Alice out. I'll be right back."

As I show them from the room, I turn and see Mom standing there in the middle of the rug, looking like a princess.

Celia meets me in the hallway on my way back. "How did it go?" she asks.

"Great! Oh, Celia, really great! Mom's walking around the room. It's amazing! Let's go see her."

We rush back to the library. But Mom is back in bed, on her side, the covers right up to her neck again, her mouth open, sound asleep.

"I can't believe it!" I tell Celia. "She was up! She was standing right in the middle of the room! There was life back in her!"

A rumbling snore from under the bedclothes interrupts me. Stooping down, my face next to hers, I shake her shoulder gently.

"Mom? Mom?"

Her left eye opens and glares up at me.

"Mom, what about the energy?"

In her deep gravelly voice, she replies, "He took it with him."

death

Death is not the end.
It is merely a transformation.

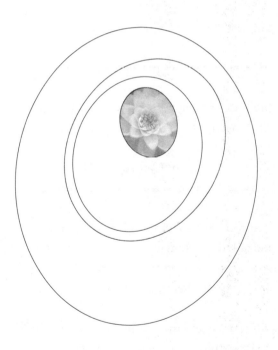

I run my hand over my mother's lifeless feet. She did it. She did the impossible. She died.

I caress her little turned-up toes, still pointing up to heaven. I can't believe it. I never thought she could die.

"Mom," I wail, "I tried to get here. I didn't make it. I'm so sorry, I wanted to be with you."

I look down at her face; the lines on her face that showed struggle and pain and sadness had all but disappeared. She looked so young, so peaceful.

"Where are you, Mom? Where did you go? Can you still hear me?" Looking up at the ceiling of her hospital room, I ask, "Are you still here somewhere? Can you see me?"

It's November 27, 1993, Laura Hawn's eightieth birthday, and, as destiny would have it, also her death day. Mom and I always shared our birthdays. They were just one week apart. Her presents are still sitting on the floor of my living room, waiting for her to come home again, but she never will.

"She went very peacefully," the nurse tells me. "When we were washing her this morning, we said, 'Happy birthday, Laura.' Her eyes looked up at us and twinkled. But then, Goldie, she closed her eyes softly and her body shut down. I think she was waiting for her birthday to finally let go."

I sit on the edge of the bed and touch her body. I whisper, "Mom, you did it! You died." A strange sensation fills me. Up until now, I've been afraid of death and dying. When I was younger, I would have night-mares that my mom would die and I would get into bed with her. I decide to lie next to my mother for the last time. I stroke her hair, and tell her, "Mom, if you can do this, if you can die, then so can I."

Patti comes running in breathlessly, looking more like a child than I have ever seen her. She probably ran as many red lights getting to the hospital as I did. There we stand, two little girls at the foot of our mother's bed, clinging to all that we have left: each other.

At Mom's funeral, the rabbi tells us that when a person dies on their birthday it's very auspicious because a cycle has been completed. This brings me calm and makes me happy, knowing that Moses died on his birthday, so there we are. So did Laura Hawn.

It has been said that it takes a year to fully recover from the death of a loved one. I know this will be the longest year of my life and I am right. For a full year, I can feel only intense sadness. Whatever I do, I'm unable to fix it. Even my children sense that I'm not the same. I question what I'm doing. I ask myself who I'm now performing for. Pleasing my mother was my dance in this life, and, with Mom gone, I have to reevaluate everything that I am. I know that no one will ever love me the way my mother did.

I spend hours in my meditation room, reading books about death, about the mysteries of life. It brings me solace, because I'm having difficulty understanding where the vibrant spirit that was my mother has gone. I read about Buddhism; I read about the Kabala. I read essays by great mystics, as well as pop culture books about talking to heaven. I even dabble in quantum physics, trying to understand the true nature of life. This is the real beginning of my mystical journey. Feeling my wanderlust rising, I need some time to travel to the most mystical land I know. And to the one city that brings me the most peace.

Now I'm in the back of a wobbly old rickshaw on the streets of one of the oldest cities in the world, Varanasi, the "City of Light"—also known as the "City of Death." An orphan for the first time, I've come to this place to heal.

I'm headed for the holy ghats, the great riverbank steps where pilgrims come to purify themselves in the sacred water of the Ganges. It is also where they come to burn their dead on funeral pyres. The nearer I get, the more the air around me is filled with the scents of sandalwood and incense, hot ash and candle wax. Fire and water play such an important part in the life of the Hindu.

Trundling through labyrinthine alleys where I can hardly tell night from day, I pass scores of old people sitting in doorways, happily waiting to die. Devout Hindus, they believe that if they die in Varanasi they will attain instant *moksha,* or enlightenment; they will be free of the continuous cycle of life and death. And so they come, in their hundreds, to live out their final days.

A little farther on, I come across two families carrying their dead wrapped in shrouds, singing mournfully all the while. Their loved ones will be burned on the ghats, and their ashes scattered on the river by a Brahmin priest.

Still farther, I'm suddenly caught up in the middle of a wedding ceremony spilling out onto the street. The laughing bride and groom wear candles on their heads and garlands of flowers around their necks. Musicians play as they parade through the streets. Those around them skip and reel, dance and cry out their joy.

Reaching my destination, I walk down to the river's edge where people are praying, while others bathe. Women wade in fully clothed, their saris floating out all around them like the overlapping petals of an exotic flower. There are bodies waiting to be burned, as tourists look on. A group of young children are lighting devotional candles and launching them out onto the water on green lotus leaves.

I sit on the banks of the river watching the life of this city unfolding before me, just as it has unfolded for centuries. It is early evening now, and the sun is setting behind me so that everything is bathed in an ethereal light. Across the water, the gilded turrets on the pavilions and temples, palaces and terraces glint back at me. Golden. This truly is a City of Light.

Returning to my hotel as darkness falls, I make an appointment for the next day with the astrologer with the piercing dark eyes who still sits in his little room just beyond the elevators. I first met him in 1980, when I came here to heal after the breakup of my second marriage.

"Your career is going to go up, and up and up," the astrologer predicted in 1980. "You'll meet a man, you'll fall in love, and you'll have a boy child." I received this information hungrily, gladly. He gave me hope for yet another chance of creating my perfect home with the white picket fence, and a loving father for my children.

The astrologer was introduced to me by Papu, an adorable little street urchin I'd adopted as my guide. "Where now, Mrs. Goldie?" Papu asked me back then, grabbing my hand. "You want see other astrologer?"

"No, Papu." I laughed. "Thank you. This one was just fine."

Papu was my guardian angel on that early journey to heal. Indefinable in age, but probably not much older than thirteen, he was someone I first met when I was lost, in the midst of the madness of Varanasi. He came running up to me out of nowhere and tugged at my hand. Pulling on my skirt, he pestered me with "Mrs., Mrs., Mrs.!" I looked down at this beautiful Indian child, staring back up at me with his big black eyes and dirty face, and my heart melted. He was wearing long raggedy pants and a frayed orange T-shirt smeared with dust. There were no shoes on his grubby feet. He was holding a palette of holy colors that he wanted to sell.

"Please, please, Mrs., you buy?"

I shook my head.

"What do you want, then? You want buy rugs?"

"No, no thank you."

"You want buy silks?"

"No, I'm fine."

"Then you want guide? I will be your guide."

As I tried to cross the street, he ran ahead of me holding the cars back with his hand and shouting, "Stop! Stop!" He was clearing the way, protecting me fiercely. Papu was so tenacious, he wouldn't let me go, so I surrendered, and I fell in love. Before I knew it, I was sitting in his uncle's silk shop, buying silks. Then I was somewhere else, looking at rugs. He pushed cows out of our way as he led me into temples; he haggled with the rickshaw drivers on my behalf. He took me to his astrologer.

After another long day together exploring the city, I asked him, "When was the last time you ate a hot meal, Papu?"

He shook his head. I could see his ribs sticking through his T-shirt. I wondered where he slept, if he had family, how he lived.

"Come with me," I told him, stepping toward the hotel.

"Not in there, Mrs. Goldie. Not allowed."

"Why not?"

He didn't answer. I suppose it was the caste system at work.

"We'll see about that, Papu," I said, grabbing his hand.

I led him into the hotel until a senior member of the staff barred our way.

"Madam, you cannot bring him in here!"

"He's my friend," I replied coldly. "We'll be dining together tonight."

Without another word, I showed Papu into the restaurant and watched him devour probably the biggest meal he had ever eaten.

Ah, dear Papu. I wonder where he is now. We kept in touch for a while, but we lost contact over the years.

Feeling nostalgic, I pick up the telephone and call home to make sure my children are all right. It is good to hear their voices and to know that they are happily carrying on their lives without me for a while. I go to bed feeling more peaceful than I have felt in months.

T he following morning, I hail a rickshaw and take a journey to see another old friend, whose company I feel the need for. The rickshaw driver knows the way. He pedals me through the tight grid of alleys in the Old City, wherein beats the real heart of Varanasi. Life is so robust here. People live their lives on the street. Parents and grandparents take care of their grandchildren. Women wash their clothes and their babies side by side. Everything is out in the open. Everybody shares. People and animals jostle together for space and air. Cows literally parade before us aimlessly while we wait for them to pass or squeeze past them apologetically.

I'm embraced once more by this wave of sensuality, of color, smells, images, religion and cultures. Admittedly, some of the smells are putrid, but mostly it's frangipani and jasmine. It is those scents I choose to remember. I smile at the children; I wave at the mothers and grandmothers we pass. They wave back and smile, their faces open and loving. I so love being lost here, just another anonymous face in the crowd.

I'm on my way to my friend Brij Gupta's guesthouse he runs with his mother, father and brother Sanjay. Our rickshaw weaves through the streets, a mass of humanity going in various directions. We dodge cows, and policeman standing in the middle of the street directing what looks like total chaos. I feel like Alice in Wonderland.

At last I reach my destination, climb down from my rickshaw and walk up to the door of the Sun Hotel guesthouse, feeling very exhilarated to see Brij after all these years. The door opens. There, Brij sits in his wheelchair, backlit by the sun flooding through the window behind him.

"Goldie!" he cries, his face lighting up. "I don't believe it! I had no idea you were in town."

He pats the seat beside him in the cramped room he shares with his family, and I take it eagerly, so happy to see him again. His mother appears in a beautiful pink sari as if by magic, kissing me warmly on both cheeks. She makes us tea and crackers, and we sit together in this room full of sunlight and love.

"So, dear Brij, how are you?" I ask, trying to ignore how brittle he looks. His unusual angle in his wheelchair suggests that his spine has grown even more crooked since I last saw him. Dark-haired and extremely handsome, he still cuts a dashing figure in his crisp white shirt and slacks.

"I'm well, dear Goldie, very well," he lies. He draws on his ubiquitous cigarette, elegantly held in an ivory holder. "Did you receive the poetry I sent you?"

"Yes, Brij, I did. It was so beautiful. Thank you. Are you doing much other writing?"

"Not so much," he says, his eyes flickering with momentary sadness.

I think back to the first time I met Brij. A woman at my hotel told me about him. "Brij Gupta is extremely intelligent, fluent in many languages and a foreign correspondent for *Der Spiegel*," she said. "But one day he dove into two feet of water, thinking it was deeper, and is now a paraplegic and unable to work. He loves visitors. It would really cheer him up. It would be so wonderful."

I remember being struck immediately by how beautiful Brij was, and what an amazing spirit he had. I sat with him for hours, talking and sharing our lives. He writes such beautiful poetry about the light in Varanasi and the spirituality of this ancient city. His poetry is so optimistic; it comes from deep within the heart of a man who has lost everything, yet who has so much. I treasure every word.

Now I have come to see him again in the hope of restoring some of my own natural optimism, which I have lost recently.

"So how are your dear children, Goldie? How is your family?" he asks.

"Kurt and the kids are great, Brij, but I'm not doing so well. I just lost my mother."

"Oh, I'm so sorry, Goldie."

"I know. I just feel like there's this huge void now."

He nods and listens patiently.

"I've been trying to make sense of what I'm feeling. Part of me feels like it has died too."

"It has," Brij offers simply. "You've lost the last person who validated you—the one person who you could really please and make proud. You have to validate yourself now, Goldie. It's up to you."

I sit and stare at his beautiful face, listening as his words fade to silence in the still air around us. Nobody can validate me now but myself? He has such wisdom.

He then reaches across to a record player and puts on a song by Barbra Streisand. He sits in rapture for a moment, eyes pressed shut; he listens to the words and then stares up at me. "Dance with me," he instructs. I am stunned, not knowing what to say.

"Oh, okay," I reply, thinking I'll just stand before him and maneuver his wheelchair in little circles. I reach for the arm of the chair.

"No, no. Hold me; hold me up," he says. Using his powerful arms to heave himself from the confines of his wheelchair, he beckons me to stead him on his feet.

"Oh, but, Brij, I can't," I cry. "I'll drop you," I say in abject fear.

"No you won't, Goldie. You are much stronger than you think."

He balances himself on his feet, clamping his arms tightly around me. I put my arms around his torso for support. I am shaking. Behind us, Barbra sings: "People, / People who need people / Are the luckiest people in the world . . ."

And so we dance. Even though I am afraid, we dance. Even though he is so heavy, we dance. And with each tiny step, I say a prayer that I won't collapse under the full weight of Brij Gupta. I see a little mouse scurry across the floor by our feet and escape into a well-worn hole. As Brij rests his body against mine, he whispers, "See, Goldie? See how strong you are?"

The spell between us is broken when the door opens and Brij's brother Sanjay walks in.

"Goldie!" Sanjay cries with delight as he helps me settle Brij back into his wheelchair. "How marvelous to see you!"

We chat for a while, but we can both see that Brij is tiring.

"How would you like to come on the River Ganges with me this evening, Goldie?" Sanjay asks on an impulse. "Some friends of mine have hired a boat and would be delighted if you'd join us."

"Oh, I don't know . . ."

But Brij catches my eyes and smiles broadly. "Oh, but you must go, Goldie! It will be wonderful! Come back and see me tomorrow."

Sanjay and I sit side by side in the back of a rickshaw in companionable silence. My heart is full of the comfort his words have given me. I was right to come here. I was right to try to open the windows of my mind and soul. I have taken the first important step away from my grief. I'm allowing a little of this amazing Indian light to flood those darkest corners of my heart.

Stepping from the rickshaw as Sanjay pays the driver, I suddenly hear a voice: "Goldie Hawn?"

My heart sinks. Oh no, not now! Not here. I don't want to be Goldie Hawn. I want to be a stranger walking alone, peaceful with my thoughts. I put my head down and keep walking toward the ghats, trying to ignore the voice.

"Goldie? Goldie Hawn?" The voice is nearer now, and has taken on an urgent tone.

Sighing heavily, deeply dismayed at being recognized here of all places, I turn to see a man in his mid-twenties standing a few feet apart from a group of other Indians, their foreheads devotionally streaked with sandalwood.

I try to muster a smile.

"You're Goldie Hawn!" the young man states, his eyes bright.

"Yes . . . Yes, I am," I reply softly.

"Mrs. Goldie! It's me, Papu!" he cries, rushing forward. "You remember! The boy who met you many years ago! You helped me. You called me your friend. Mrs. Goldie, I have prayed for your long life every day!"

I stare openmouthed at the man before me. Try as I might, I cannot recognize anything of the little boy I once befriended in this adult's face. But I know from the sandalwood on his forehead that he is a devout man. I can also tell from the tears in his eyes that he is speaking the truth.

"Papu? I can't believe it! I can't believe it! You're all grown up!"

He runs to me, and I hug him with all my might.

"How in the world did we come to be on the same street?"

I can speak no more. The synchronicity of our meeting on this auspicious day overwhelms me. My guardian angel has been returned to me. Our paths have crossed once more.

Sanjay coughs and steps forward shyly, so I introduce him to Papu.

"Then you must come with us tonight on the boat, Papu," Sanjay tells him, smilingly. Pointing the way with his hand, he insists. "Please, my dears, come."

Papu takes my hand just as he did when he was a little boy, following Sanjay to the river. "Thanks to you, Mrs. Goldie," he says, grinning broadly, "I'm now a very wealthy man. I have my own silk shop. It was your faith in me that made me successful."

"No, Papu," I correct him. "It was your faith in yourself."

"Here we are," says Sanjay, pointing to a beautiful double-decker boat moored to the riverbank. He and his friends have hired musicians to play for us, and the beautiful Hindu music of sitar, flute and tabla calls to us from across the water.

As I pull off my sandals and step aboard the boat, the sitar player puts down his instrument and scatters rose petals before my bare feet. He leads me to the top deck, which is covered in rugs and pillows. He takes rose oil and rubs it on his hands, gently massaging the oil into my hair and my skin.

Sanjay's friends join us, and we push off from the riverbank as the musicians begin to play. There is no motor, just the sound of paddles gently slapping the water. I lie back on the pillows and rugs, inhaling the oil, soaking up the golden light. I can feel my joy awakening from deep inside me.

We drink chai as the musicians play a Hindu song I recognize. Before I know it, I'm singing along: "Hare Krishna, Hare Krishna, Krishna Krishna, Hare Hare."

Boy, I think, laughing, if my mother could see me now!

I can almost feel Moses looking down on me from heaven. "So what are you, Goldie Hawn?" he is saying. "A Jew or a Hindu?"

"I dunno," I reply. "I think I'm a little bit of everything. All faiths can be beautiful."

I stare across at this moving tableau: the funeral pyres, the flames and billowing smoke, the flesh and bones of those who've died becoming the air that we breathe. Nearby, inside the tall, thin houses on the edge of the river, babies are being born. On the doorsteps, men and women are waiting to die. All around me is the full circle of life and death, and all of the inevitables, emerging from creation and destruction simultaneously. A beautiful sense of calm fills me at my acceptance of this endless cycle. I am beginning to understand. My mother's death is all part of this same divine process.

What are we mourning? What are we running from? Death is the one inevitability in life, yet so many of us, especially in the West, are uncomfortable with it. Certainly in my house, we never discussed it. My parents never spoke of death, and even to the very end my mother refused to say, "I'm going to die." And yet she did. We all do.

During this healing journey, I sensed some divine force had brought me to this mystical city to find the answers I was seeking to questions in my life, forcing me to focus on questions about death and to immerse myself in a culture that so embraces it. By rejecting the normal Western reaction of being so afraid of dying, I came to believe that it is vital that we come to terms with death, especially our own, in order to live out the rest of our lives fully and consciously.

Know that you are going to die, then back up and live each day with that truth in mind. Wake up each morning happy to be alive.

oxygen

*Oxygen is the unseen element of our universe
that awakens our body, mind and spirit.
Without it, we die.*

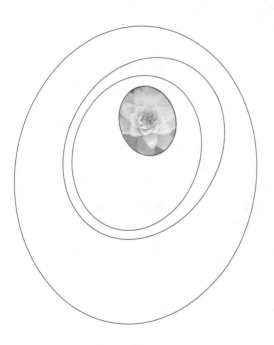

I feel as if I'm in a Garden of Allah as I push my way through overgrown banana trees and ferns to find the half-hidden door to the motel in Hollywood, California. The place looks like something out of the *Sunset Boulevard* era.

Hacking my way through to the entrance and up the stairs, I think, Goldie, do you really want to do this? Maybe this transformational breathing session is too much of a left turn . . . even for you.

After knocking on a door, I stand before it, toying with the idea of running away. But before I can, it opens, and I come face-to-face with a woman whose luminous smile reassures me.

"Hi! Come on in," she says, leading me into a room lit only by candles and filled with crystals and incense. She seems pretty normal, I think. Soft-spoken, she is sweet and soothing. "This way," she says, and takes me through to a bedroom. "So now why don't you start by loosening your clothing and making yourself comfortable. Lie down on the bed and relax. I'll just fetch a glass of water. I'll be right back."

I sit on the edge of the bed and look around. The curtains are sheer and a little bit grubby, but I can just about see through them out onto the Hollywood Hills. My breathing guide returns with the promised water, and sits next to me on the bed.

"So this will help my prana, my life force?" I ask.

"Yes, in a way. Now, we're just going to start with some deep breathing, so lie down."

"Oh, okay."

"We'll go deeper and deeper with the breathing, and you'll soon begin to have some strange physical sensations."

"I will?"

"Yes. Now, whatever happens, I want you to keep with it. Don't be afraid. It can get pretty intense, and if you feel like you have to stop, then stop, it's okay. But it's best if you just keep rolling. Don't worry, I'll guide you through it."

"Er, okay," I say nervously. "But this is going to be, like, fun, right?"

She doesn't answer me. Instead, she just presses my arm with her hand and makes me lie back on the bed.

"All right, now, Goldie. We'll start with a quick inhale and then a puff out, forcefully. Like this." She demonstrates. "We'll do that a few times, and then we'll start to pant, but with each breath it will become deeper and more rhythmic."

"Okay." I do as I am told.

In through my nose and out through my mouth, deeply through the diaphragm, pushing my ribs sideways, feeling them move.

In . . . out . . . in . . . out.

A tingling sensation starts behind my eyes, and I feel slightly dizzy.

In . . . out . . . in . . . out.

I'm breathing to her rhythm, not mine. After about ten minutes, I start to feel a strange buzzing in my head, and then I start to get scared. What's this going to do to my brain? I think. What if I hyperventilate and pass out? I am understandably afraid of reaching an altered state.

"Keep going, Goldie. That's it. Keep breathing, just like that."

I'm dizzy. I'm nauseated. I'm trying to get all the air out before I breathe new air in. Worse, I'm beginning to feel unbelievable pressure on the top of my head. It feels like the whole world is pressing down on me.

In . . . out . . . in . . . out.

Continuous heavy breathing. The pressure gets worse and worse. It now feels as if I have a hundred pounds on top of my skull.

What's going on here? I ask myself. This is heavy-duty. I must be crazy. My head feels as if it will explode. But there is no respite. The woman urges me on and on with ever more fervor.

In . . . out . . . in . . . out.

"Keep going, Goldie, keep going!" she coaches, kneeling beside me now on the carpet, her fists clenched in encouragement. "Soon you'll be out and free!"

In . . . out . . . in . . . out.

"Free?" I pant. "But I'm already free!" Touching the top of my head, I groan. "Oh, there's so much pressure here."

In . . . out . . . in . . . out.

Finally, I can't take it anymore. "No!" I say, breaking the rhythm and sitting up. Panting, I tell her, "I'm sorry but that's just too much."

"It's okay," she says, but I can see her disappointment.

"I need to use the bathroom," I say, getting up rather unsteadily.

Staring in the mirror, I try to pull myself together. All right, Goldie, you're going to go through this now. Just do it. This won't kill you.

I open the door, flop back on the bed and go for it. I start breathing heavily again and very quickly return to my earlier state. Once again, I feel like my head is in a vise.

"Oooh, but it really hurts," I complain, having second thoughts.

"That's okay," she says. "Don't worry. That's completely normal when you're experiencing rebirth."

"Re . . . birth?!" I pant between breaths, looking up at her. "Wait a minute! Are we rebirthing me?"

"Yes, Goldie! Yes! Can't you feel it?" she replies, more breathless than I am. "You're pushing down and pushing down! You're going through the birth canal! Can't you feel the squeeze on your head?"

My hands clamped to the top of my head, I cry, "Yes, already! But when the hell am I going to get out of here?"

Suddenly, I know what it is that I'm feeling. Pushing, pushing. In, out, in, out, in, out. Puffing, panting, my cheeks filling with air and emptying. The pain and pressure on my head excruciating.

"I can't stand much more of this!" I whine. "It hurts too much."

"Keep going!" she shrieks. Her eyes radiate her zeal. "You're almost there!"

"I am?" I carry on, chiefly because I figure this is my only way out of wherever it is that I am. In and out . . . in and out . . . gasping, fighting for every breath.

I have no idea what to expect next. Nothing prepares me for what follows. Suddenly, there is the most tremendous sense of exhilaration. All the pressure in my head melts away. I can feel it all so powerfully: the struggle of childbirth—the pain—followed by the sheer elation of emerging out into the world, of merging with the earth, with the air, with life.

I'm laughing and laughing, and crying, and laughing some more. I'm feeling incredible joy. I have come into this world, and all I keep saying through my tears is, "I'm so happy to be here. I'm so happy to be here."

True or false, whether it was real or imagined or just all in my mind, I was faced with a new perception of myself that day—that I loved being born. It's something I have always innately felt, I guess—that from the very beginning, I have had some joyful connection to being here in this world.

Since that day, I try to wake up each morning feeling equally reborn, ready to meet each new day with the possibility of doing it better. I seek to return to that joy of just existing, of being here and now in the moment, so safe and pure and sound.

But what was even more amazing for me was the realization that birth is not that much different from death as a transition: it has the same feelings of letting go, of going back, the joy and relief of returning home. The moment a new child bursts into the world and fights for its first gulp of breath is as awesome as the moment of one's final breath.

In my mind, I'd experienced coming out of not just any birth canal but that of my own mother's. Now, even though I was fifty years out of her womb and she had taken that final breath, I'd been able to summon up the experience of being born to her again. The connection to her was still so alive. Just because I couldn't see her or touch her didn't mean that she was no longer there.

This was such an important lesson for me to learn in this long and painful process of healing. I had lost my mother. But I could still feel the strength and purity of the umbilical link between us.

empty nest

The chickens leave the nest,
one by one, leaving us alone.
Why is there no warning?

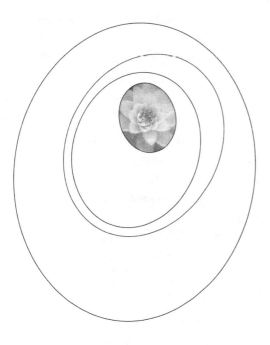

You got everything, Ollie?" Kurt asks as he peers into the back of Oliver's 1972 blue Bronco.

"Yeah, Pa," he yells back, his head deep inside the trunk, squashing his last duffel bag among his books, records, sports gear and prized fishing rod. We stand by the side of the road outside our home watching helplessly as he packs his belongings into his car for his first-ever move away from home.

"Oh, I almost forgot, your sheets are in the dryer," I say, dashing back inside the house to grab the soft sheets that he loves so much. I roll them up, tuck them unceremoniously under my arm and run back out to the car. "Here they are, honey. You can't leave without these."

"Thanks, Mom," he says, smiling his crooked smile at Pa as if to say, Gee, Mom and her sheets!

"Humor me," I say. "It's not every day your son goes away to college."

So, here we stand, Kurt and I, in the middle of the street, watching our oldest child leave home. Braving it out, on the verge of tears, we make jokes, trying to act normal. After all, this is as it should be. We prepare our children to leave and seek a life of their own. I recall that day I left home, and the strength my mother and father showed. Only it's me now. The roles have reversed.

Just then, John, Oliver's friend who lives across the street, comes running toward the car carrying all of his bags. His mother, Lorraine, runs after him with some snacks she's prepared for the journey.

"Johnny's all ready," she says as she puts the snacks in the car. "Isn't it amazing that they're going to the same university? How lucky is that?"

We all lock eyes and telepathically share the memories of car pools, sleepovers, lost walkie-talkies and—as they grew older—the late-night calls checking on the safety of our boys. But we say nothing. John and Oliver have been friends since they were seven years old, and now they are off together to experience the next chapter of their lives. Only they are going it alone.

"Okay, then," Oliver says, emerging one last time from the trunk into the sunny California morning, his disheveled hair framing his shining face. "That's about it. I guess it's time to go."

I look at him standing tall before me. Seventeen. Hands thrust deep in the pockets of his jeans self-consciously, not sure of what to do next. There is an awkward silence as if an angel is flying overhead. All I can think of is my tiny baby in that hospital, his heartbeat fluttering irregularly on the monitor above his cot, my hand pressed tenderly on his chest while I prayed for his life, so long ago.

I try to speak, to say something funny and glib like my father would have. "Don't pick your nose in public. And remember to put the butter back in the icebox." But I can't find the words. I squeeze Kurt's hand, knowing that he is feeling the same way. Where did the time go? How did Oliver speed through his childhood at such a pace? At this moment, we both want to turn back the clock and start all over again. Kate, my energetic firecracker of a daughter who ignites a room with her power and strength, is following hard on his heels. But, no, I can't allow myself to think about that. It's too unbearable.

I am happy that she is at school right now, for I fear her heart couldn't bear to witness Oliver's departure. Wyatt, also in class, is spared from this defining moment. I can still see him at Oliver's graduation, holding on to his big brother for dear life, saying, "I don't want him to go." Then Ollie too, in his cap and gown, holding Wyatt close to him and lamenting, "I won't see him grow up." Our family unit is being disrupted and rearranged by the inevitable growing pains of life.

Oliver is his own person now, stepping out into the world just as I had, as we all have to. He is about to find his way, seeking his own unique path on his own life's journey. The umbilical cord is about to be stretched farther than it has ever had to stretch before. I can already feel it tugging at me deep inside.

"Come on," John calls out from the other side of the Bronco, "let's get on the road. I want it to still be light when this damn car breaks down." He makes us laugh, breaking up my melancholy.

His mother pats him on the back. "Bye-bye, Johnny." She seems to be in much better shape than Kurt and me.

"Okay, then, guys, you'd better get going," Kurt says, letting go of my hand. He takes Oliver in his arms and squeezes him close with all his might. "Go get 'em, honey."

I love how Kurt calls Oliver "honey." I love how physical and loving he is with the children. Watching them embrace, I recall the first time Kurt ever laid eyes on Oliver. He met Oliver when he was only six years old, at a baseball game in San Diego, a year before he met me. Serendipitously, Kurt happened to be one of the ballplayers. He noticed the shy young boy sitting all alone on the bench. He sat next to Oliver and asked him if he wanted to play catch, and he did. They've been playing catch ever since.

I feel like my heart is shattering into a thousand tiny pieces. Now it is my turn. Taking a deep sigh, I bury my head in Oliver's chest and try desperately not to cry. "Way to go, Ollie, you did it. Have fun, honey." I'm trying to remain as upbeat as I can.

He knows I'm faking it. He gently takes me by the shoulders and says, "It's okay, Mom. I'll be okay. Boulder's not that far away, and I'll be back all the time."

"I know, I know." I can't help but remember how I tried to console my mother with the same naïve chant: "I'll be home soon, Mom. I'm not going away forever." But I was going away forever, and so is Ollie.

"Bye," I finally say, with a smile that doesn't quite reach my eyes. "Be careful, okay? Don't drive too fast. Oh, and don't forget to call when you get there."

Kurt takes my hand and squeezes it hard. Hang on, the squeeze is saying. Keep it light, and just hang on a little longer.

Oliver jumps in the driver's seat and starts to turn the key in the ignition. John—my "fourth son"—jumps in the other side. Oliver starts the car, then leans out the window. "Gentlemen, start your engines." He laughs.

Oliver takes one last look at Kurt and me, standing arm in arm in the street. I know he is capturing this snapshot moment in his memory, just as I had done. Now it's my turn to stand and wave.

Oliver guns the engine, lays some rubber for laughs and peels out down the street. He is the joker, just like his grandfather, Rut, always breaking the tense moments with a flourished smile.

Kurt and I lean against each other, waving and smiling, smiling and waving, until our son's car finally disappears from view. John's mother, Lorraine, is across the street waving too. Catching her eye, we laugh at ourselves and wander back to our respective homes. The energy has distinctly changed.

Kurt and I walk quietly through our front door, unable to speak just yet.

Taking my hand, he leads me upstairs to Oliver's bedroom. Pushing open the door against a tide of abandoned sneakers, jeans and T-shirts all heaped on the floor, we walk in and sit on his bed. Looking around at his belongings—his picture of Kurt and himself white-water-rafting in Colorado, a marlin he caught that we had stuffed, a photo of me holding him when he was a baby, an old fisherman's lamp I bought him, trophies from karate and his hockey stickers—we sit in silence, letting the tears flow, wallowing unashamedly in the sadness of this passage in life.

"I can't imagine Oliver not being here," Kurt says softly.

"Me too, honey. Me too."

Being a mother has been my finest and most joyous role, other than that of being a daughter. I loved being surrounded by my kids, in the house, all day, every day. I loved the activity, the busyness, the constancy of it all, the mealtimes, the snuggling, the middles of the night, the "Mommy! Mommy!" I loved being the one who had all the answers.

I loved the way they looked up to me with those big eyes, so adoringly, so uncensored, with so much raw love. I was the queen of the universe.

When they were little, I'd flash forward and try to prepare myself for the moment they'd leave. I imagined what fun it would be helping them fix up their first home, watching them fall in love, get married and have babies of their own. But nothing prepared me for the pain of this moment. The empty-nest syndrome is real. Everything changes. My father once said that when we kids left the house, we took the oxygen with us. Now I understand. Starved of my life force, my arms felt weak and useless with nothing to nurture, nothing to hold.

Thrown back on our own resources, we are forced to reexamine the parts of ourselves that we put on hold while our kids were growing up. We have to reexamine our relationship to ourselves. Who are we now? What are the things we sacrificed along the way?

"I lost me," the character played by Susan Sarandon railed in a movie I did called *The Banger Sisters*. How many of us understand that feeling? We have to ask what we care about now, what our passions are. The most frightening aspect for many people, especially women, is the "What happens now?"

And, of course, one of the most important questions we are faced with at this time is the nature of our relationship with our partner. Losing our children to their new lives leaves us naked. We have only each other now. It can be very frightening to stand there stripped bare, trying to remind ourselves of the person we first fell in love with. Sometimes panic can set in. Some of us flee our relationships in denial, sensing our own mortality, fearing that the stopwatch ticking away to our old age has now begun.

But it doesn't have to be that way. Not if we keep this most inevitable of moments clear and alive in our minds while we are raising our children. We must make sure that we don't wake up only when they're eighteen years old and leaving home and it's too late. The key is to continue to find places to enjoy each other and have fun as partners while the children are still growing. To make sure we don't sacrifice every single living breath for the children. We need to take special time every year, even if only an occasional night at a hotel. We need to say to our kids, "Mommy and Daddy are going to play now. You've got your sandbox; we need ours." Believe me, they'll cope. Not only will our relationships be healthier, but our kids relish Kurt's and my time alone together, because it makes them feel secure knowing that their parents are still in love.

Faced with this time in my life, I once again remembered the words of my father. "What did you learn today, Go?" he used to say. I'm still trying to learn something new every day. Sad as it is to lose our children to the world, it allows us to set out on a whole new path. It gives us a chance to satiate our curiosity, to embrace life's magic and all of its unanswerables. To be fired up by the things that excite and ignite us. There is so much still to learn, to see, to experience and to feel.

Wonder has not left the building.

After one of my meditations, I wrote the following:

My breath fills me with light that permeates my cells
    with divine protection.
I awake alone.
My nest is empty of my vessels of love.
The family that I call mine are gone.
One by one they have detached from my cord of nourishment,
    of unconditional love.
Life is changing, always renewing as it spins into timeless space.
Sadness sets in for moments at a time, then evaporates
    as quickly as it came.
I sit alone, experiencing my quietude in a sun-filled room
    surrounded by loved ones, seen and unseen.
I tingle with light.
I can feel the new skin on my body refining its glow,
    and the future feels more like the past.
I recall each of my pregnancies. I feel the divine dancing
    of the millions of cells growing within me.

The gentle caress of universal love.
The magic brew of life.
How perfect is man and his potential.
What a privilege to be born human.
All I ask is how I can serve in gratitude.

smile

Giving back is a path to joy.

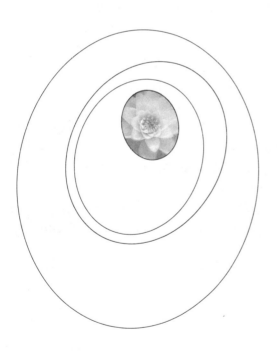

One smile can mark you forever. It did me. I met a little boy in Lima, Peru, who melted my heart, and took me on an unexpected journey to the heights of joy as well as to the depths of despair. Another left-hand turn.

It is unusually chilly in Lima. I arrived last night from Los Angeles, at the request of an organization called Operation Smile, which travels the world helping children who need reconstructive facial surgery. I've always wanted to give in some way to this special charity that flies volunteer doctors to third world countries to help deformed children whose cultures sometimes believe they have been touched by the devil.

"Yes," I finally said to the call, "I can go." The charity gave me the option of traveling to Vietnam, Africa or Peru. The Lima dates were the only ones that fit my schedule, and, happily, Kurt, Oliver and Boston were able to join me.

The plan is to go on to some of the ancient Incan sights I've always wanted to see. But what we found first in Lima was greater than any anthropological site. We found a human spirit, so alive, so joyful, and yet also so damaged and so scared.

We are on our way to meet the doctor from Operation Smile who will perform the surgery. One by one, we peel out of the elevator of our hotel, jet-lagged and bleary-eyed. He is waiting for us, sitting in the lobby in his overcoat, sipping coffee.

"I hope we're not late," I say apologetically.

"No, not at all," he says, rising to shake our hands. "But we should get going. There are two hundred kids waiting for us at the hospital."

"Two hundred? Are you going to operate on all of them?"

"No." He smiles sadly as he opens the door to the van and we all shuffle in and sit down. "The children you're about to see are all suffering from some sort of facial deformity. Some are far worse than others, and some we simply can't help. But the majority, we hope to do something about, eventually."

It's misting and gray outside as our van weaves its way through the wet streets of Lima until we reach the old hospital. It is run-down and cavernous, and reminds me of the old hotel in Livorno, Italy, where I first met my loving friend Aldo. Inside the grubby hallway, with its green paint peeling off the walls, the acrid smell of antiseptic cuts the air. It feels as cold and unwelcoming as the Peruvian winter.

Walking down a long corridor, we glance into the many empty rooms. Simple cots are cramped together and lined up against the cold wall, just waiting to bed the sick. I am so grateful that at least part of our family is together for this experience. It is unlike anything we have ever done together before. The vacations we took before were always to places with beautiful white sandy beaches, or we rode bikes through France, or we went to England, making fun excursions to the Tower of London atop a red double-decker bus. It is good to be here, very good.

We can hear the children before we can see them. Trailing toward a wide, open hallway, the noise of laughing, screaming and excited chattering greets us.

"Prepare yourselves," the doctor warns.

Rounding the corner, we are met with a wall of faces and sound. The children let out a huge cheer, squealing and clapping and pressing forward to meet us. A camera crew turns on their lights, the paparazzi start snapping away, and everyone jockeys for position in the melee.

I spot a young boy's face behind all the others in the crowd. A dark, middle-aged woman, perhaps an Operation Smile volunteer, is lifting him up. He's waving his hands wildly at us, or so it seems. His mouth is

smile

extremely deformed, but he has the widest, most compelling smile I have ever seen. Beams of light burst out of his mouth. His eyes dance with happiness. Shy and self-conscious he isn't. His electricity, his aura, his joy is so blinding that, for a moment, I can see nothing else.

Spotting us from across the room, he extends his arms with great zest toward Kurt and me. As if pulled by a magnet, we are drawn to him, sharing in his joy. What power this little Incan child possesses! The boys follow us as we cut through the crowd to be practically attacked by his hugs and kisses. His mouth is unable to close because of the severity of his condition. His sloppy kisses lift my heart. He has Kurt and I in a tight headlock, both his arms clamped around our necks, laughing and kissing one and then the other. We look at each other and smile. We are clearly falling in love with this very tenacious spirit.

I can tell from the guttural noises the boy is making in his throat that he cannot speak. "What's his name?" I ask the woman who was holding him.

"Juan Carlos," she says. "He's quite something, isn't he?"

"Are you his mother?" Kurt asks.

"No, I run the orphanage where he lives in Trujillo. I told him he was too old for this surgery, when he saw it on television. He saw the pictures of the other children who'd been helped. He became most insistent. I had to borrow a truck and drive all the way here. It is very far. But Juan knows how to get what he wants."

I am shocked that Juan is an orphan; he seems so happy. I wonder if he is like this all the time. "Are his parents dead?"

"No, he ran away from home when he was four years old because he was so badly beaten. His family were very ignorant and thought he was possessed by the devil. He lived on the streets for at least two years, we think. He only came to us when the police picked him up."

The more I hear, the more attached I become to this child. I look at his tattered clothes. I see that he has no shoes. Suddenly, I want to do everything I can to help him. I wave the doctor over, who is talking to some volunteers, and introduce him to Juan.

Juan takes his arm and puts it around his neck and kisses him. "Wow, what a grip!" the doctor laughs.

"Listen," I tell the doctor. "I know you've chosen a little girl. But if we choose another child, will you operate on her anyway?"

"Yes." He nods.

"Then I'd love Juan to be our child too."

The doctor speaks quickly in Spanish to the woman who brought Juan to the hospital, and the smile falls from his face. He leads us away to another part of the room. Although Juan has also melted his heart, it seems he is too old for the charity's work. "Juan is seven, and we only operate on those under seven," he explains. "That age was chosen because it makes the recovery easier, and because we have to stop somewhere."

"Please?" I plead. "He isn't much older than seven, and they may not know his true age anyway."

"We'll see."

We are whisked off to another part of the hospital to meet the other children who are going to be operated on today. It is excruciating, meeting these kids who have been rejected from birth, and who, feeling like freaks of nature, have been so badly damaged psychologically that they may never integrate fully into society. All the while, though, I can't stop thinking about Juan.

Coming back to the children, Juan is still waiting there, still beaming that smile of his. I turn to the doctor and press my hand on his arm. "So, what's the answer?" I ask.

He pauses, looks from Juan to me, and back again, and then sighs. "How can I possibly say no?"

When all the necessary paperwork has been completed and the doctors are ready, we escort Juan to the operating room for his surgery. He is such a brave little soldier, seemingly completely unafraid. We all have to dress in green scrubs, which are not my outfit of choice. The worst part is that I have to wear a horrible green hat and tuck my bangs up under it. Looking in the mirror, I now know the reason I never got the part of a Copa girl when I was dancing in New York: my forehead is so high when you pull the hair back from my face. Throwing caution to the wind, and looking pretty much like my father, I come out, take one look at Kurt in his hat and laugh. He doesn't look so hot either.

The cameras of a documentary crew rolling, the four of us looking

smile

like goodness knows what, we don masks and gloves and help get Juan ready, who is so happy and excited he can hardly contain himself. Kurt lifts him into his arms and carries him in.

The doctor tells me, "Goldie, would you please sit here? And, Kurt, can you put Juan in Goldie's arms?"

Juan is so happy to be plopped into my lap. He throws his arms around my neck, kisses my face, bounces up and down in my lap and can't wait to get started. We're all standing around looking at him and laughing, bubbling over with happiness and expectation. It couldn't have been more different than my childhood experience of having my tonsils out at seven and being terrified of the sterile, seemingly hostile environment of the operating room.

My nose wrinkles at the horrible smell in the room, which only reminds me of that bad memory. I can see from Boston's and Oliver's faces that they can smell it too. "Is something leaking?" I ask the anesthesiologist.

"No." He laughs. "It's just the gas. Here, try to get Juan to put this mask on his face, but go gently—kids are often very frightened by this part."

Someone tells Juan in Spanish what's about to happen.

The anesthesiologist needn't have worried. Even though the mixture smells bad, Juan grabs that mask and sucks in with everything he's got. There isn't an ounce of fear in this tough little street kid. He looks up at me with an expression that says, Aren't I doing good? The more he breathes in, the heavier he becomes in my arms, all the light and life and energy dripping away from him. When I can feel the full weight of Juan's body, as he gives in to the gas, Kurt helps the doctor lift him off me and lays him, deadweight, on the operating table.

The surgery begins. My family gathers round while the anesthesiologist sits at Juan's head monitoring vital signs. I look at my children and Kurt, our eyes meeting above our masks, with looks of amazement that we are really here, sharing this moment. This is a most unusual Monday morning.

Now that Juan's face is in repose, we are able to see for the first time just how disfigured he is. We want him to be helped even more. We all participate in our own way. The doctor calls for a scalpel, and Oliver hands it to him. I give him the scissors he asks for. We watch in awe as he takes the scalpel and begins to cut into Juan's face, sculpting a new mouth.

Over the next two hours, we watch in fascination as the doctor moves what there is of Juan's palate, bringing his massive top lip down, and cuts into his flattened nose. With delicacy I can hardly believe, he creates a brand-new mouth, a new nose, a completely different appearance. I wonder if Juan will ever be able to smile as big again.

As he's stitching Juan up, the surgeon says, "This will make him look better, but, unfortunately, he'll need more surgery, and he still won't be able to speak clearly. But at least he won't be so persecuted."

When it's all over, Kurt picks Juan up, and, as we all follow, carries him down the hallway to the recovery room and lays him in his bed. The surgery complete, it is time for us to say good-bye. Although I knew this moment would come, it suddenly feels terribly hard. I am already so attached to this child. Oh, Goldie, I scold myself, you're being a hopeless romantic. Straighten up and fly right. You've done your bit; you've all done a good thing. Now walk away.

But I hear myself telling the doctor, "Please, I want to know what happens to Juan. I want to pay for his second operation. Can you contact me and let me know what happens to him?"

He readily agrees.

Each of us kisses Juan's head as he is rousing, restlessly, and say good-bye. Taking our leave, we back up, watching him being tended by the nurses, and prepare ourselves to say farewell to all these wonderful volunteers who make the work of this charity possible.

But I still can't get Juan out of my mind. When we've said good-bye to everyone, and, just before we are due to leave, I run back to his room to see him one last time. He is groggy now, and in considerable pain. His eyes are deeply unhappy. His mood is aggressive and uncooperative and full of anger. I am as affected by his pain as I was by his joy. For the first time, I see a different side to this tormented child, the part he hid from us behind his seductive smile.

．　．　．

Our journey continues, and we travel to all the places we have wanted to see. Machu Picchu, the Valley of the Gods, and thirteen thousand feet up to Cusco, where we meet the oldest living Incan, a shaman, who gives us blessings in a holy cave. Everywhere I go, I see Juan's face. He is so of this land and of the spirit of Peru. I have sensed his incredible spirit and exuberance from the beginning, but the more I see of this extraordinary country, the more I understand who he is.

The people of this mountainous land worship the sun. Juan has reminded me of the sun from the moment I saw him. He has such a deep connection to this ancient form of worship, and I suddenly want him to see all this with me one day, to know what his roots are, who his tribe is and what he belongs to. I want him to reconnect to his spiritual life, having had so little spiritual life in his formative years. And I want to be with him when he does.

Over the next six months, I am in constant contact with Operation Smile. They tell me of Juan's progress, and let me know when he's ready for his second operation, which will enable him to speak. I ask them what I can do to help. "Could you host a fund-raising dinner at your home?" they ask. I agree immediately.

In my backyard, I create a vibrant celebration of life. I invite musicians from around the world and from all different cultures, and the theme is laughter and joy. It is a great turnout, the music is fabulous, and everyone is dancing and having fun. The event is covered by *In Style* magazine, and we raise a lot of money for this charity.

But then something even more extraordinary happens. At the end of the evening, I have to stand on a stage and speak to the invited guests about my special relationship with Juan. I am then supposed to introduce a slide show of the charity's good work.

"Okay, everyone," I say when the film is over, "now's the time to dig deep. Someone will be coming round to your tables with special envelopes, and Juan and I and all the other little children would be very grateful if you could find it in your hearts to make a donation."

There is a general hubbub, and people nod at me and smile.

"Can someone bring in the envelopes, please?" I call into the microphone.

Suddenly, in the doorway to the house, I see a face. It is Juan, carrying a tray full of envelopes, working his way toward me down the aisle.

"Oh my God!" I cry, my hands to my face. "I can't believe this!"

Juan abandons his tray, runs forward, jumps up on the stage and hugs me as tightly as he did the first time we met. I hug him back just as fiercely. Trying to get the words out, I say, "This is Juan, everybody! This is my little Juan!"

He rests his head on my shoulder and looks up at me. I can't stop kissing his face, his beautiful new face.

The Brazilian band begins to play, and everyone jumps up to dance, including Juan and I. Kurt comes up onto the stage and lifts Juan onto his shoulders. The Mardi Gras troupe escorts our happy little procession into our home, drumming, dancing and jumping gaily all around us. When we reach the open doors of our house, the drummers circle around Juan with fire in their eyes and start drumming just for him. Juan, in his little pair of corduroy pants and a little dress shirt, loves all the attention. Jumping down from Kurt's shoulders, he twirls and spins, jumps and twists for them; he beats his hands on their drums and he laughs and laughs and laughs.

Dr. Magee, one of the mainstays of the charity, comes up behind me and taps me on the shoulder.

"You tricked me!" I tell him, laughing.

"He's been in your son Wyatt's room playing on the computer for the last four hours."

"He has? Oh my God! Well, anyway, this is the best trick that's ever been played on me." Kissing him, I add, "Thank you."

Juan's journey after that night is a bit of a bumpy one. Dr. Magee, the head of Operation Smile, decides to take him to his home in Virginia and operate on him himself, starting the complicated repair of the hole in the roof of his mouth.

Juan flourishes there at first. He is under the foster care of a wonderful couple, and he learns to fish and skate. With the help of speech therapists, he learns English and attends a regular school. His adoptive parents are deeply religious, and he learns to read Bible books. They have their own little girl, but they are happy to keep Juan in their home—for a while. We e-mail back and forth, and I keep abreast of his progress. They send me photographs of him as he turns into the all-American boy. It is a good time, and all of us are filled with hope.

I go to another Operation Smile fund-raiser in Washington, D.C., and the family arranged for Juan to come up and meet me. I can't wait to see him. It is a very grand affair, with ball gowns and tuxedos, terribly formal, and held in a beautiful gallery. I see this little boy dressed in his first tuxedo walking toward me, looking more handsome than I could possibly imagine, and I smile as big as he used to. The little frog has turned into a prince—my prince. So self-possessed, he takes my hand and escorts me to my table as my date. He is articulate, speaking English, and looking fabulous. Staring at him, almost unable to believe it, I am so proud. I know I have done something good here.

A comedian comes on the stage and does an opening act. He is very funny, but Juan and I seem to be the only people laughing. Juan gets every joke, laughing in all the right places. He becomes so overjoyed, so delighted that this man is making us laugh, that he jumps up, runs onto the stage and gives him the biggest hug, right in the middle of his routine. Sitting watching him, like a proud mother, I am overjoyed. This child has so much potential for love, and, at last, he is able to express it.

But, sadly, Juan's problems are more than skin-deep. His years of rejection, abuse and fear have taken a heavy toll on his young psyche. He soon begins to test his new foster parents with an uncontrollable temper and violent tantrums. Their e-mails become increasingly desperate.

I am in our summer cottage in Canada when I hear the news that Juan has been flown back to Peru. He has been returned to the orphanage in Trujillo. His American belongings—his clothes and his toys—have been packed away so that the other children can't steal them.

The news devastates me.

"Juan was brought here because of us," I tell Kurt inconsolably. "He was the center of all our hoopla. He became the poster boy for Operation Smile. I feel responsible. I won't give up on him. I have to go see him."

In Lima I am met by Paola, a twenty-five-year-old volunteer who has helped organize Juan's return. Accompanied by two psychologists, we journey by plane to Trujillo to find our troubled boy. We arrive at the orphanage, a former convent, which sits slumped in the middle of the small town, dilapidated and sad. Hundreds of children run wild in the cloisters and corridors, with no one apparently in charge.

"We have come to speak with Juan," Paola tells a woman we finally find in a kitchen.

"He's not here," she replies. "He's in the mountains on a field trip. I don't know when he'll be back."

Shattered by the news, I take myself off to a bar in the town's square. Sitting there, sipping strong coffee, I laugh at myself. What are you doing, Goldie? You've come all this way, and you may not even find him.

Paola draws up in a car and rolls down the window. "We've found him, we've found him! Come on."

Armed with illegible directions, we wind our way up through the hills, toward a mountain pasture. Seeing scores of children playing in the pasture, we bring the car to a halt. Getting out, I can see kids playing soccer, running wild. Others are swinging on an old tire, attached to a tree. My eyes scan right and left, looking for Juan. Finally, frustrated, I yell out his name: "Juan! Juan!"

I suddenly spot him, surrounded by his friends. He looks up, stops what he's doing and runs toward me. He slams into my body and throws his arms around me the way he always did. Hugging him back, I can't speak.

But it doesn't last long. Juan pulls away quickly and runs back to play with his friends. He doesn't want to abandon them; he doesn't want to be different. So we wait for him to finish playing. When he eventually comes back, more shyly this time, I bend down and ask him, "It was your birthday last week?"

He smiles.

"Did you have a party?"

smile

He shakes his head.

"Come on," I say, holding out my hand. "Let's go and buy you a birthday cake."

We drive back to Trujillo and take him to a bakery. Juan won't speak to me; he won't speak English and Paola translates.

"But you can speak English, Juan," I remind him.

He just smiles and stares out the window, saying nothing. We tell him to pick out a birthday cake, and he has such fun choosing the one he wants. Then, speaking only in Spanish, he tells Paola he wants to take it back to the orphanage later and share it with his friends. Sitting at a table, we laugh and play and draw pictures with crayons. Juan draws a picture of himself with a big smile on his face and only one arm. He draws a picture of me with all my arms and legs and a smile on my face. He then connects the two of us with a little red squiggly thing that emerges from the top of his head and links to the top of mine.

"What's that, Juan?" I ask.

"Love," he replies in English, without looking up. It is the only word he's spoken to me all day.

Taking the picture from his hand, I press it close to my heart and smile. "I love you too, Juan."

We return to the orphanage with his birthday cake in its box untouched. We all gather around and sing happy birthday, and Juan shows off the wooden top that I bought him. When there are only crumbs left on the plate, he grabs me by the hand and takes me to the dormitory where he sleeps. Furtively, just like a little Russian girl did once before, he reaches under his bed in his special corner of the room to show me his hidden treasure. They are books, Bible books, brought all the way back from Virginia.

All too soon, it is time for us to go. I turn to him, a lump in my throat. "Juan, I have to go now."

He doesn't say anything, so Paola translates.

"Juan, look at me." I bend down and stare into his face, locking eyes. "I want you to understand something, Juan. Even though I don't live near you, I will always be here for you. Do you understand me?"

He looks away.

"No. Look at me. Do you understand what I'm saying to you, Juan? You can trust me. Do you believe me?"

He nods.

"All right, then." I kiss him. God, it is so hard to leave. "Good-bye, sweetheart." I walk away, and turn around to see him one last time, but he is gone.

I leave Juan, and I leave Paola, and I leave the psychologists who have promised to work with him to help him control his anger and his fear.

Back home, I keep in constant touch with Paola, who is trying to find new adoptive parents for Juan. I send Juan a computer, and money for computer lessons. I pay for him to have more speech therapy to improve his communication skills. Paola works tirelessly to get Juan adopted. She fights endless bureaucracy, filling in multiple forms, and she parades him before countless parents who are looking for a child. But nobody wants him. Nobody wants a nine-year-old boy who can't speak properly and who has serious emotional problems.

Finally, Paola calls me up one day. "I don't know," she tells me, half laughing, "maybe I'm crazy, but I'm so in love with Juan, I'm going to adopt him myself. I know I can help him."

"Are you sure about this, Paola? This is a lot for a young girl like you to take on. I mean, this is a huge commitment."

When Paola tells me she is sure, I promise that I will give her all the help I can, that my love and bond with Juan extends to her now too. I pay for her apartment. I pay for his schooling. We speak constantly, and I offer every encouragement and incentive I can. This has to work. It must.

Juan moves in with Paola and her mother as she carries on with her regular job at the bank. Her volunteer work for Operation Smile continues, and Juan participates eagerly. He sees a child psychologist and a speech therapist every week, and he thrives under Paola's love and attention. Things are not easy for her, but both of us refuse to let go of the optimistic belief that this child has so much potential that we will overcome any obstacles to his success.

The following summer, I invite Juan to our lake cottage in Canada. We have so much fun together, I can hardly wait to get up and play with him each morning. We fish for hours and take paddleboat rides. We fly across the lake on our Ski-Doos and wave runners and watch movies together at night. He makes a plaster likeness of his face, so that I can keep him with me always. His little face that he is now so proud of.

One day, we take a wild Ski-Doo ride in the middle of the lake, him sitting behind me, his arms around me holding on tight. Jumping the waves, the wind takes my hat. I switch off the motor to see where it went, and, without a moment's hesitation, Juan jumps into the deep, cold lake and swims for it. Holding it triumphantly up in the air, my little street urchin swims back with hat in hand. He climbs back up onto the Ski-Doo like an athlete and squashes it, dripping, back on my head. My little Juan, my helpless little boy whom I thought I was protecting, is suddenly my hero.

That night, our last, I get into bed with him and stroke his back, just as Mom did for me. I want to give him some of the love he never had, some of the independence and the security. His English is getting better and better, and we begin to talk more and more.

"What happened to you when you lived on the streets, Juan?" I ask him gently.

A cloud passes over his face.

"Did people treat you badly?"

He looks up at me with the eyes of an old man, and I know the answer.

"When was the best time?"

"Night."

"Really? Why?"

"Because no one could see my face."

Our time together over, I take him back to New York to be reunited with Paola, where he undergoes a frightening transformation. Gone is the happy little boy on the lake. In his place is a child who completely flips out. Going on a walk in Central Park with Paola, he throws a tantrum in the street, kicks her, runs away from her and threatens to leave her forever. They return to my apartment hardly talking, Paola in floods of tears, Juan pale and silent.

"I can't take much more of this," she sobs.

I see the look of anxiety on her face, and it just kills me. I understand,

I understand completely. His fear and anger are so deeply embedded into his fiber. I wonder if she's going to make it. This isn't going to be easy.

Kurt sees what's happening and takes Juan's hand. He asks Paola to translate. "You can either control your emotions and stop ruining every-thing or you can go back to the way your life was on the streets," Kurt tells Juan firmly. "It's up to you." Juan listens to him quietly. "Now I want you to apologize to Paola."

Shamefaced, he does as he's told, and behaves much more courte-ously for the rest of the time they are there. A little discipline goes a long way. He and Paola fly home the next day on much better terms.

Over the next year, I speak regularly on the telephone with Juan, and I can tell his English is improving all the time. I know he is still having problems with his anger. I know that he is testing Paola constantly. The older and the bigger he gets, the more frightening his outbursts become. He is now living with Paola's mother in Lima, and Paola is attending the London School of Economics, chasing her dream to work full-time with underprivileged children and build a secure life for her and Juan.

When she calls to tell me she's going to be in Washington, D.C., to work for the World Bank and that Juan is flying up to join her, I drop everything and jump on a plane. Arriving at my hotel, I get all dressed up as if I'm going on a date. Sitting by the telephone, waiting for the two of them to arrive, I have butterflies in my stomach. It's been a year since I've seen Juan, and I wonder what will happen.

When the telephone rings, I jump on the elevator, run to the lobby and there they are. Juan looks so handsome, all dressed up in a little V-neck sweater and a shirt and tie. He is at least two inches taller, much more mature, but not quite as demonstrative as he used to be.

He first takes my hand and then Paola's, and the three of us walk into the dining room and sit down for dinner. He handles himself so beauti-fully, winning over all the waitresses with his seductive personality. I also notice that he is much deeper, more contemplative, perhaps because of his therapy and self-reflection. For the first time, we talk about serious things.

Sipping his Coke, he looks up at me and says, "Where does anger come from?"

I explain to him in the best way I know how about fear and what happens to us when we are afraid and how it changes into anger. "Fear is not a good thing," I tell him. "The fear of having to go back to where you came from, the fear that someone is going to leave you, or not love you anymore. That can make you very angry. And often fear can turn into anger, Juan."

He looks at me with those big eyes of his with a wisdom way beyond his twelve years. "Do you believe that we have white angels and dark angels in our hearts?" he asks.

"Yes, I do, Juan. We're only human. It's how we deal with them that matters."

"I want to get rid of my dark angels," he says, his voice almost a whisper.

Placing my hand on his, I look into his face. "One day you will, Juan. I truly believe that." Paola and I look at each other and share a knowing look. "All you have to do, Juan," I add, "is trust that you are loved."

He looks up and smiles his new smile at me. It is a good smile. It is a nice smile. It's a hopeful smile.

I was taught it is our moral duty to give back something to this world, to say thank you for our gifts. I can still hear my mother say, "For every dollar you make, honey, I want you to give at least ten cents to the needy." Donating money to charity is one way of giving back, and it is a good way, but sometimes it can feel hollow, and you don't always really know if it's going into the proper hands.

Personally, I like to have more of a hands-on experience. It's not all altruistic. I guess I feel, selfishly, that if I can help one or two children directly, then I'm getting something from it too, a new love experience and—perhaps most important of all—a shot of humility for me and my family.

I involved my children in Operation Smile from the outset, to try to make them appreciate their own great good fortune, which landed on them through absolutely no effort on their part. Being born to wealthy and famous parents can have its own problems unless we make our children see that this is not so for everyone.

I want them to cultivate compassion by going out and standing in somebody else's shoes. I want them to interface with people who don't have what they have, or who have been damaged, physically or psychologically. It is a wonderful way of developing a compassionate heart, which is something that is good for everyone. If everyone cultivated more compassion in their lives, the world would be a very different place today.

My involvement with those I have come to care for along the highway of my life has been deeply rewarding, but it has also offered me a salutary lesson. It has taught me to accept that life doesn't always have a fairy-tale ending—it just isn't that neat. Sometimes, you'll find that there really is nothing more you can do for the people you're trying to help, that you have done all you can, and at least you've given them some good memories before you walk away.

The problem is that when you build a personal relationship with a child like Juan, it's so vitally important to follow through. It isn't in my nature to walk away from difficult situations. I see Juan more and more. At this time, he lives in my beloved India with his adopted mother, Paola. I like to call her my angel from heaven. Juan just turned thirteen. His English is impeccable now, his sense of humor is flourishing and he has become a great student. There are still many of life's challenges ahead of him. That's where we come in. As long as I am able to, I will continue to try to save one life from the agonies of this world.

The doctors may have fixed Juan's smile, but they can do nothing to fix his heart. Perhaps no one can. But as long as I am able to, I will continue to try.

lotus

*How can we count our moments of joy one by one? Isolated
from one another? They should accumulate and be
worn throughout life like a mantle of wealth
in which we can drape ourselves,
at any given moment.*

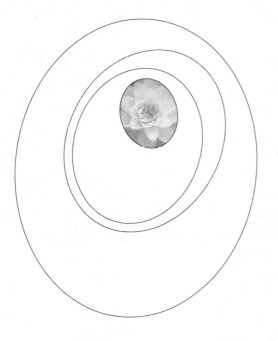

postcard

I am ushered into a lovely room with a low table, at which I sit, cross-legged on the floor, with my son Oliver, and my stepson, Boston. I quiet my mind and inhale the pungent incense and listen to the bells of the monastery gently ringing out all around me.

Looking out the window, I see the snowcapped Himalayas towering over us. We are in Dharamsala, India, nestled into the foothills of these majestic mountains. Our breath makes clouds of steam as we exhale.

A monk in orange and maroon robes appears at the back of the room and steps through a soft Tibetan curtain that covers the doorway. It is the color of saffron. He has a young and gentle face, which lights up the room.

"I am Kutenla," he tells me.

We all nod shyly and say hello.

I have been told that Kutenla is a man of wisdom and prophecy and incredible kindness. I feel so privileged to meet him. We have walked into his world, another world, the Nechung Monastery, a beautiful Buddhist temple in the most heavenly of settings.

Kutenla is the current Nechung Oracle. Chosen by the Dalai Lama and deemed to be a reincarnate of the original Oracle of 750 A.D., he is the spiritual protector of the Dalai Lama and the Tibetan government in exile. Several times a year, he adorns himself in an elaborate costume weighing more than seventy pounds and a huge hat weighing more than thirty. Despite being almost crushed beneath the weight, he goes into a spirited, trancelike state during which he dances and speaks his wisdom.

Having had a normal childhood in the Tibetan Children's

Village, a Montessori school that I help support, he had a hidden purpose that none suspected. But as a young monk, he suffered severe headaches from which he could find no relief. Then one day he had what looked like an epileptic seizure. Much to his own surprise, he began to recite ancient Tibetan that no one had ever taught him. The Dalai Lama heard of this and appointed him the new Oracle. Now here we are being granted an audience.

I am living a mother's dream, on this most special of journeys with my sons. Boston, a practicing Buddhist and a Buddhist scholar in his final year at the university, is very much into his stance, wanting to share his knowledge. Oliver looks more at peace than I have ever seen him.

When Kutenla first walked in, I was shocked. I expected to see an old, wise mystic, not this young, round-faced, joyful man. He sits down and takes tea with us and asks us about our day. We feel aglow, sitting in this place of peace, with the sound of chanting and bells coming from the temple, and monks coming and going noiselessly. We are ripe and alive and in awe, our hearts and minds open to the unknown. I love witnessing my sons' experience, as much as I am enjoying my own.

"I understand you have something to ask me," Kutenla says with a warm smile.

"I do," I say, nodding reverently. "I would like to know what 'joy' is to you. How would you describe it? Of all the people I have ever met, the Tibetans are the happiest. They seem to have a secret of some kind."

Kutenla looks at me and laughs his big, open laugh. "Let me see if I can explain this," he says, resting his hands on his knees and looking for all the world like a young Buddha. "I believe that we are born with the seed of joy."

"You do?"

"Yes. Every human being comes into this world wanting happiness and not wishing to suffer."

His words ring so true to me. I think of my childhood wish to be happy, or further back to my own bubble of happiness that I was born with. I can't help but think of those who try to attain levels of happiness through an altered state, and how that usually only ends with sadness.

"You see, we believe that through the quieting of the mind we are able to separate what is real and what isn't, what is ego and what is truth. It is like making butter; you keep churning and churning until the cream begins to separate. You must really work at churning a chaotic mind, learn to separate your thoughts from your true nature, and become a witness rather than a party to your destructive emotions. What you are left with is a natural state of joy."

I smile. "Is that like nirvana?"

He laughs. "Not exactly nirvana, but to become a bodhisattva . . ."

"Excuse me, what's a 'bodhisattva'?" Oliver asks.

Boston interjects, "A bodhisattva is someone who has taken the vow to act for the benefit of all sentient beings. To take a vow of a bodhisattva is a promise to help others through compassion, wisdom and understanding. You arrive at freedom by understanding your deeper nature, and, when you are free, you can feel joy."

Kutenla smiles and nods, impressed. Boston glows with happiness.

"This is all fine and well," I say, "but it seems to me there is so much sorrow in the world, even for those who have deep faith and belief. How do we transcend our deepest pain?"

Kutenla smiles a smile that warms the chilly room. "We have a saying: 'The lotus grows in the mud.'"

" 'The lotus grows in the mud'? What does that mean?"

"The lotus is the most beautiful flower, whose petals open one by one. But it will only grow in mud. In order to grow and gain wisdom, first you must have the mud—the obstacles of life and its suffering."

"That's a beautiful metaphor," I say wistfully, "and an interesting teaching in itself."

"The mud speaks of the common ground that we humans share, no matter what our stations in life," he says. "Whether we have it all or we have nothing, we are all faced with the same obstacles: sadness, loss, illness, dying and death. If we are to strive as human beings to gain more wisdom, more kindness and more compassion, we must have the intention to grow as a lotus and open each petal one by one."

Kutenla unravels his mala, or tiger's-eye prayer beads, from around his wrist and opens my hand. Closing my fingers around his mala, he looks me in the eye. "This is my gift to you," he says. "Don't lose it."

Smiling, unable to speak, I nod my gratitude.

"All you need," Kutenla tells me as he stands to go, his eyes gentle, "is the intention and the wish to be happy, and it will be so."

mothers and daughters

*After my son Wyatt was born, the first face I
saw was my daughter Kate's. "Mommy,
Mommy," she said with a sigh, "I'm
so glad I'm the only girl."*

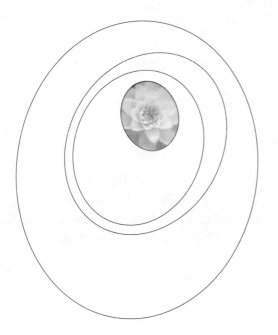

postcard

Demeter, the Greek goddess of the harvest, loved her only child, her daughter, Persephone, so much that the earth flowed with abundance and bloomed all year. Then, one day, Persephone was kidnapped by Hades, lord of the underworld, and dragged to a place that was frightening and unknown. Demeter was so distraught at losing her vibrant daughter to Hades that she mourned for a full year. Without her blessing, the ground turned to dust, and every growing thing withered and died, and the people starved. Fearing for the earth, Zeus, the king of the gods, ordered Hades to return Persephone to her mother.

Reunited, the two women wept for joy. The sun shone again, and their tears of happiness watered the earth, making everything bloom once more. But Hades, hopelessly in love with Persephone and determined to have her back, tricked her into eating a pomegranate seed, which doomed her to return to the underworld forever.

But wise Zeus arranged a compromise: Persephone would spend half the year with Hades and half with Demeter. And so every spring when Persephone is returned to Demeter, the earth is filled with abundance and love. And every winter when the ground opens up and Persephone returns to the darkness, Demeter mourns. The leaves wither, die and fall from the trees, and a cold descends on the earth, reflecting her grief.

There are many different interpretations of this mythical story. Some see it as an explanation for the seasons. Others see it as a metaphor for the depth and potency of the relationship between mother and daughter. The way I look at it, it describes the joys and the agony of having a daughter and letting her go, watching her become her own person and experiencing her life on her own terms.

I have always loved the Persephone story. I'm touched by Demeter's sorrow, and feel badly for her poor daughter, consigned to a life apart from her mother and away from the light. But of these two deeply connected women, I think my heart goes out to the mother, Demeter, the most.

Even in the real world, a mother can be all-powerful, and she is the one person who can make her family flourish. She dotes lovingly on her daughter, and identifies with her in a way she can't with her son. All her juices are flowing; she feels alive—she feels the vitality in her and in her girl child. She is present and relevant and omniscient. Such is the bond between a mother and daughter.

But when that daughter grows up and begins to lead her own life, a mother can feel bereft. The daughter moves into her own shadowy underworld, just as Persephone did, only in the real world it is secrets and boys and sexual discovery. A mother may be left behind, thinking, But I'm not done yet. I still have something to say but you're not listening. I still have something to give but you're not receptive to it. And so I have no one to nourish anymore. What do I do for the rest of my life?

When Kate left home, I indeed felt bereft. I'd walk into her bedroom and cry when I saw her things: the beautiful books she'd read, the perfume bottles, all of her makeup in her bathroom. I missed her so much that I wanted to keep everything just as it was. And then, very soon afterward it seemed, she got married, and suddenly she was a woman, somebody's wife.

I relished this time for my daughter. I found joy in her joy, but I couldn't help but feel the power of these emotions. I wonder how I would feel if my life wasn't so rich, full of love and so rewarding. I have pondered the effects of my success at such a young age on my own mother, wondering if she felt left out or abandoned. Could my youthful luster have made her feel less luminous and not as useful? I recalled times when I scolded my mom for coming into my home and rearranging my dishes; I accused her of trying to live my life. Oh, how hard I tried to separate myself from her, to become my own person and stand on my own two feet. Now I ask, Did I secretly devastate her and leave her more saddened and alone?

I was only guilty of what all girls do. In order to become real individuals, they don't want to be like their mothers. But now that I have experienced the loss of my own girl child to the great seduction called life, I have true compassion for both mother and daughter in this passage. That's all it is, a passage. It isn't lasting, and, if handled well, it moves into a healthy friendship that only grows and grows. But letting go is a most important first step: letting go of roles and the power we have had all of our lives as mother and daughter; letting go, and having faith that the lessons learned will be remembered. It's not easy, but it is necessary, unless you want to be a mother who has to be "dealt with" instead of a mother who is free and fun.

My mother was never fully realized as a woman despite being the brightest one at the party, the most beautiful, the sexiest and probably the smartest. She could have been the star. Everywhere she went, she drew people to her, and lit up like a lightbulb with them. But her life was not as she wanted it to be. She didn't get to be the luminary she should have been. She gave birth to two powerful daughters, one of whom just so happened to figure out how to dance and act and ended up being the sort of performer she probably would have loved to be.

When Patti and I had children of our own, my mother, like Demeter, knew that her procreating days were over, and it hurt. I remember one day when I took her to the drugstore to buy some new lipstick. Quite frail by then, she spotted a young woman outside wheeling her baby across the street and she stopped and stared wistfully. "Oh, how I envy her," she said. It took me a moment to understand what she meant, and then the truth of her statement hit me hard. I got a lump in my throat, knowing that one day that would be me saying that.

But I don't think I truly understood how Mom felt until my Katie became pregnant. I was so happy for her, so filled with excitement, knowing that she was embarking on this most magical of journeys. The maternal torch was being passed, and I bowed my head in reverence. I was filled with such awe that this little baby girl that I still held in my heart and my mind was having a baby of her own. It was like watching creation happening right in front of my eyes, with great facility and grace. It was the continuation of the process that had started in my womb.

Everyone told me how great it would feel to be a grandmother—"The most wonderful feeling in the world," I heard over and over again. I thought to myself, How could it be any more fabulous than being a mother to my own children? Besides, I still had a teenage son to nurture and cherish at home, my beloved Wyatt. It was sheer joy watching my daughter feel the feelings I had when she was growing inside me. I loved every moment of sharing all of the physical and emotional changes in Kate, of being able to identify so closely with the experience and compare it to my own.

The wonderful day arrived; my grandson, Ryder Russell, burst forth into this world. I could barely contain myself. But was I really a "grandmother"? A word that had so many connotations of old age and decrepitude. My son Oliver decided I should be called "Glam-Ma," which I thought was quite brilliant and made us all laugh so hard.

Someone said to me jokingly, "Well, now, Goldie, you've got a new baby." I thought, My God, what a dangerous thing to say. My baby? This isn't my baby; this is my daughter's baby. He is all hers.

I try to be mindful of the fact that my children came through me, that I am just a vessel, and I cannot claim their lives. Their journey is clearly their own. My grandchild came through my daughter's body, and so the circle goes, the circle of life.

Katie will always be my baby girl, just as I was for my mom, no matter how old she was. Daughters never really leave their mothers, and thank God for that. I couldn't imagine my life without her to share it with. Like Demeter, I may shed many tears along the way about losing her to her other life, the part I don't know about, her living away from me and being the person she can't be with me. But, as with Demeter, when my daughter walks back into my world, the sun shines and my heart fills once more with love and light, giving me a whole new reason to feel joy.

And to think that I also have Oliver, my sage, my guru; tender Wyatt, my Zen master; my spirited grandson, Ryder; and my spiritual cohort, my stepson, Boston—to bless my life as well. Kurt is my love and my heart, and my work is now taking me in directions I could never possibly have dreamed of. With all of these remarkable lights in my life, I can honestly say that I wake up now with more energy and zest than ever before. As a mother, as a daughter, as a lover, as a sister, as a friend, I'm filled with such joy and excitement at the prospect of new opportunities for this perhaps most interesting segment of my life's blessed journey.

Every day I ask myself, wondering aloud, "What does the future hold for you now, Goldie Hawn?" And the best thing of all is, I just don't know.

text photo captions